MULTI-OWNED HOUSING

Multi-owned Housing
Law, Power and Practice

Edited by

SARAH BLANDY
University of Leeds, UK

ANN DUPUIS
Massey University, New Zealand

JENNIFER DIXON
University of Auckland, New Zealand

ASHGATE

Published by
Ashgate Publishing Limited
Wey Court East
Union Road
Farnham
Surrey, GU9 7PT
England

Ashgate Publishing Company
Suite 420
101 Cherry Street
Burlington
VT 05401-4405
USA

www.ashgate.com

British Library Cataloguing in Publication Data
Multi-owned housing : law, power and practice.
1. Housing management--Law and legislation--Cross-cultural studies. 2. Comparative law.
I. Blandy, Sarah. II. Dixon, Jennifer. III. Dupuis, Ann, 1946-
346'.0434-dc22

Library of Congress Cataloging-in-Publication Data
Blandy, Sarah.
Multi-owned housing : law, power and practice / by Sarah Blandy, Ann Dupuis and Jennifer Dixon.
p. cm.
Includes bibliographical references and index.
ISBN 978-0-7546-7566-2 (hbk) 1. Common interest ownership communities--Law and legislation. I. Dupuis, Ann, 1946- II. Dixon, Jennifer (Jennifer E.) III. Title.
K738.B58 2010
346.04'2--dc22
2009052465

ISBN 9780754675662 (hbk)
ISBN 9781409408956 (ebk)

Mixed Sources
Product group from well-managed forests and other controlled sources
www.fsc.org Cert no. SGS-COC-2482
© 1996 Forest Stewardship Council
FSC

Printed and bound in Great Britain by
TJ International Ltd, Padstow, Cornwall

Contents

List of Figures

List of Tables

List of Contributors

Professor Rachelle Alterman holds the David Azrieli Chair in Architecture/Town Planning at the Technion-Israel Institute of Technology and heads the Center of Urban and Regional Studies there. A planner and lawyer, Dr Alterman has written numerous publications on comparative planning law, property rights, and planning theory, and is the founding president of the International Academic Association on Planning, Law and Property Rights.

Sarah Blandy is a Senior Lecturer in property law at the University of Leeds. She has led and contributed to many empirical research projects and has written widely on housing and property law issues from a socio-legal perspective, including both academic publications and practitioner papers.

Dr Michael Bounds is an Associate Professor (adjunct) with the Urban Research Centre at the University of Western Sydney and a Director of Cambridge Examinations, Australia. He was formerly Director of the Australian Housing and Urban Research Institute at the Universities of Western Sydney and of New South Wales with the Urban Research Centre. He has undertaken extensive research into public housing in Australia and the UK and is the author of a number of books, articles and reports on housing, urban development and on urban social theory.

Dr Kelly Cassidy is a Senior Research Fellow in the Tourism, Leisure, Hotel and Sport Management department at Griffith University (Gold Coast Campus), Australia. She has researched and written on strata title management for both academic and industry audiences, and was a member of the organising committee for the 2005 and 2007 *Strata and Community Title in Australia for the 21st Century* conferences.

Dr Alice Christudason is an Associate Professor teaching real property law at the National University of Singapore whose research interests include strata and real estate law as well as educational pedagogy. She is actively involved in legislative reform, including invited representations before Singapore's Parliamentary Select Committees on the Land Titles (Strata) and the Building Maintenance and Strata Management Bills. She is the lead contributor to *Halsbury's Laws of Singapore: Land* and has published widely in various international journals.

Professor Jennifer Dixon is Professor of Planning and Dean, National Institute of Creative Arts and Industries, University of Auckland, New Zealand. With Ann Dupuis, she undertook research on the operation of bodies corporate in the Auckland region that led to the first review of the Unit Titles Act 1972. Professor Dixon is Chair of the Centre for Housing Research, Aotearoa, New Zealand.

Dr Ann Dupuis is Associate Professor of Sociology at Massey University, Auckland, New Zealand. Her research and publications in the field of urban studies focus on housing wealth and inheritance, urban intensification, urban governance issues and gated communities.

Professor Chris Guilding works with Griffith University's department of Tourism, Leisure, Hotel and Sport Management. His research and publications now have a particular focus on strata titled property management, and he has acted as chairperson for the Griffith hosted *Strata and Community Title in Australia for the 21st Century* conferences held in 2005, 2007 and 2009.

Dr Evan McKenzie is Associate Professor in the Political Science Department of the University of Illinois at Chicago and is an Adjunct Professor at the John Marshall Law School, where he teaches the law of condominium and homeowner associations. He is the author of *Privatopia* (Yale University Press 1994), one of the earliest and most enduringly influential books on common interest housing and homeowner associations, as well as numerous book chapters and articles on common interest housing. His current research focus is on the ways American municipalities promote the creation of private residential governments, and the consequences of such practices.

Professor Douglas S. Robertson is an expert in Scottish private housing, especially flatted property. He is head of the Department of Applied Social Science at the University of Stirling. His comparative research was highly influential in the introduction of the Commonhold and Leasehold Reform Act 2002. Current research interests focus on the governance implications arising from recent property law reforms, namely leasehold and commonhold reform in England and Wales, and Titles and Burdens and the Law of the Tenement reforms in Scotland.

Marjorie van Roon is an environmental scientist and Senior Lecturer in Planning at the University of Auckland. Her current research focus is on ensuring the ecological functionality of urban areas, both greenfield and brownfield, including those undergoing intensification, and she has published widely on these topics.

Cathy Sherry is a Senior Lecturer in the Faculty of Law, University of New South Wales, Australia. She teaches property, equity and trusts, children and the law and a postgraduate course on Strata and Community Title. She researches high-rise and master planned communities and has a particular interest in the effect of the built environment on children's well-being.

Dr Feng Wang is an Assistant Professor in the School of Public Economics and Administration, Shanghai University of Finance and Economics. Her research interests include neighbourhood governance, organizational behaviour and theory, and public and nonprofit performance management. She has published internationally on these topics. She co-ordinated the *International Conference on Community Governance: Multi-Cultural Perspectives* in Beijing, 2007.

Dr Jan Warnken teaches planning and environmental law and environmental assessment and management at the Griffith School of Environment, Griffith University, Gold Coast, Australia. He has contributed to many research projects commissioned by government and industry bodies, and his publications include journal articles, book chapters and industry reports on sustainable tourism issues with a focus on strata and community title management.

Dr Ngai Ming Yip is Associate Professor in the Department of Public and Social Administration of City University of Hong Kong, and is also a registered professional housing manager. His research interests include private housing governance, neighbourhood and urban governance at grassroots level, and social and spatial segregation. He has published widely on housing and urban issues.

List of Cases by Jurisdiction

England and Wales

Barton v Accent Property Solutions Ltd, Eton Court Management Company Ltd, and Graycliffe Homes Ltd LRX/22/2008
Eltham Properties Limited v Kenny LRX/161/2006
Kok Hoong v Leong Cheong Kweng Mines Limited [1964] AC 993
Rhone v Stephens [1994] 2 AC 310
Tulk v Moxhay (1848) 2 Ph 774

Hong Kong

Uniland Investment Enterprises Limited v The Incorporated Owners of Sea View Estate & Ors [1999] 4 HKC 141

New South Wales

Community Association DP No 270180 v Arrow Asset Management Pty Ltd and Ors [2007] NSWSC 527
Hudson Property Group Pty Ltd v Community Association DP 270238 [2005] NSWCA 374
Owners – Strata Plan No 51487 v Broadsand Pty Ltd [2002] NSWSC 770
Yedway Pty Ltd v Owners Corporation of Strata Plan 62871 [2009] NSWSC 8

New Zealand

Paparoa Farmlands Limited and Rodney District Council RMA 623/99

Scotland

Hanover (Scotland) Housing Association Limited and Others against John Reid and Margaret Reid [2006] CSOH 56

Singapore

Cortina Development Store Pte Ltd v MCST Plan No 557 (STB No. 17 of 1991)
Leong Siew Cheng v Subsidiary Proprietors (1st Respondent) and MCST Plan No 647 (2nd Respondent) (Unreported, STB No. 28 of 1989)
Management Corporation Strata Title Plan No 980 v Yat Yuen Hong Co Pte Ltd & Anor [1993] 1 SLR 555
Sumitri M Menon v MCST Plan No 335 (Unreported, STB No 8 of 1989)
Tan Jui Meng v Hoong See Chye and Tan Lem Yee [2005] SGSTB 1
Tan Siew Tian v Lee Khek Ern Ken [2008] 3 SLR 64

USA

175 East Delaware Condominium Association v Hinojosa (1997) 287 Ill.App.3d 886
Apple II Condominium Association v Worth Bank and Trust (1995) 277 Ill.App.3d 345
Avila South Condominium Association Inc. v Kappa Corp. 347 So.2d 599 (Fla. 1977)
Bernardo Villas Management Corp. v Black (1987) 190 Cal.App.3d 153
City of Ladue v Gilleo (1994) 512 U.S. 50
Committee for a Better Twin Rivers v Twin Rivers Homeowners' Association (2007) 192 N.J. 344
Marsh v Alabama (1946) 326 U.S. 501
Nahrstedt v Lakeside Village Condominium Association (1994) 4 Cal. 4th 361
Portola Hills Community Assn. v James (1992) 4 Cal.App.4th 289
Raven's Cove Townhomes Inc. v Knuppe Dev. Co. Inc. (1981) 114 Cal.App.3d 783

List of Statutes by Jurisdiction

AUSTRALIA

Corporations Act 2001

Queensland

Body Corporate and Community Management Act 1997
Body Corporate and Community Management Regulations 1997

New South Wales

Strata Title Act 1961
Strata Schemes (Freehold Development) Act 1973
Environmental Planning and Assessment Act 1979
Community Land Development Act 1989
Community Land Management Act 1989
Strata Management Legislation Amendment Act 2008

CHINA

Organisational Law of Urban Residents' Committees 1989
Regulations on Real Property Management 2003, amended 2007
Property Rights Law of the People's Republic of China 2007

HONG KONG

Multi-Storey Buildings (Owners Incorporation) Act 1970
Building Management Ordinance 1993
Building Management (Amendment) Ordinance 2007

IRELAND

Planning and Development Act 2000

ISRAEL

Note: Official (but legally non-binding) English translations of Israeli laws are available but only of legislation enacted up until the early 1980s. Later legislation and subsequent amendments to the earlier legislation have not been officially translated.

Planning and Building Law 1965
Real Property Law 1969
Common Condominium Regulations annexed to the Real Property Law 1969 *(no English translation available)*
Law of Sale (Apartments) 1973

NEW ZEALAND

Incorporated Societies Act 1908
Land Transfer Act 1952
Charitable Trusts Act 1957
Trustee Companies Management Act 1967
Companies Act 1969
Unit Titles Act 1972
Fair Trading Act 1986
Resource Management Act 1991
Companies Act 1993
Privacy Act 1993
Public Trust Act 2001

SINGAPORE

Land Acquisition Act 1985
Planning Act 1998
Land Titles (Strata) Act 1999
Building Maintenance and Strata Management Act 2008

UNITED KINGDOM

Town and Country Planning Act 1947
Housing Act 1980

England and Wales

Law of Property Act 1925

Rentcharges Act 1977
Landlord and Tenant Act 1985
Landlord and Tenant Act 1987
Leasehold Reform, Housing and Urban Development Act 1993
Housing Act 1996
Commonhold and Leasehold Reform Act 2002

Scotland

Town and Country Planning (General Permitted Development) (Scotland) Order 1992
Abolition of Feudal Tenure etc. (Scotland) Act 2000
Title Conditions (Scotland) Act 2003
Tenements (Scotland) Act 2004
Housing (Scotland) Act 2006

USA

Uniform Condominium Act 1977, amended in 1980
Condominium and Cooperative Conversion Protection and Abuse Relief Act 1980
Uniform Common Interest Ownership Act 1982

Arizona

2003–04: House Bills HB 2177; HB 2379; HB 2380; HB 2381; HB 2402; HB 2478; HB 2492. Senate Bills SB 1125; SB 1137
2007–08: HB 2440

California

Davis-Stirling Common Interest Development Act 1985
2002–03: Assembly Bills AB 512; AB 1836; AB 2376; SB 1682 (fused with a companion Bill) AB 2598; AB 567; AB 1921

Florida

Condominium Statute 2008
2004: Senate Bills SB 1184; SB 2984
2007: House Bill HB 995

Acknowledgements

Rachelle Alterman thanks her colleague, Dr Danny Ben Shahar, with whom she collaborated on some of the economic aspects referenced in her chapter, and the many people interviewed for this research in Israel and Florida. Special thanks are due to The Continental Group Inc., its CEO, Mr Tom Roses (at the time the president of the property management division), and his staff who were very generous with their time. She also commends Mr Ilan Leibowitch who was a Member of the Knesset in 2005 and cooperated on a draft legislative amendment that did not proceed.

Sarah Blandy's research was funded by the Office of the Deputy Prime Minister's New Horizons Research Programme (*Gated Communities in England*, with Rowland Atkinson, John Flint and Diane Lister, 2002–2003); and by two grants from the British Academy (SG3925 *Tenure and Rights in a Gated Community* 2001–2002, and SG45089 *The Role of Legality in Multi-occupied Residential Settings* 2007–2008). She would also like to thank all those who gave up their time to be interviewed, and the Land Registry for providing information about commonhold registrations.

Jennifer Dixon, Marjorie van Roon and Ann Dupuis would like to thank the New Zealand Foundation for Science Research and Technology for financial support of the Learning Sustainability and Low Impact Urban Design and Development research programmes.

Douglas Robertson's comparative research was funded by the Joseph Rowntree Foundation. He would also like to acknowledge the help, assistance and enthusiasm of Scott Wortley, School of Law, University of Edinburgh in keeping him right on legal concepts and terminology used in Scots property law.

Ngai Ming Yip acknowledges the financial support of the Research Grant Council of Hong Kong (CERG project CityU 1264/04H).

Chapter 1
Introduction

Ann Dupuis, Sarah Blandy and Jennifer Dixon

Origins and Rationale

This book is an international, interdisciplinary, edited collection that explores the issues of private governance and management of multi-owned housing developments. In particular, it addresses the relationship between law and power and how this is expressed in practice. In bringing together contributions from a range of countries and contributors, new and critical insights are raised for housing researchers and practitioners engaged in the fields of sociology, planning, law, urban and housing policy, property and environment management.

In recent years multi-owned housing developments (which include high- and low-rise apartment blocks, mixed commercial and housing sites, as well as collectively-managed individual dwellings in planned communities), have become increasingly common in many areas of the world. The topic is timely, given that multi-owned developments are largely an urban trend and that in 2007, for the first time, the global urban population exceeded the population living in the countryside (United Nations Population Fund 2007). Although continuing urban growth is forecast to be particularly rapid in less developed regions, nonetheless in Europe and Northern America the percentage of the population living in urban areas is estimated to reach 80 per cent and 87 per cent respectively by 2030. This rate of growth almost certainly means increasing political pressures to promote more intensive and sustainable forms of urban development, leading to higher density housing and to a greater proportion of residential development in the form of flats and apartments. This type of housing is attractive to government at national and local levels because it is seen to reduce urban sprawl and to enable inner city regeneration. Owners and residents are also becoming educated to appreciate the advantages of multi-occupied housing which, in many cases, promise them access to a better location and more extensive facilities than would be available in more traditional urban forms. Hence, demand is also growing.

Multi-owned residential housing is, however, more (and more complicated) than a collection of individually owned homes. In this type of development the individual dwelling, often referred to as a 'unit' or 'lot', might consist of an apartment, flat, or house. As well as purchasing a dwelling, each owner also acquires certain rights over the common property and facilities, which can include grounds, internal roads and parking, leisure and retail facilities, even schools and places of worship. Individual rights over the common property can amount to full ownership of an undivided share, or merely a right of access. The advantages of sharing the cost and responsibility for maintenance, security and the common property are offset by the inherent difficulties in this collective arrangement. In practical terms, who will manage the common property? In legal terms, who will own it and what rights will others have to it? In terms of urban development, does the local state have the power and capacity to regulate this type of housing at the outset and/or to intervene if subsequent problems arise from the breakdown of collective responsibility? From a sociological perspective, critical questions are raised concerning the impact of legal entities on the quality of the day-to-day lived experiences of owners and residents.

This book addresses these and other issues from an international and interdisciplinary approach. An international perspective is needed to draw out the essential themes and emerging issues in the relationship between law, power and practice in the context of multi-owned developments. The challenges of balancing the competing demands of development, management and regulation of this kind of housing are common to all countries, although the contexts (legal, social or cultural, political and institutional) vary widely. An interdisciplinary approach is needed as the multi-faceted issues raised by these sites are addressed in practice by urban and housing policy-makers, legislators and the courts, planning officers, and property lawyers, as well as by those more closely involved: the developers, professional managing agents, and owners. The book reflects the fact that multi-occupied housing has provoked academic discussion from a variety of disciplines, notably law, planning, sociology, economics and the environmental and political sciences.

The rationale for this collected volume, therefore, is to provide a sound conceptual basis through which the complex issues of governance and management of multi-owned housing can be examined across different jurisdictions. Drawing on notions of power, law and practice, it reveals the complexities of developing, living in, and governing this form of housing. The inspiration for this book was the 2005 Gated Communities Conference in Pretoria, South Africa, *Territory, Control and Enclosure*, where the editors presented a conference paper which drew on our respective analyses of multi-owned residential developments in England and New Zealand (Blandy, Dixon and Dupuis 2005). The conference paper was developed into a journal article for *Urban Studies*, 'Theorising power relationships in multi-owned residential developments: Unpacking the bundle of rights' (Blandy, Dixon and Dupuis 2006).

Our research at that point identified the key actors involved in multi-owned housing as the developer, the professional managing agent (also known as corporate manager, management company, etc.) and the owners – as both purchasers of individual dwellings and as owners of rights in the development's collective property. We also developed a theoretical framework to explain the similar empirical findings in both England and New Zealand: that residents in multi-owned developments were experiencing frustration and dissatisfaction. It was initially surprising when residents told us in interviews that they felt powerless, and that the developer or managing agent exercised significant control over the site, over financial concerns such as levies and even over behaviours and activities residents could and could not engage in. Our respective academic backgrounds in law, planning and sociology led us to develop an interdisciplinary approach to understanding how apparently neutral legal frameworks can disguise a real imbalance of power, usually at the expense of the residents, in different jurisdictions.

Conceptual Analysis

We drew on the idea, widely accepted in common law jurisprudence, that property rights may be seen as 'a bundle of powers, capable of being mentally contemplated apart from one another and capable of being separately enjoyed' (Maine 1881: 158). This analysis is helpful in understanding how rights 'work' in the context of multi-owned housing, as it allows for more than one owner of rights in the same property and for differentiated rights to be the subject of separate contracts between two or more of the interested parties. Our theoretical approach is to analyse which rights are transferred between key actors through the life-course of a multi-owned development, and at what points. This makes transparent the exercise of power and helps to explain why certain actors benefit from these transfers and why others are left disadvantaged.

Making use of sociological insights into the nature of power and how it may be used by different parties in the life cycle of a multi-owned development, we developed the concept of 'critical legal events'. These are the points at which particular rights – of ownership, development, occupation and management, for example – are transferred or allocated to one or more of the parties involved in the site. These critical legal events typically include initial purchase of the site; the establishment by the developer and their advisors of the legal entity established to govern and manage the common property; the transfer of individual dwellings to new purchasers; and the on-going management and operation of the site, usually (but not always) by managing agents on contract to the residents as a collective legal entity. These legal entities, known as bodies corporate, home owners associations, common interest developments, residents associations, and so on in their particular jurisdictions, are crucial in framing the day-to-day management and maintenance of commonly-owned property.

The analytical framework that has been the driver for this book is underpinned by a particular understanding of the law (for further details, see Blandy, Dixon and Dupuis 2006). Rather than accepting the law as a neutral framework, we adopted Bourdieu's (1987) concept of the juridical field. The actors who are able to control this field, through access to lawyers and to influential politicians, can make sure the law is used to their advantage. This approach has much in common with Foucauldian discourse analysis, which holds that knowledge is power, and that knowledge is discursively produced through language (Foucault 1980). Power can be exercised by actors with access to 'legal practice and legal language [which] are structured in such a way as to prevent the acquisition of such knowledge by any other than a highly trained elite of specialists' (Goodrich 1987: 7), and this is particularly relevant to multi-owned housing, as most purchasers are unable to understand the highly complex legal frameworks which are often couched in extremely technical language.

International and Interdisciplinary Approach in Context

The contributors to this book are each recognized scholars in their own disciplines, which include environmental science, law, management and tourism studies, planning, political science, sociology, housing and urban studies. Their chapters provide analysis drawn from research in Australia, China, England, Hong Kong, Israel, New Zealand, Scotland, Singapore and the US. Each of the chapter authors has responded in a different way to the challenges posed by multi-owned residential developments, partly due to the range of disciplinary backgrounds represented here. However, the main reason is that each chapter reflects the authors' research into the most pressing real-life issues which arise from this type of housing in their respective jurisdictions. Starting with a common analytical framework designed to tease out relationships of power between the key actors has therefore produced a rich and varied collection of material reflecting the best of current research and analysis on this topic.

Each chapter author provides contextual information about multi-owned housing developments in their particular jurisdiction, before addressing more specific issues. A wide range of dwelling types is presented in the chapters, including: single family houses; low-rise/walk up apartments; high-rise towers; and large planned and gated communities. A similarly wide range of uses is discussed; from the purely residential, to mixed uses with commercial and retail premises and tourist accommodation. In the same vein, the extent of the typical 'common property' also varies widely, from merely a shared external shell of the building to something far more extensive; as do the types of facility or services provided for owners, from basic ground maintenance to very luxurious leisure and other facilities. We also asked contributors to consider, where relevant, the attitude of the planning authorities to multi-owned developments. In some areas, notably in the US, collective management of residential areas is welcomed by municipalities because it increases local taxes while reducing demand for publicly funded services (McKenzie 1998). Our own research initially focused on owners (Blandy, Dixon and Dupuis 2006) but we also recognize that planners have a potentially important role to play as key actors in the development phase of these sites (Blandy, Dixon, Dupuis and Parsons 2006).

Legal Considerations

Each of the countries considered in these chapters has a different history in terms of its law relating to multi-owned housing developments, but all are common law jurisdictions. The problems raised by multi-owned housing are, of course, by no means confined to common law countries and solutions based in common law have now been adopted by countries with a different legal tradition (for example, homeowner associations are now established in many post-Soviet countries: Tsenkova and Lowe 2003). However, we sought contributions from scholars researching these issues in common law countries to avoid language difficulties and to ensure a shared starting point in the property law regime of England and Wales. The exception here is the chapter dealing with Scotland; in fact the recently reformed Scots property law framework was unique, being based on feudal relationships rather than on a civil law regime (in which ownership is absolute rather than a 'bundle of rights').

As Clarke has observed, the 'problem of finding an acceptable device to regulate relationships in communal-living situations is one that has had to be faced by all common law jurisdictions … In most cases the devices are found wanting and inadequate, leading to reform and statutory solutions being introduced or proposed' (1998: 385). These common law devices include leasehold, still very much in use in England and Wales; tenancies in common, the basis on which high-rise buildings in Hong Kong are owned; and co-ownership in common, historically used in New Zealand from when large plots were first sub-divided. Although statutory solutions have a shorter history, the first Australian strata title legislation was passed in New South Wales as long ago as 1961 and condominium legislation had been adopted by all the US states by 1967. The selected jurisdictions here illustrate differing approaches to legal frameworks for multi-occupied sites. In England and the US, their development has been enabled by using diverse property law models, while Australia has taken a legislative approach in establishing a statutory framework for strata titles, and this has been followed in other jurisdictions including Singapore.

In contrast, each chapter in this volume also addresses the country-specific contexts in which the law is operating and looks specifically at practice 'on the ground'. These contextual details make it possible to combine analysis at the state level, at the 'intermediary level of legal implementation and enforcement, and at the micro-level of citizenry' (Banakar 2009: 81), so that richer comparisons can be made between the various legal approaches adopted to address these issues. This volume therefore goes beyond a comparative legal text as it combines critical perspectives from sociology, urban planning and other disciplines with research into current practice at every level.

Unravelling the Complexities of Private Urban Governance

Each chapter provides fresh insights and sheds light on issues which are also addressed elsewhere in the collection, to build up a full picture of law, power and practice relating to multi-owned housing developments in common law countries across the world. Sarah Blandy's chapter is concerned with multi-owned residential developments, a rapidly growing housing sector in England and Wales. Here, leasehold remains the predominant and remarkably versatile legal framework, although statutory alternatives are now available. Blandy shows how developers retain their powerful position as initial freeholder of the site, setting up the legal framework which best suits their interests, and discusses the impact which this has on the experience of residents. Douglas Robertson's chapter on Scotland examines the recent major reforms to what was Europe's last feudal property system, which affect the owners of multi-owned private flatted property representing some 30 per cent of all Scottish home occupiers. However, developers still retain the choice of which legal framework to adopt. Robertson argues that throughout the reform process the interests of developers and managers have been allowed to take precedence over those of the residents.

Evan McKenzie's chapter explores the crucial issue of whether private contract law is adequate for resolving disputes between owners and powerful residents' associations which undertake quasi-judicial, public functions. McKenzie lays out the US legal framework for common interest housing, examines emerging regulatory trends in three states: Arizona, California and Florida and offers an assessment of the political power dynamics that drive the competing law reform agendas. Given that common interest housing is such a large share of the new housing stock in the US, the stakes riding on these reforms are enormous. Based on her own research into condominium towers (high-rise residential buildings), Rachelle Alterman's chapter compares two types of condominium law: 'simple', as represented by the law in Israel; and 'enhanced', as in the US state of Florida. This increasingly popular type of building involves particularly high costs, increasing over time, and higher probabilities for free-riding by some residents. Alterman considers whether either type of law can be effective in ensuring adequate long-term financing for maintenance, in different economic and social contexts. This chapter highlights the role of local planning authorities in Israel, which are attempting to compensate for lack of regulation by requiring that developers should contract with a property management company.

Alice Christudason, Ngai Ming Yip and Feng Wang discuss multi-owned residential developments in Asia: Singapore, Hong Kong and China respectively. In Singapore and Hong Kong there is a similar shortage of land and consequent state encouragement of high density housing. Christudason's chapter focuses on conflicts between minority residential owners and majority commercial owners over decisions to sell mixed-use buildings, in the context of urban regeneration. Her case study indicates that the current legal framework offers little legal protection for minority owners, and the chapter assesses recent reforms in light of this imbalance of power. Ngai Ming Yip suggests that problems with the management and governance of multi-unit residential developments are especially severe in Hong Kong, where there is an inadequate legal infrastructure for multiple ownership. Yip argues that in areas like Hong Kong, where civic society is still relatively underdeveloped, it is more difficult for communal governance to take root. A highly concentrated power structure, and the bias of the state towards economic development (and hence towards developers), can marginalize small owners in multi-ownership properties. Feng Wang's chapter discusses the very topical issues arising from the development of new residential neighbourhoods in China, a phenomenon occurring over the last decade. This chapter sets out the regulatory environment for the management of newly developed neighbourhoods and analyses the imbalance of power relationships among developers, property management firms, residents' committees and homeowner associations. Wang's research sheds light on the operation of law in a fast-changing environment in which owners find themselves outmanouevred by developers and the newly established property management firms.

The next three chapters discuss a variety of issues in multi-owned housing in Australia. Michael Bounds discusses legal arrangements associated with property ownership in multi-owned developments in Sydney, New South Wales. In assessing the implications of these arrangements for residential satisfaction, Bounds argues that satisfaction can be high for residents in multi-owned housing. This position is contrary to the views of many critics of medium-density development still evident in Australia, which Bounds suggests derive from a variety of continuing anti-urbanist sentiments. His research indicates that home type and the characteristics of a neighbourhood's residents are much more important factors in residential satisfaction than housing density. However, the key issue is one of control, which distinguishes multi-owned housing from individual home ownership; the case studies illustrate how owners are disadvantaged in dealing with developers. The implications of recent reforms are also considered.

Cathy Sherry's chapter highlights the ability of developers in New South Wales to cause bodies corporate (the collective legal entity to which owners must belong) to enter into long-term contracts in the early stages of the development, when the developer as owner of all or most of the units controls the body corporate. The chapter outlines a recent Australian case on the sale of long-term management rights by a developer, to illustrate the successes and failings of both specific legislation dealing with multi-owned housing and the use of more general principles of common law to achieve a just result for the owners. The chapter also compares developer abuses through long-term management contracts and leases, in the United States in the 1960s and 1970s and in contemporary New South Wales, to demonstrate that developer practices across time and jurisdictions are uncannily consistent. Kelly Cassidy, Chris Guilding and Jan Warnken examine the phenomenon of multi-titled tourism accommodation in Australia and, like Sherry, focus on the sale of management rights in this type of development. Their chapter also outlines challenges arising in the sector, with particular importance attached to power issues between the stakeholders in multi-titled tourism accommodation and the attempts through detailed legislation to address these issues.

Ann Dupuis and Jennifer Dixon identify a number of new forms of entities being created by New Zealand developers in place of strata title. There is a lack of a robust regulatory framework so that effectively practice is ahead of law. This chapter reports on current research into the emergence of these new entities and identifies some critical issues in respect of owners' rights and likely long-term prospects for good governance. Following on from this Jennifer Dixon and Marjorie van Roon's contribution examines models of the private governance of sustainable design features in multi-owned residential housing developments in New Zealand. The chapter explores issues of public and private rights and responsibilities and considers whether contractual arrangements that are created both to implement local government requirements and enable owners to manage these features require more active oversight by regulators and policy-makers.

Themes and Issues

Themes and issues traversed in the book can be loosely grouped around the critical events discussed above. The first theme focuses on the power of developers and their legal advisors in shaping long-term governance. Some jurisdictions now attempt to control very strictly the type of legal framework which must be adopted for multi-owned housing developments. However, even here there is evidence that through their superior access to the 'juridical field' developers can make use of these rules to their own advantage. Across a number of other jurisdictions which still permit some degree of freedom in designing legal frameworks, developers are now creating new forms of entities using legislation which was not specifically designed for the purpose of governing and maintaining multi-owned developments, and therefore lacks the built-in protections found in 'fit-for-purpose' legislation. In New Zealand, for example, there is no government agency charged with oversight of these 'proto-institutions', as we have termed them to reflect their emerging status, and no central database to provide information on how many of these entities have been created. In yet another group of jurisdictions, the existing common law legal frameworks have always permitted considerable flexibility in drafting, and developers continue to make the most of these opportunities.

As many of the chapters in our text demonstrate, the power of the developer is widely perceived to be problematic in a number of countries. In particular, this power can extend to embedding lengthy contracts for managing agents which new owners find difficult to change, depending on the rules governing their voting rights. There are some signals that this power is being constrained, but developers in effect have a 'long reach' in the shape of the entity they create, in that the rules and regulations embedded in the legal entities governing multi-unit housing can last long after the developer's involvement is over. In addition, there is usually no oversight from regulatory bodies in terms of providing checks and balances for the owners-to-be. This is somewhat ironic, given the controls on the physical design and development of buildings typically exercised by local government in issuing building and planning consents.

A second theme highlights the marginalized status of owners and residents. As noted above, the first generation of owners are not consulted in the creation of the legal entity which governs their development. Two key issues arise as a consequence. First, purchasers with no previous experience of legal entities are often poorly informed and have little awareness that they are taking on a new set of ownership responsibilities. Legislation has often been murky about the new roles and responsibilities that owners and residents are entering into, although more recent initiatives in some countries are providing important clarification in this regard with increasing emphasis in new legislation on the need to educate purchasers and new owners. Second, the lack of knowledge at the outset often puts owners and residents in a weak position on a day-to-day basis. In some countries it is clear that managing agents, simply by virtue of their expertise, are more informed about operational and legal matters. This places managing agents in positions of considerable strength in relation to how they deal with owners' committees whose members are inexperienced in dealing with the intricacies of law and its application to their entity. In other jurisdictions, notably in the US, it is the position of owners in relation to homeowners' associations that is particularly problematic. These associations have wide-reaching powers, including that of foreclosure, placing ill-informed and inexperienced owners at a great disadvantage in their dealings with them. A different imbalance of power which has not previously received much attention is highlighted in the chapters dealing with Singapore, Hong Kong and Queensland: the conflict between groups of residents, rather than between owners and the developer, property managing agent, or corporate entity.

A third theme relates to the broader context within which multi-owned housing sits. While matters of physical location and urban design are typically determined by local government statutory plans, public or private agencies pay little attention to the social aspects of these developments and the formation of new communities. Often the rhetoric of plans and glossy promises of a carefree urban future are not realized in practice, with long gaps before the necessary social and physical infrastructure in the wider neighbourhood is implemented to make these places work well for residents. Complexities of daily living for owners and tenants in relation to the management of their development can be exacerbated by these wider issues of urban development that constrain liveability for residents, and over which they have little control.

A fourth theme relates to the way in which maintenance of multi-owned residential developments is assessed, and paid for by owners, and whether this is regulated or monitored in any way. In some countries, local authorities may require developers to contract with a management company, but this is by no means universal, and may introduce further problems in terms of the relationship of power between residents and management company, as discussed above. Issues of equity for successive generations of owners in relation to funding long-term developments can be fraught. Related to this theme is a concern about the lack of oversight of the contractual agreements set in place once entities are created. Therefore much rests on the expertise and knowledge of local governments, professional advisors and developers in the creation of a suite of arrangements to manage developments over the long term. Of critical importance is the role of local government in evaluating proposed developments and ensuring that appropriate conditions and mechanisms are put in place to address management and maintenance issues that fall within the local government mandate. This issue demands not only careful prior scrutiny of proposed developments, but long-term monitoring to ensure that conditions are being adhered to and appropriate modifications are being made where necessary. If arrangements for the private, collective maintenance of multi-owned developments fail, this has serious consequences for the whole locality, not just for the resident owners.

An emerging aspect of this theme centres on the inclusion and arrangements for the management of sustainable design features, such as areas of retained indigenous forests or wetlands, rain gardens and swales, in multi-owned sites. Inclusion of such features is seen as a means of enhancing local sustainability while reducing environmental and infrastructure costs for local governments and communities. A potentially significant shift in responsibilities and funding from government to the private sector is taking place. However, some critical issues are emerging in respect of their day-to-day management, particularly in relation to maintenance, liability and performance, and longer-term prospects as a means of improving sustainability of the local environment.

Concluding Comment

Our intent for this book has been to provide interdisciplinary, international and illuminating perspectives on the complex interrelationships of power, law and practice in relation to the governance of multi-owned residential developments. The contribution of scholars from a range of disciplines and a variety of countries enhances the core argument of the book. The framework of the critical events in the life cycle of the development process provides a coherence to this text. Despite the differences in context and jurisdictions, what is striking about the content of the chapters in this volume is the commonality of experiences across countries. The embedded power of the developer strongly contrasts with that of owners and residents. The legal mechanisms pertaining to multi-owned housing developments, rather than being neutral instruments, can operate in ways that inhibit the opportunities for positive future change. The role of the state in regulating the governance of multi-owned developments is highlighted through the very different approaches taken in the countries which have been researched by the contributors to this book. Practice, the day-to-day interactions of the key actors, exemplifies the conflicts and contradictions inherent in the various instruments that impinge on the private governance of multi-owned residential developments. The chapters that follow shed further light on these concerns.

References

Banakar, R. 2009. Power, culture and method in comparative law. *International Journal of Law in Context*, 5(1), 69–85.

Blandy, S., Dixon, J. and Dupuis, A. 2005. *Unravelling a Bundle of Rights: Pitfalls and Prospects in Multi-owned Housing*. Paper to the international conference Territory, Control and Enclosure: The Ecology of Urban Fragmentation, Pretoria, South Africa, 28 February–3 March, 2005.

Blandy, S., Dixon, J. and Dupuis, A. 2006. Theorising power relationships in multi-owned residential developments: Unpacking the bundle of rights. *Urban Studies*, 43(13), 2365–83.

Blandy, S., Dixon, J., Dupuis, A. and Parsons, D. 2006. The rise of private residential neighbourhoods in Britain and New Zealand, in *Private Neighbourhoods: Global and Local Perspectives*, edited by G. Glasze, C. Webster and K. Frantz. London: Routledge, 190–205.

Bourdieu, P. 1987. The force of law: Toward a sociology of the juridical field. *The Hastings Law Journal*, 38(5), 814–53.

Clarke, D. 1998. Occupying 'cheek by jowl': Property issues arising from communal living, in *Land Law: Themes and Perspectives*, edited by S. Bright and J. Dewar. Oxford: Oxford University Press, 377–405.

Foucault, M. 1980. *Power/Knowledge*. Brighton: Harvester Press.

Goodrich, P. 1987. *Legal Discourse: Studies in Linguistics, Rhetoric and Legal Analysis*. London: Macmillan.

Maine, H.S. 1881. *Village-communities in the East and West: Six Lectures Delivered at Oxford.* London: John Murray.

McKenzie, E. 1998. Homeowner associations and California politics: An exploratory analysis. *Urban Affairs Review*, 34(1), 52–74.

Tsenkova, S. and Lowe, S. (eds). 2003. *Housing Change in Central and Eastern Europe.* Aldershot: Ashgate.

United Nations Population Fund. 2007. *State of World Population 2007: Unleashing the Potential of Urban Growth.* New York: United Nations Population Fund.

Chapter 2
Legal Frameworks for Multi-owned Housing in England and Wales: Owners' Experiences

Sarah Blandy

Introduction

This chapter is concerned with multi-owned residential developments in England and Wales (for Scotland, see Robertson, Chapter 3). First, the context in terms of trends in the numbers and types of multi-owned residential developments is set out. Critical legal events in the life-course of these sites are then identified, following the approach of Blandy, Dixon and Dupuis (2006). This analytical approach alerts us to *when* rights are first acquired, by *whom*, and *which* rights are then subsequently transferred, helping to make transparent the power relations between the key actors: local planning authorities, developers, managing agents, and homeowners. The first three critical legal events: obtaining planning permission, acquisition by the developer of freehold ownership of the site, and the management rights contract between the developer and managing agent, are not strictly sequential and often overlap. The purchase of individual dwellings, obviously the most important event so far as the owners are concerned, is merely the fourth critical legal event and occurs at a point when power relations between the developer and managing agent have been firmly established by the previous critical legal events. Further critical legal events may include subsequent transfers of the freehold title to the site, and transfers of management rights. The pattern varies for each development, according to its unique legal framework.

The chapter explores the wide range of legal frameworks which are available for these developments in England and Wales, and owners' experiences of them. The most common frameworks are variants of rentcharge and leasehold, both derived from common law; commonhold is now available as a statutory alternative. Development companies (usually referred to here as 'developers') are in a very strong position as initial freeholders, able to determine the legal framework and thus control subsequent critical legal events, with a few exceptions where legislation enables residents to acquire rights against the freeholder's wishes. The choice of legal framework depends on how the developer hopes to make a profit out of the site: as a long-term investment or from quick sales to individual owners (Clarke 2006). The 'Type 1' framework is used where the developer retains ownership and control of the site, deriving profit from charging the individual owners for providing management services. In a 'Type 2' legal framework the developer will transfer the freehold on completion and sale of all the dwellings in the development to another party, often for a nominal sum. The developer's focus here is on profiting from sales of the new dwellings to individual owners. An early sale of the whole site (the fifth critical legal event) enables the developer to avoid difficult confrontations over problems of poor workmanship and the like, which may emerge after the individual dwellings have been purchased at the fourth critical legal event.

Once a legal trajectory has been set in motion by the initial critical legal event, it is difficult to change its direction in favour of a different party. The link between critical legal events and power relations between the key actors has been highlighted in three separate studies with which the author was involved. In 2001 the first purchasers in a new, multi-owned, gated development were surveyed as they moved in, and a few months later follow-up interviews were carried out with eight households (see Blandy and Lister 2005). The relevant legal documents were analysed, and the developer and planning officers were interviewed (see Blandy and Parsons 2003). Material from this study will be identified in this chapter as 'GC 2001–02'. In 2002–03 a national survey of planning authorities was undertaken to determine the extent of gated communities in England (see Atkinson, Flint, Blandy, and Lister 2003). As part of this study, legal documents were analysed, and interviews carried out with lawyers for four leading development companies, and with 12 residents from four case study areas. Material from this study will be identified in this chapter as 'NS 2002–03'. More recent research, so far unpublished, includes interviews with over 40 residents in eight sites with differing legal frameworks and analysis of their legal documents. Material from this study of multi-owned residential developments will be identified in this chapter as 'M-ORD 2007–08'.

The experience of residents in multi-owned developments is crucially important in understanding the relations of power between the key actors. Excerpts from interviews and other data from the three studies are used to illustrate how residents are affected by the developer's initial choice of legal framework and by longstanding relationships between developers and managing agents. The position is also considered whereby residents collectively acquire legal control of the site, either because that arrangement suited the developer, or because the residents exercised a statutory right to do so. The chapter concludes by examining recent developments which may improve the position of homeowners in multi-owned residential developments.

Multi-owned Housing in England and Wales: An Overview

It is not possible to assemble a full picture of the number and types of multi-owned developments in England and Wales from the official data available. However, it is clear that fewer 'traditional English' detached houses are being built, in a period when home ownership in England has rapidly increased from just over half of the housing stock in 1971, to just over 70 per cent in 2006 (Communities and Local Government 2009a). By 2007/08 the percentage of flats (apartments) built had increased to 45 per cent of all dwellings, compared with 1991/92 when 79 per cent of new dwellings were houses and only 21 per cent flats (Communities and Local Government 2009b). Residential density has also increased, from an average of 25 dwellings per hectare between 1996 and 2002, to 41 dwellings per hectare in 2006 (Communities and Local Government 2008). The recent growth in gated communities, found by the national survey in 2002 to number at least one thousand in England (Atkinson et al. 2003), has also contributed to the increase in multi-owned developments, whether comprising flats or houses.

Data on tenure provide some indication of the extent of multi-owned residential developments in England and Wales. Freehold and leasehold are the only tenures available: Law of Property Act 1925. Freehold is the closest to absolute ownership, whereas leasehold interests are created by the freeholder and are always time-limited, even though some leases extend for 999 years or more.[1] When the period of a long lease comes to an end, the land reverts to the freeholder. In effect, a leasehold owner is buying the right to use the freeholder's land for a defined period of time, in exchange for payment of a (usually very small) annual rent, known as ground rent. Leasehold therefore encompasses both a property right and a contract. In 2006/07, 89 per cent of home owners in England owned a freehold house; 4 per cent a leasehold house; and 7 per cent owned a leasehold flat (Communities and Local Government 2009a). Almost all of these one million leasehold flats are found in horizontally divided, multi-owned residential developments; English property law cannot cope with 'flying freeholds', where the property is not attached to the ground. Houses in multi-owned residential developments may be freehold or leasehold, so it cannot be concluded that leasehold tenure for houses necessarily means they are located in a multi-owned development.

In these sites the obligation to pay for maintenance of common property is usually shared between the owners of the individual dwellings, imposed and enforced through inserting a covenant (a legal promise) into the freehold property title of each dwelling, or into the terms of its lease. There are two types of covenant: positive, which *require* specific action, for example to contribute to the maintenance of common parts and facilities; and negative covenants which *prevent* specific actions, for example building an extension to a house. The important distinction between the two types of covenant in England and Wales is that negative covenants are said to 'run with the land', meaning that they are enforceable against both freehold and leasehold owners, whether the original owner who entered into the covenant or a successor in title. However, in relation to freehold land, a positive covenant only binds the person who entered into it. When that property is sold or is inherited, the covenant is not enforceable against the new freehold owner. In the words of Gray and Gray (2009: 246), this is one 'of the scarcely credible features of the modern law of freehold covenants' which has been reluctantly re-confirmed in recent case law.[2]

1 In this chapter 'leasehold' is used to mean long leasehold of 21 years or more rather than shorter periods, which are usually referred to as 'tenancies'.

2 *Rhone v Stephens* [1994] 2 AC 310.

In contrast, leasehold tenure enables enforcement of positive covenants against both current and successive leasehold owners: *Tulk v Moxhay.*[3] Rights and obligations are created through the leasehold contract, which typically sets out which party will be responsible for maintenance and insurance of the land and any buildings on it, and how this will be paid for. This explains the predominance of leasehold for multi-owned developments in England and Wales, in contrast to the US, for example, where under common law homeowners' associations can enforce both negative and positive covenants against freehold owners of individual houses and apartments (see McKenzie, Chapter 3).

As a final point, co-ownership in England and Wales is restricted to no more than four co-owners by the Law of Property Act 1925, so frequently whole sites are owned by a corporate legal entity in the form of a residents' management company. In many other common law jurisdictions there is no limit on the number of individuals who may co-own property, making it simple in legal terms to set up multi-owned residential developments (see Yip, Chapter 7; Alterman, Chapter 5, for example).

Legal Frameworks and Key Actors

There is no statutory requirement in England and Wales that any particular legal framework must be adopted for multi-owned developments. Examination of legal documents from a range of these developments, undertaken by the author in the three studies outlined earlier, indicates a wide variation in legal frameworks. Property rights are distributed between key actors in different permutations at different points in the life-course of each development. English property law does not include the concept of absolute ownership, so the 'bundle of rights' is capable of being divided in different ways. Rights of ownership may be separated from the right to manage; more than one person can own rights in land simultaneously; and the length of time over which any right may be exercised can be determined into the future. Company law and contract law may be used in addition to property law to achieve the best solution. This flexibility makes the ability to manipulate the legal framework in one's own interests a decisive tool. It is important to look behind the formal legal relationships to investigate which party controls the decision over which legal framework to adopt, and to examine the implications of this decision for future relations between the parties. Attention now turns to the key actors in multi-owned developments.

Planning Authorities

There is no evidence that local planning authorities in England and Wales actively encourage multi-owned housing developments for fiscal reasons (unlike

3 (1848) 2 Ph 774.

the position in the US; see McKenzie, Chapter 4), but these sites fit neatly into current planning policies encouraging higher density and avoidance of suburban sprawl (Communities and Local Government 2006). When deciding on planning permission applications from developers, local planning authorities must take into account guidance from central government that favours developments which make more efficient use of land, preferably between 30 and 50 dwellings per hectare (Communities and Local Government 2006). Thus multi-owned developments, whether city centre apartment blocks built on derelict land, or redevelopment of an existing building, usually find favour with planners – particularly if they are prestigious 'landmark' developments which will enhance the municipal profile. In 2006, 75 per cent of new or converted dwellings were estimated to have been built on previously developed land (Communities and Local Government 2008a). These denser developments represent a higher profit for the developer from the same land area, and are also popular with purchasers seeking convenience, onsite facilities and security.

Nonetheless, planning authorities sometimes prove awkward over issues of design or require that the development include some low-cost housing. Large development companies can afford the services of expert planning lawyers, which means that they are often able to out-manoeuvre planning officers in the important early negotiation stage of obtaining planning permission, ensuring that no onerous planning conditions are imposed (see Blandy and Parsons 2003). Further, local planning authorities rarely consider arrangements for the ongoing management and maintenance of multi-owned developments, or whether the legal framework will be effective in ensuring their sustainability (see also Alterman, Chapter 5; Dixon and van Roon, Chapter 13). Changes of freehold ownership of such developments are typically built into the legal framework, and may occur frequently, as discussed in the next section. Therefore any developer with whom the planning authority negotiates planning consent and conditions can soon be out of the picture, but a survey showed that this possibility did not concern the vast majority of planners (NS 2002–03).

Developers

Once successfully through the critical legal events of obtaining planning consent and acquiring freehold land, the developer can choose which legal framework to adopt. Many of the largest housebuilding companies have their own legal departments to draft the appropriate legal documents for their multi-owned developments; others buy in the services of leading legal firms or use the legal services offered by professional property managing agents (NS 2002–03).

Reputable builders and developers are keen to create successful developments which will provide attractive examples when marketing new developments to potential purchasers. Professional property managing agents are contracted for the management and maintenance of these developments. The relationship between developer and agent is therefore extremely important, often longstanding and embedded in business practices which pre-date the management arrangements for a particular development, and enshrined in legal forms (NS 2002–03). Contract law governs the transfer of the right to manage from the developer to a tried and trusted managing agent, and it is also common to discover from company law analysis that these two key actors are linked in a complex web of subsidiary companies (see also Yip, Chapter 7).

Professional Property Managing Agents

In addition to providing property management services, some of the larger property managing agents also offer legal services to developers, as already mentioned. These services usually comprise the drafting of all legal documentation, and providing company secretarial services and directorships (NS 2002–03). The agent is therefore able to control the way in which the management of a development is set up and to ensure that they remain involved. Depending on which legal framework is adopted, the agent might be contracted to provide management services for the freeholder, for a residents' management company, or might later even acquire the freehold of the development. Given these influential roles, it is instructive to consider the views of agents about residents' involvement in management. One in-house lawyer for a managing agent said that they encourage the formation of residents' associations and that 'democracy is alive and well'. In contrast, another reported that his organisation did not favour:

> resident management companies – they have a habit of being hijacked by a small committed group. Most of our residents are not bothered about day to day management, anyway. There are some particular individuals [who] can stir up a lot of bad feeling for no good reason (Interview with lawyer for professional property managing agent, NS 2002–03).

Complaints by residents about the cost and quality of management services have a very long history, prompting regular consideration of whether and how managing agents might be regulated. The government recently rejected the idea of a full licensing regime (Department for Transport, Local Government and the Regions, 2002), so managing agents remain at best self-regulated. The Royal Institution of Chartered Surveyors (2009) has produced a voluntary *Service Charge Residential Management Code*, approved by the Secretary of State under the Leasehold Reform, Housing and Urban Development Act 1993, but there is no sanction for non-compliance.

Owners: Individual and Collective Actors

Whether buying property as an investment or as a home, the purchasers of individual dwellings in a multi-owned development do not enter the picture until after the developer has already established its legal framework. The owners' relatively weak position is further exacerbated by a lack of reliable information about the legal framework they are buying into. Research has found that sales agents were unable to provide relevant information to purchasers about levels of service charges, or details about how developments would be owned and managed (NS 2002–03), while interviews with recent purchasers indicated they had received few or no details from their solicitors about the legal framework for the development (GC 2001–02). In order to complete the purchase, each would-be owner must sign non-negotiable legal documents drafted by the lawyer for the developer or for the managing agent. Typically these are complicated and lengthy (often around 30 pages) with multiple schedules. This respondent's comment speaks for many owners' experience of what, for them, is the most important critical legal event: 'Well, I wasn't very happy about it but I just had to sign' (Interview with resident, GC 2001–02). The study also found that, several months after moving in, most owners remained uncertain about the legal framework for their development and, in particular, about which of the key actors was responsible for management of the common parts and how this was to be paid for (GC 2001–02).

This confusion is understandable because many of the varied legal frameworks for multi-owned residential developments in England and Wales place owners in two legal positions simultaneously. They are individual purchasers and members of a residents' management company, which can be considered as a key actor in its own right. The complexities facing owners with dual roles are exemplified in the notes provided to *Table S322: Whether accommodation is owned freehold or leasehold* of the Survey of English Housing 2006–07, which record and explain the assumptions which the data compilers had to make. For example, 17,000 respondents 'claim to own freehold of building but don't receive ground rent and are therefore assumed to own a share of the freehold'; 96,000 respondents 'claim to own freehold of just own flat but this is extremely rare and are therefore assumed to own a share of the building freehold'; and at a time when only 16 small commonhold developments had been registered, 12,000 respondents claimed commonhold ownership of their flat (Communities and Local Government 2009a: Notes to Table S322). In other words, well over 100,000 owners simply did not understand their individual and collective property rights.

The chapter now examines residents' experiences in developments with differing legal frameworks, concentrating on the three major legal categories (estate rentcharge schemes, leasehold and commonhold). Other ingenious legal solutions to the problem of freehold covenants certainly exist (see Gray and Gray 2009: 248–9; 251–3), but legal frameworks not widely used or only applicable to very small developments are not included here for reasons of space. Table 2.1 summarizes the range of legal frameworks discussed in this chapter, providing a guide to subsequent sections.

Table 2.1 The Major Legal Frameworks for Multi-owned Developments in England and Wales

Legal Framework	Property Rights of Individual Owners in Respect of Their Own Dwellings	Owners' Rights over Common Property, and Type of Collective Organisation for Owners
A. Estate Rentcharge Scheme	Freehold	Rights of access. Residents' association, with no collective legal status.
B. Traditional Freehold/Leasehold Structure	Leasehold	Rights of access. Residents' association, possibly with statutory recognition.
C. Freehold/ Leasehold Structure with Residents' Management Company	Leasehold	Rights of access. (i) Company established by developer to take on management rights and obligations. (ii) Statutory Right to Manage Company (flats only).
D. Residents' Management Company as Freeholder	Leasehold	Freehold ownership. (i) Company established by developer to acquire freehold of the whole development. (ii) Company established by leaseholders for collective enfranchisement (flats only).
E. Commonhold	Freehold	Freehold ownership. Commonhold Association.

Source: Contstructed by author.

Estate Rentcharge Schemes (A, Table 2.1)

Rentcharges are a long established common law mechanism now governed by the Rentcharges Act 1977. Estate rentcharge schemes are used by at least two large housebuilding companies for multi-owned developments of freehold houses (NS 2002–03). A rentcharge is analogous to an obligation by the owner of each individual dwelling to make regular payments to the 'rent owner'. A right of entry, amounting to the right to repossess the dwelling, is annexed to the rentcharge deed which must be signed every time an individual dwelling in the development is transferred to a new purchaser. This right of entry can be exercised by the rent owner if any covenant is breached, thus making both negative and positive covenants enforceable against both first and successor owners even if freeholders (see Bright 1988).

The developer's intentions determine how subsequent critical legal events will unfold following purchase of the dwellings in a rentcharge scheme (NS 2002–03). In a Type 1 rentcharge scheme the legal documents include a covenant requiring owners to pay both a fixed annual rentcharge and a variable rentcharge. The developer remains the rent owner of the fixed rentcharge, but assigns the right to the variable rentcharge – designed to cover the maintenance and management costs for the common parts of the development – to a managing agent, through a separate contract requiring the agent to provide management services for the development. In contrast, in a Type 2 rentcharge scheme, once the site is completed the developer transfers the rentcharge rights to a managing agent who 'deals with the legal side of things' (Interview with developer, NS 2002–03). The individual owners in both variants of estate rentcharge schemes are freeholders, but collectively can exercise little control.

Some rentcharge schemes are drafted to allow a voluntary residents' association to acquire the right to manage on a majority vote, after a specified number of years following the sale of the last dwelling. In practice, according to a managing agent for such schemes, this right had been rarely requested and only for small developments which the agent was happy to hand over, there being little profit to be made from managing such sites (Interview with agent, NS 2002–03). Research into a larger development, built by a different developer, found that there a residents' association had been formed because of the freehold owners' frustrations with the professional managing agent. They felt at the mercy of the agent, and their complaints included that the agents' charges:

> are too expensive for what they provide … They have failed to deal with issues raised by residents. They refused to come to the residents' association Annual General Meeting. They are not strong enough at enforcing the residents' covenants (Interview with committee member of voluntary residents' association, NS 2002–03).

However, the legal documents provided that the agent was also the rent owner, with rights granted by the developer before the individual dwellings were purchased, and committed the owners to this particular managing agent for at least five years.

Leasehold (B, C and D, Table 2.1)

Traditionally, before statutory interventions provided some consumer protection for owners, the terms of a lease would include obligations by the leaseholder to pay to the freeholder ground rent and service charges representing each leaseholder's share of the costs of managing and servicing the common parts. The freeholder was free to decide on the extent of repairs and maintenance, levels of service charge, and whether to take on responsibility for the provision of these services or to contract them out. The problems for leaseholders included their powerlessness to require repairs to be carried out, to prevent works which they considered excessive or unnecessary being carried out, and inability to challenge unreasonable service charges. A leaseholder who failed to pay ground rent or the service charges levied by the freeholder, or to comply with other obligations contained within the lease, faced the draconian sanction of forfeiture of the leaseholder's property (known as 'foreclosure' in most other jurisdictions).

There is clearly an inherent imbalance between freeholder and leaseholder at the latter's expense, apparent in the terminology used in legislation giving lesaeholders rights, which refers to them as 'tenants', for example the Landlord and Tenant Acts 1985 and 1987. Yet leaseholders buy and sell their legal interest in property on the open market in the same way as freeholders, and consider themselves to be property owners (Cole and Robinson 2000). The longstanding campaigns for leasehold reform dating from the nineteenth century, and the piecemeal legislation which eventually resulted, are summarized in Blandy and Robinson (2001). For example, the Landlord and Tenant Act 1985 now requires freeholders to consult with leaseholders before signing repairs and maintenance contracts. However, in practice, the case of *Eltham Properties Limited v Kenny*[4] illustrates the cavalier attitude still displayed by some freeholders and their managing agents. In this case, elderly leaseholders were informed by letter that they could inspect the estimates for work to be undertaken to their apartment block, at the managing agent's office – some ten miles away. The Lands Tribunal considered this to be unacceptable. However, such ploys are common, and are seldom challenged by browbeaten leaseholders who lack the organisation, time and money to do so.

The Commonhold and Leasehold Reform Act 2002 is the most recent of 27 attempts to address leasehold problems over the previous 100 years. It was introduced because the government recognized that 'the protection afforded by the law remains incomplete and the remedies available to leaseholders are unduly difficult and costly to use'; and the need 'to give leaseholders effective redress against abuses by landlords or managing agents' (Lord Chancellor's Department 2000: v). Despite the many attempts at reform, some leaseholders still face an uphill struggle to enforce the statutory rights now guaranteed to them, against a resistant freeholder.

Traditional Freehold/Leasehold Structure (B, Table 2.1)

This long established two-party structure provides an ideal Type 1 framework for a development company which envisages retaining a long-term interest in a multi-owned residential development. Each leasehold owner is given rights of access over the common parts of the site owned by the freeholder, and in return enters into enforceable covenants to contribute to the maintenance costs. Two developments which illustrate contrasting experiences of this structure for the resident leaseholders are now outlined and analysed.

The first example is provided by a block of over flats built nearly 100 years ago, a classic example of a Type 1 leasehold framework where the freeholder's profit is

4 LRX/161/2006.

made from providing management services. The freehold title has changed hands many times since the original developer owned it. The right to manage has usually been contracted to managing agents closely associated with the current freehold owner. The lengthy struggles between these particular leaseholders and their freeholder over a number of issues were researched by Cole and Smith (1994) who recorded that the rights of the leaseholders to consultation over service charges, repairs and maintenance were largely ignored. Despite very high service charges, over the years a lack of adequate maintenance had led to physical deterioration. The leaseholders' other statutory rights, including rights to be informed about any forthcoming sale of the freehold and to gain rights of consultation for a properly formed residents' association, were seen by the freeholder as an infringement of his own property rights and were withheld from the leaseholders until the freeholder was forced through litigation to concede them (Cole and Smith 1994).

The leaseholders' residents' association now has a good working relationship with the managing agent currently contracted by the freeholder, which has considerably improved matters for them (M-ORD 2007–08). Nevertheless, in recent interviews leaseholders clearly expressed their still powerless position in terms such as 'I wouldn't venture to say that we get a lot of say, we're just told that they [the managing agent] are going to do this, that and the other' (Interview with residents' association committee member, M-ORD 2007–08). These leaseholders have never felt on sufficiently strong ground to apply to the Leasehold Valuation Tribunal for a determination of the reasonableness of service charges, as is now their right under the Housing Act 1996.

The second example of the traditional freehold/leasehold structure is entirely different. It is a recently built development of 35 dwellings, both houses and flats, with a large building at its centre designed for collective use, described as a 'co-housing development' (see also Dixon and van Roon, Chapter 13). Its otherwise very conventional lease requires that purchasers commit themselves to the ideal of co-housing, although it is debatable whether this covenant is legally enforceable. The freeholder of the site is a company registered in the name of the property developer who was the driving force behind the development. He gathered a group of people who wanted to live more communally and were prepared to contribute to the purchase of the whole site, and drove the project through to completion. All residents, including the developer, were committed from the outset to attending meetings at which all decisions would be achieved by consensus, and to rotas for collective cooking and gardening duties. It is clear that this development runs on trust, rather than by reference to the unequal legal relationships of freeholder and leaseholders enshrined in the lease, or based on the developer's control of the critical legal events. These co-housing leaseholders have collective control along with responsibility for the whole site. The imbalance of power usually associated with leasehold has been circumvented and the development is very successful, although extremely demanding of the leasehold residents' time as they are carrying out duties usually contracted to a managing agent as well as communal domestic tasks.

Residents' Management Companies in the Freehold/Leasehold Structure (C [i], Table 2.1)

Particularly in large developments there has been a recent trend to draft leases making the leaseholders rather than the freeholder responsible for the management of the whole site (Association of Residential Managing Agents 2009). In this legal framework a residents' management company (a legal entity comprising all the leaseholders) is created by the developer as a separate critical legal event which takes place before the individual dwellings are purchased. The developer determines the rules of the company, including membership, voting arrangements and so on. It may be limited by shares or by guarantee and must comply with the (not particularly onerous) requirements of the Companies Act 2006. Usually, development companies ensure control of the residents' management company for the first year or two by granting themselves a 'golden share' which enables them to outvote the other members of the company, the owners.

The residents' management company is included as a third party in the lease between the freeholder and each leasehold purchaser of an individual dwelling. Each new leasehold owner has no choice but to become a member of the company on purchase of their home. The lease gives the residents' management company no ownership rights, but obliges it to keep the building in good repair and properly insured, for which services the company may charge the leaseholders. However, only the freeholder has the right to collect ground rent and enforce covenants, so the leaseholders collectively are given responsibility without control. Further, the residents' management company is under the developer's control in the crucial early stages of the development and can be committed to a long-term contract with the developer's chosen professional managing agent (see also Sherry, Chapter 10).

The advantages of this legal structure from the point of view of the developer and managing agent are well illustrated by *Barton v Accent Property Solutions Ltd, Eton Court Management Company Ltd, and Graycliffe Homes Ltd.*[5] In this case the Lands Tribunal held that there was no legal relationship between the managing agent Accent and Mr Barton, an individual leaseholder who was dissatisfied with Accent's services and charges, so he had no right to bring proceedings against Accent. However, nor could the Eton Court Management Company (comprising all the leaseholders) claim against Accent as the service charges complied with the contract between those two actors. Thus the leaseholders were left without a remedy, even though the contract with Accent had been entered into at a time when the residents' management company had been under the control of the freeholder rather than the leaseholders.

A more extreme instance of this imbalance of power was found when researching another multi-owned development. Here the housebuilding company as original freeholder had 'pre-sold' the site to a professional managing agent, on terms that no transfer would take place until the building phase was completed

5 LRX/22/2008.

(M-ORD 2007–08). These two key actors, developer and managing agent, were also linked through a complicated series of subsidiary companies. The contract between the managing agent and the residents' management company was signed at a time when the developer still controlled the company. The leaseholders purchased and then moved in to their homes, and building defects emerged soon afterwards. New leasehold directors of the residents' management company were sought and appointed, although one active resident said that she had 'refused to take part in the board of directors because it was just a complete sham' as the developer still retained a golden share (Interview with leasehold resident, M-ORD 2007–08). The new leasehold directors slowly realized 'that the managing agent we kept instructing to do "x, y and z" in relation to [the developer] had actually been appointed by them … they will inevitably be ineffective if they're tied in to this relationship' (Interview with residents' management company director, M-ORD 2007–08).

The covert pre-sale exacerbated the leaseholders' position, as the directors of the residents' management company found it almost impossible to get rid of the managing agent who was now also the freeholder of the site. The links between the developer as original freeholder and the managing agent, established through contract law and company structure, had ensured that these leasehold owners were in a very weak position indeed.

Statutory Right to Manage Companies for Leasehold Owners of Flats (C [ii], Table 2.1)

Where the multi-owned development is a block of flats, freeholders who do not set up a residents' management company of the type described above risk having a statutory Right to Manage company imposed on them by the leaseholders. The Right to Manage was originally introduced by the Landlord and Tenant Act 1987 and a no-fault version was brought in by the Commonhold and Leasehold Reform Act 2002. Unlike residents' management companies established by a developer, both the form (limited by guarantee rather than by shares) and the internal rules of these Right to Manage companies are prescribed in the legislation, together with standardized company documentation of around 20 pages.

Management may seem an important right for dissatisfied leaseholders, as it effectively prevents freeholders from profiting through unreasonable service charges. However, unless all the leaseholders are committed to the time and effort involved in setting up and running a Right to Manage company, efforts are probably doomed to failure. Recent research into a small development, where 17 leaseholders out of the total of 21 had expressed interest in setting up this type of company, found a common problem: 'there are always a number of people who just don't take any notice, aren't interested, you can't contact them' (Interview with leaseholder chair of voluntary residents' association, M-ORD 2007–08).

Nevertheless, about 2,000 statutory Right to Manage companies are currently registered. Registration as a company is just the first step; there are no data available on whether these companies are now actually managing their developments having successfully completed the complex and potentially expensive procedure for acquiring the Right to Manage. The block of 200 leasehold flats which formed the first case study in the previous section provides an example of the difficulties involved. The leaseholders there failed to observe the detailed procedural rules, and were challenged by their freeholder. A Leasehold Valuation Tribunal found against the leaseholders on technical grounds, so they not only failed in their attempt to acquire the Right to Manage but were also ordered to pay the freeholder's legal costs.

Even if the Right to Manage is established, freeholders retain some power through having rights to membership of the company entitling them to vote on service charges, and must be consulted about proposed maintenance and repairs. Further, a statutory Right to Manage company cannot enforce leasehold covenants as the legislation specifies that any breaches must be reported to the freeholder, and it cannot exercise powers of forfeiture as these are retained by the freeholder. Thus, although this statutory right promises a measure of control to leaseholders suffering from ineffective or abusive freeholders and managing agents, its ability to resolve their difficulties is limited.

Residents' Management Companies as Freeholders

This section explores the legal frameworks that enable owners collectively, as a residents' management company, to acquire not just the right to manage but the freehold of the whole site, thus becoming responsible both for its upkeep and for enforcing covenants. Official data, albeit based on the very questionable tenure survey responses already discussed, suggest that around one-third of owners of leasehold flats now have freehold rights to the whole building (Communities and Local Government 2009a). This particular distribution of the bundle of rights results either from the developer's Type 2 intention to sell the freehold interest at a very early stage, or from the leaseholders exercising their statutory right to 'leasehold enfranchisement'. Each mechanism will be discussed in turn.

Developer-driven Residents' Management Companies (D [i], Table 2.1)

The resident's management company is established by the developer with the same control as described earlier in relation to similar companies with management obligations. In this framework, however, the developer covenants in the lease to transfer the freehold of the site to the residents' management company following sale of all the dwellings, whether flats or houses. It is usual for this type of residents' management company to be placed under the control of the developer (or of the managing agent by agreement with the developer) for a fixed period of one or two years following sale of the last dwelling on the site, through a golden share guaranteeing one more vote than the sum total of the votes allotted to leaseholders at any point during this period. It is also common for the first officers of the company during this period to be employees of the freeholder or agent.

The residents' management company could be described as a legal shell at this stage, with its officers appointed by the developer and/or managing agent. By the time that leaseholders take over control of the company, the original managing agent contracted by the developer will be firmly ensconced (see also Sherry, Chapter 10). Although the residents' management company may be technically free to appoint a different agent, research has shown this often proves difficult (NS 2002–03). One problem is that at the critical legal event when the leaseholders collectively acquire the freehold, the new owners have yet to develop a collective identity and may be unable to reach agreement over the tasks involved in terminating the original contract and finding another agent to take over.

Research (M-ORD 2006–07) has uncovered a variant of this legal framework, in which the developer set up a residents' management company and, once the building phase was completed, transferred the freehold of the site to a professional property managing agent already contracted to provide management services. The lease contained an optional right for the residents' management company by majority vote after two years to purchase the freehold from the agent. The managing agent encouraged this course of action, standing to profit from sale of the freehold. Although some leaseholders were not in favour, they were outvoted. The managing agent then incorrectly advised the residents' management company officers that the minority leaseholders could be forced to contribute to the cost of purchase by adding large sums of money to their service charges. This action was contrary to express terms in the lease, but until the minority leaseholders paid their 'arrears' their properties would be unsaleable. At considerable expense, one leaseholder obtained legal advice and forced the residents' management company to back down under threat of legal action; he then attempted to recover his legal costs from the managing agent. Although the County Court judge was sympathetic, the leaseholder lost the case because he, as an individual, had no contractual relationship with the managing agent, nor did the agent owe a duty of care to him but to the residents' management company. A series of pre-determined critical legal events at which property and contractual rights were transferred between the key actors had ensured that the negligent managing agent was protected and the individual owner placed at a disadvantage.

Although there are of course many well-established residents' management companies which own the freehold and run their developments effectively, developer-driven acquisition of the freehold by a residents' management company cannot provide an automatic route to harmony. In any multi-owned residential development run by the leaseholders, there is potential for a clash between individual and collective interests, because once the residents' management company has acquired the freehold as the developer intended, the covenants must be enforced by neighbouring owners. Case studies undertaken for the national study of gated communities provided several examples of this situation. One resident leasehold owner complained that 'three individuals in particular attempt to rule the residents with a rod of iron'; another said that the board members of his residents' management company 'took a very hard line', sending formal letters over alleged breaches of covenant rather than resolving issues face to face, which had caused other board members to resign and had led to 'the destruction of any community spirit' (Interviews with residents, NS 2002–03).

Collective Enfranchisement by Leasehold Owners of Flats (D [ii], Table 2.1)

This second type of residents' management company as freeholder of a multi-owned development often results from leaseholders uniting in the face of freeholder abuse. The Leasehold Reform Housing and Urban Development Act 1993, gave leaseholders (of flats only) the right to 'collective enfranchisement'. They may purchase the freehold even against the wishes of a freeholder who had envisaged retaining a long-term Type 1 interest in the development. Collective enfranchisement requires the leasehold owners to initiate a critical legal event by establishing a residents' management company to acquire the freehold of the block of flats on behalf of the leaseholders and to take on responsibility for the management and maintenance of the common parts. Large professional property management companies frequently act on behalf of leaseholders in these transactions, drafting the relevant legal documents in such a way that power is reserved to themselves by providing officers and directors for the residents' management company.

Considerable determination is needed by leaseholders to enforce collective enfranchisement against a potentially resistant freeholder. Research found that the essential ingredient for successful acquisition of the freehold was an active residents group with a continuing commitment to the 'consultation and co-operation that come with ownership' (Cole, Gidley, Robinson and Smith 1998: 58). Resident satisfaction was then high, even in larger developments where a managing agent was employed (see also Bounds, Chapter 9), but conflict was likely if owners failed to put collective interests before their own (Cole et al. 1998). Recent interviews with leasehold residents of a large house converted into five flats, who had formed a residents' management company and acquired the freehold ten years previously, provide some insights into how resident freehold and management can work in practice (M-ORD 2007–08). Each flat in this building has a single share in the company. There are no formal company meetings. Financial contributions to maintenance and repairs are agreed over a drink: 'if we were reduced to looking at the lease, we'd be in serious trouble' (Interview with secretary of residents' management company, M-ORD 2007–08). Such informality suits this very small multi-owned residential development, where close relations between the individual owners mean that management issues can be dealt with on the basis of trust.

However, the records of Leasehold Valuation Tribunals and the Lands Tribunal indicate many cases where the conflict between enfranchised leasehold owners is as serious as conflicts between leaseholders and freeholder. As in all leasehold frameworks, obligations in the form of positive covenants remain enshrined in the lease. But in the previous two types of leasehold framework which have been discussed here, the covenants would be enforceable by the residents' management company in its role as freeholder rather than by an outside freeholder or managing agent acting for the freeholder. This can lead to serious difficulties, especially when flats are sold on and the new owner is unaware of the legal framework that applies to the block. The Association of Residential Managing Agents reports that it 'regularly receives calls from "disgruntled" lessees [leaseholders] about the management of their building. Very often it turns out that the lessee lives in a building owned or run by a company in which they are a shareholder' (Association of Residential Managing Agents 2009:1).

Commonhold (E, Table 2.1)

Commonhold had been promoted as a potential solution to leasehold problems for many years before it was finally enacted (see Law Commission 1987). However, rather than bringing leasehold tenure to an end, the Commonhold and Leasehold Reform Act 2002 introduced an alternative form of landholding: the freehold estate in commonhold land, which has been described as:

> an alternative to long leasehold ownership of flats and other interdependent properties … similar in concept to condominium title in the USA, strata title in Australia, unit titles in New Zealand and similar arrangements in Europe and South Africa (Department for Constitutional Affairs 2004: paras. 5 and 7).

The Act sets up a new legal framework for multi-owned developments, in which freehold of the common property is owned by a commonhold association, a company limited by guarantee governed by the Companies Act 2006, of which all individual purchasers (termed unit-holders) are members. Each unit-holder owns the freehold of their commonhold unit, making their legal status similar to that of owners in estate rentcharge schemes, not the 'inferior' status of a leaseholder. The problem of positive freehold covenants is dealt with by making all unit-holders subject to the same statutorily defined rights and obligations, which also apply to all future unit-holders. Unlike leasehold, where each developer's lawyer draws up tailor-made leases and other documents for that particular development, the commonhold legislation provides for standardized legal documents. These are very lengthy: the Commonhold Community Statement alone runs to 36 pages, plus four Annexes, hardly easy reading for potential purchasers.

The commonhold legal framework envisages owners as equals. Unlike freeholders in the leasehold framework, or rent owners in estate rentcharge schemes, commonhold associations have no power of forfeiture or right of entry, but must take ordinary debt enforcement procedures to recover outstanding financial contributions (see also Alterman, Chapter 5). There is provision in the Act for a dispute resolution procedure to resolve issues between the commonhold association and unit-holder(s), although no detailed scheme has yet been approved.

Developers' lawyers interviewed at the time the Act was introduced were not keen to abandon their familiar leasehold or rentcharge schemes in favour of the new commonhold structure (NS 2002–03). As one put it: 'I accept that rentcharges and the positive covenant system are archaic, but at present they seem the best option' (Interview with development company in-house lawyer, NS 2002–03). Some concerns seemed ill-founded, as the Act safeguards developer interests (see Van Der Merwe and Smith 2005). Further, non-members of the commonhold association may hold office as directors, and commonhold is not subject to the hard-won statutory rights of leaseholders to consultation and challenge, making it theoretically possible for a developer to commit the commonhold association at an early stage to a lengthy contract with its favoured managing agent. Yet the initial resistance by developers to commonhold continues; at the time of writing Land Registry records include only 19 commonhold registrations, predominantly small developments of which three were set up by the same lawyer who is enthusiastically committed to commonhold (see Hopkins 2005). No conclusions about residents' experiences can be drawn from so few instances, although interviews undertaken with residents in two commonhold developments indicate that they were concerned with buying the home they wanted, rather than with collective ownership or management: 'this commonhold lark doesn't worry me at all, so long as all we have to do is pay our money' (Interview with commonhold resident, M-ORD 2007–08).

The unpopularity of the commonhold legal framework with developers confirms the analysis put forward in this chapter: that developers' control of the all-important first few critical legal events enables them to manipulate the legal framework to their advantage. While a choice remains, developers and their lawyers will continue to prefer tried and tested flexible legal frameworks.

Attempts to Redress the Imbalance of Power

The chapter has now explored the experiences of owners in estate rentcharge schemes, in the different leasehold frameworks – whether created by developers' lawyers or by statute – and in commonhold developments, but the story is not yet over. Provisions of the Commonhold and Leasehold Reform Act 2002 are still belatedly coming into force, adding further reforms of the leasehold system to those outlined above. For example, freeholders and managing agents must now provide more financial information to leaseholders. Proposed amendments to the legal documentation for statutory Right to Manage companies are currently out for consultation; mainly to ensure conformity with the Companies Act 2006, but also to amend the current voting provision which 'would appear to have the effect of unjustifiably distorting the voting arrangements' in favour of freeholders (Communities and Local Government 2009c:14).

One of the underlying causes of an imbalance of power between the key actors is the lack of information available to purchasers of dwellings in multi-owned residential developments. The government has therefore helpfully published *Residential Long Leaseholders: A Guide to Your Rights and Responsibilities* (Communities and Local Government 2008b). The guide is 148 pages long, giving some indication of the complexities of leasehold as well as making it unlikely that the intended audience will read it. Other efforts to provide information include a new statutory requirement that a summary of rights and obligations must accompany every demand for payment issued to a leaseholder. The first page of every Commonhold Community Statement must state: 'This document is important. It creates legally binding rights and duties. It is recommended that anyone affected by it should take appropriate advice'. LEASE (the Leasehold Advisory Service) has been funded by the government since 1994 to provide free legal advice to anyone affected by legal issues related to residential leasehold and commonhold. During 2007–08 LEASE received over 500,000 visits to its website, and 30,000 enquiries, of which the overwhelming majority (79 per cent) were from leaseholders (LEASE 2009), a further indication of the level of demand for information.

Yet, however well informed, the purchaser of a dwelling in a multi-owned development has little choice but to sign up to the legal framework already determined by the developer at a previous critical legal event. The Office of Fair Trading is responsible for ensuring compliance with the Unfair Terms in Consumer Contracts Regulations 1999, in which 'consumer' is widely defined as an individual not acting for the purposes of his or her trade, business or profession. It has recently investigated the fairness of the standard lease used by McCarthy & Stone, the largest UK provider of multi-owned retirement accommodation. The Office of Fair Trading ruled unfair a requirement that leaseholders pay to McCarthy & Stone 1 per cent of the price on any subsequent sale of their property (The Office of Fair Trading 2009a). McCarthy & Stone will not enforce this term in existing contracts, and have removed it from future leases. Another seven standard terms considered to be unfair will be amended, with the Office of Fair Trading reserving its position on a further seven provisions pending any further complaints or evidence of unfairness. In September 2009 it announced a further investigation into the same issue, and has issued formal written notices to 26 other retirement home providers (The Office of Fair Trading 2009b). These activities of the Office of Fair Trading are welcome, particularly if they pave the way for further investigations into standard terms used by other large developers of general, rather than retirement home, multi-owned accommodation.

Conclusions

Individual owners find themselves in the weakest position of the key actors in multi-owned residential developments, as a result of early critical legal events which are under the developer's control. This holds true across virtually all legal frameworks. Planning authorities need more information about the consequences of particular legal frameworks to make the most of their power to intervene at a vital stage of development, and methods of regulating managing agents should be put in place. Leasehold reform legislation, particularly those provisions giving collective rights to acquire the freehold or to manage, has secured some improvements. However, no amount of additional rights – or information about those rights – will rectify the inevitable imbalance of power between the leaseholders and the developer as initial freeholder.

The government has promised to encourage the adoption of commonhold, but no date has yet been set for the publication of its promised consultation paper, designed to 'identify any changes that need to be made to the commonhold legislation to address any actual or perceived barriers to take-up' (House of Commons 2009: Column 982W). Until then, England and Wales will remain 'the last major common law jurisdiction persisting in using leasehold tenure for the sale and purchase of homes, and all the trumpeted benefits of a commonhold system will be denied to the majority' (Clarke 2006: 90). One solution, long argued for by leasehold campaigners, is the enforced transfer of freeholds of multi-owned developments to leaseholder-owned management companies (Clarke 2006). This would certainly break the powerful hold of freeholders, but is unlikely ever to be introduced due to the same entrenched property interests which have held back leasehold reform over many years (Blandy and Robinson 2001).

The dual nature of owners' roles (individual and collective) in multi-owned developments are inherently problematic. Reported cases and research provide many examples of conflict between residents' management companies and individual owners, caused by lack of engagement or by the heavy-handed enforcement of covenants, although not to the extent experienced in the US (see McKenzie, Chapter 4). Larger sites, unless the owners are prepared to take on maintenance tasks themselves, as in the co-housing development described earlier, require a managing agent; this allows another key actor considerable power through the contracted right to manage. Collective management by residents may be simpler in smaller developments, but can lead to extremely bitter and personal disputes between owners who continue to live in close proximity.

At the critical legal event when the dwelling is purchased, most owners are unaware of arrangements for management and of the commitment required of them. Better informed purchasers, sales agents, and lawyers would go some way to improving the situation, but perhaps the last word should go to an owner: 'you can make laws until you're blue in the face – in the end it all comes down to how you get on with other people' (Interview with commonhold resident, M-ORD 2007–08).

References

Association of Residential Managing Agents. 2009. *Guidance Note 12: Lessees and Residents' Management Companies.* [Online]. Available at: http://www.arma.org.uk/files/ARMAGN.pdf [accessed: 17 July 2009].

Atkinson, R., Flint, J., Blandy, S. and Lister, D. 2003. *Gated Communities in England: Final Report of the Gated Communities in England New Horizons Project*. London: Office of the Deputy Prime Minister.

Blandy, S., Dixon, J. and Dupuis, A. 2006. Theorising Power Relationships in Multi-owned Residential Developments: Unpacking the Bundle of Rights. *Urban Studies*, 43(13), 2365–83.

Blandy, S. and Lister, D. 2005. Gated Communities: (Ne)gating Community Development? *Housing Studies*, 20(2), 287–302.

Blandy, S. and Parsons, D. 2003. Gated Communities in England: Rules and Rhetoric of Urban Planning. *Geographica Helvetica*, 58(4), 314–24.

Blandy, S. and Robinson, D. 2001. Reforming Leasehold: Discursive Events and Outcomes, 1984–2000. *Journal of Law and Society*, 28(3), 384–408.

Bright, S. 1988. Estate Rentcharges and the Enforcement of Positive Covenants. *Conveyancer and Property Lawyer*, March–April, 99–107.

Clarke, D. 2006. Long Residential Leases: Future Directions, in *Landlord and Tenant Law: Past, Present and Future*, edited by S. Bright. Oxford: Hart, 171–90.

Cole, I., Gidley, G., Robinson, D. and Smith, Y. 1998. *The Impact of Leasehold Reform: Flat Dwellers' Experiences of Leasehold Enfranchisement and Lease Renewal*. London: Department of the Environment.

Cole, I. and Robinson, D. 2000. Owners yet Tenants: The Position of Leaseholders in Flats in England and Wales. *Housing Studies*, 15(4), 595–612.

Cole, I. and Smith, Y. 1994. *Liberating the Leaseholder? The Prospects for Reform*. Sheffield: Centre for Regional Economic and Social Research, Sheffield Hallam University.

Communities and Local Government. 2006. *Planning Policy Statement 3 (PPS 3): Housing*. London: Communities and Local Government.

Communities and Local Government. 2008a. *Land Use Change in England: Residential Development to 2006 – Update January 2008*. London: Communities and Local Government.

Communities and Local Government. 2008b *Residential Long Leaseholders: A Guide to Your Rights and Responsibilities*. London: Communities and Local Government.

Communities and Local Government. 2009a. *Survey of English Housing*. [Online]. Available at: http://www.communities.gov.uk/housing/housingresearch/housingsurveys/surveyofenglishhousing/sehlivetables/owneroccupiersincluding/ [accessed: 4 May 2009].

Communities and Local Government. 2009b. *Housing Statistics*. [Online]. Available at: http://www.communities.gov.uk/housing/housingresearch/housingstatistics/housingstatisticsby/housebuilding/livetables/ [accessed: 4 May 2009].

Communities and Local Government. 2009c. *Consultation on Right to Manage Company Articles*. London: Communities and Local Government.
Department for Constitutional Affairs. 2004. *Non-Statutory Guidance on The Commonhold Regulations 2004*. London: Department for Constitutional Affairs.
Department for Transport, Local Government and the Regions. 2002. *Improving the Standards of Residential Leasehold Management: Consultation*. London: DTLR.
Gray, K. and Gray, S.F. 2009. *Elements of Land Law*. 5th edition. Oxford: Oxford University Press.
Hopkins, J. 2005. Soon to be Commonplace? *Property Law Journal*, 30, August, 5–8.
House of Commons. 2009. *Hansard Written Answers for 26 Feb 2009* Column 982W [Online]. Available at: http://www.publications.parliament.uk/pa/cm200809/cmhansrd/cm090226/text/90226w0019.htm [accessed: 20 July 2009].
Law Commission. 1987. *Commonhold: Freehold Flats and Freehold Ownership of Other Interdependent Buildings, Cm 179*. London: The Law Commission.
LEASE. 2009. *Annual Report 2008*. London: LEASE.
Lord Chancellor's Department. 2000. *Commonhold and Leasehold Reform: Draft Bill and Consultation Paper, Cm 3843*. London: Her Majesty's Stationery Office.
Royal Institution of Chartered Surveyors (RICS). 2009. *Service Charge Residential Management Code 2009*. London: RICS.
The Office of Fair Trading. 2009a. *Investigation: McCarthy & Stone plc*. [Online]. Available at: http://www.oft.gov.uk/advice_and_resources/resource_base/consumer-regulations/traders/3197/1/ [accessed: 12 February 2009].
The Office of Fair Trading. 2009b. *Retirement Homes Investigation into Exit Fees*. [Online]. Available at: http://www.oft.gov.uk/oft_at_work/markets/markets/retirement-homes/ [accessed: 3 September 2009].
Van Der Merwe, C.G. and Smith, P.F. 2005. Commonhold Development Rights – A Comparative Assessment. *Conveyancer and Property Lawyer*, January/February, 53–78.

Chapter 3

Disinterested Developers, Empowered Managers and Vulnerable Owners: Power Relations in Multi-occupied Private Housing in Scotland

Douglas S. Robertson

Introduction

Property ownership laws in Scotland have recently undergone a major overhaul. With the re-establishment of a Scottish Parliament, Europe's last feudal property ownership system was at long last reformed, via three separate but related pieces of legislation which all came into force in 2004: the Abolition of Feudal Tenure, etc. (Scotland) Act 2000; the Title Conditions (Scotland) Act 2003; and the Tenements (Scotland) Act 2004. Feudal title involved split ownership. Ordinarily in Scotland, as in most of Europe (although unlike in common law jurisdictions), ownership is legally absolute: that is, if a person owns something it necessarily follows that others do not. Of course, the idea of absolute ownership is somewhat misleading, given public law in relation to planning and building controls as well as private law in respect of title conditions and the law of nuisance, through which ownership is restricted in various ways. However, under feudalism the 'vassal' (the person at the bottom of the ownership chain) had *dominium utile*, or useful ownership; that is, the right to possess. The 'superiors' (any person higher up the ownership chain, right up to and including the Crown) had a controlling ownership which historically had allowed some to claim the right to demand military service from the vassal; this right was abolished in 1746 following the defeat of the Jacobite Rebellion. Superiors were, however, still entitled to regular twice yearly payments of *feu duty*, as well as (from the early nineteenth century) the right to enforce title conditions. Typically, in the twentieth century, the latter right allowed the superior to demand payment for waivers of the title conditions. This controlling ownership had no substantive content, however, other than the power to apply these economic rights (for a fuller discussion of feudal tenure see Gretton and Steven 2009).

As part of the recent major reform exercise a number of longstanding problematic issues in relation to the ownership and governance of multi-owned property were addressed. These reforms have had, however, a limited impact upon the ownership challenges presented by private ‘flatted property’, as apartment buildings are known in Scotland. Underlying legal problems have ensured that governance matters associated with multi-owned property – that is, the maintenance, repairs, other services and financial management arrangements – remain highly problematic.

Critically reviewing these reforms provides a useful means of exploring the inherent problems with the ownership and associated governance arrangements for multi-owned private property. What transpired to be a limited shift in the respective rights and powers, as a result of these recent legal reforms, amply illustrates the strength of the underlying power relations that exist within this core segment of the Scottish housing market. Fundamentally, the power positions of the three key actors operating within the multi-owned property context, namely that of the developers, of property managers and of the home owners themselves, did not alter. This was because throughout the reform process, developers’ and to a lesser extent property managers’ interests remained paramount to those of the actual owners. Therefore, in common with previous feudal property arrangements, Scots law still retains a disregard for the interests of the least powerful actors within the context of multi-owned property, the home owners themselves.

Multi-owned Private Housing in Scotland

Scotland has a long tradition of flatted living and, as a result, the country has a high proportion of flats. The most recent Scottish House Condition Survey reveals that multi-owned property accounted for 26 per cent of all Scottish home occupier properties, which equates to 270,000 properties (Scottish Homes 2003). Owner occupation accounts for 70 per cent of all Scottish housing. The rate of growth over the past few decades has been quite dramatic, with flats becoming a more significant segment of the newbuild owner-occupied market (Scottish Homes 2003). Apartment blocks were the major urban construction growth area throughout the 1990s and 2000s, especially in the two major cities of Edinburgh and Glasgow, until the economic downturn of late 2008 brought new building to a stop. Planning authorities have been supportive of such developments as they comply with sustainability ambitions and increase the local tax base. In this respect Scotland reflects more the European building tradition where apartment living is quite common, rather than that of its immediate southern neighbour England, where the traditional house with its own front and back doors remains the dominant domestic building form.

Under Scots law a flat is legally defined in the Town and Country Planning (General Permitted Development) (Scotland) Order 1992 as being any property that is a ‘separate and self contained set of premises, whether or not on the same floor, forming part of a building which is divided horizontally’. The types of property encompassed within this broad definition are wide-ranging, including modern apartment blocks, lofts, four-in-a-block housing, and sub-divided houses commonly referred to as 'conversions'; as well as the traditional Scots eighteenth and nineteenth century sandstone tenements. Tenements have been a common form of housing in Scotland since medieval times; they are buildings with two to four flats on each floor sharing a common entrance way and staircase, typically three to five storeys in height, although some are much higher. While originally much of this property had been built for rent, either privately or by a local authority, over time it has been transferred into individual ownership. For privately rented property this transfer occurred from the 1950s onwards, whereas for the council stock this was brought about by the advent of the 'Right to Buy' in the Housing Act 1980.

So in Scotland, the great majority of flats are within purpose-built blocks, reflecting the tenement tradition. Two-thirds of all flats were built before 1945 and four-fifths are in blocks with eight or fewer flats. A fifth of flat owners live in properties which were previously owned by a local authority. As flats are, in general, older property and small in scale, with a sizeable proportion having previously been in council ownership, collectively such property makes up a significant proportion of the 'bottom end' of the current housing market. The elderly and the young are typical of the demographic profile of residents in multi-owned property, and this is similar to the profile in the newer apartment blocks. What differs is their respective income: wealthier single people or couples, typically young professionals, reside within the newer property, whereas the older property tends to house poorer, older households.

Although there is a diversity of stock, the predomination of older smaller blocks means that management services focus on providing basic maintenance and occasional repair services, typically in response to a crisis. The larger scale modern apartment blocks generally demand a higher level of service, given the broader range of facilities provided. It is also worth noting that flats in Scotland often contain a mix of uses, with shops and other commercial premises on the ground floor, typically on main thoroughfares. As such properties are liable for differing proportions of the maintenance and management costs for the common elements of these blocks, this adds to the complexity of the governance task.

Legal Context

All owned property requires a registered title document, which is held by the Land Registry (previously the Register of Sasines). It is the title deeds which legally define ownership. The Land Registry is charged with ensuring that this information is accurate and properly recorded when submitted by the conveyancing solicitor registering a house sale on the Land Certificate.

Title provisions set down the physical extent of the flat (or apartment) as well as the rules detailing the rights and responsibilities that pertain to the governance of the block within which the flat is located. Individual flat owners in Scotland own the freehold of their property and are also jointly responsible for the governance of the block. The rules setting out the owners' governance responsibilities for the upkeep, management and maintenance of these common elements are detailed through the use of real burdens and servitudes.

Real burdens and servitudes are the conditions, or encumbrances on ownership, which have been voluntarily created, typically when the property as a unit was initially sold off. Real burdens allow the neighbour to restrain your use of your property: common examples include prohibitions on future building; running a business from the property; or allowing the property to be occupied by more than one family, thus preventing it being let to multiple occupants. Servitudes allow the neighbour to use neighbouring property, with access rights being the best example. In rural areas water supplies are often covered by such servitudes to allow water pipes, drainage and sewage across other properties. Such burdens have an additional utility because, unlike the position in English law, they can impose obligations to maintain property, enforceable by neighbours against each other, which are of particular value when and if enforced within a tenement ownership context. Such obligations are made the joint and several responsibility of all owners and, as they run with title, they apply equally to all future owners.

Real burdens and servitudes are set down within the title deeds, either at length within one document, or by direct reference to another deed, the so-called subsisting burdens, the most common of which is the Deed of Conditions. Such secondary deed provisions were introduced from the 1870s onwards to ensure an element of standardization in relation to the properties governance regime, as this was not always achieved in the actual title deed itself. Typically, common maintenance responsibilities are set out in such secondary deeds, as are any management arrangements to ensure decisions are able to be taken and then acted upon. Within this context, the Deed of Conditions often makes an explicit provision for the appointment of a property manager. Arrangements may also be detailed for apportioning the costs associated with instructing any works or services to be carried out.

Running in the background to these ownership contracts are long established common law arrangements, the 'Law of the Tenement', which provide for basic default provisions for all tenemental property. However, only where title deeds are silent in respect of a particular governance matter, can the common law be made to apply. If title conditions are detailed, the Law of the Tenement cannot be adopted in preference. The Law of the Tenement adopts the view that ownership within a tenement context is primarily individual, the only exception being the common close, the roof immediately above the close and the common stairs (Reid 1993). All other elements of the building are held in the individual ownership of one or other of the flat owners. So the owners of top floor flats have the ownership and responsibility for maintaining the roof immediately above their property, while ground floor flats own and have responsibility for the *solum*, the land area immediately under their floor. Ownership of external walls is divided amongst all owners, while ownership of all internal walls separates at the midpoint.

To assume that these provisions taken together result in a well thought through and supportive legal arrangement underpinning the private ownership of multi-owned property would be a mistake. A number of major and persistent problems have existed in respect of both these arrangements. The limitations and problems associated with the Law of the Tenement were well known, in that individuals are expected to take on what, in other tenemental contexts, are collective responsibilities. These concerns were set out in a critical report on the Law of the Tenement (Scottish Law Commission 1998a). The challenges emanating from poorly drafted title deed provisions, by contrast, have been less well articulated.

Common Problems

Title Deeds

Generally speaking, the older the property the shorter the title deed and, therefore, the greater the reliance upon the common law. Older title deeds typically make little or no provision for common decision-making mechanisms, thus the common law maxim that ownership within a tenement context is, for the most part, individual comes into play. This is in marked contrast with new apartment developments, which tend to have comprehensive title provisions given they are often built with various communal facilities provided, such as common grounds, lifts and, in some cases, leisure facilities, all of which demand on-going governance arrangements. The presumption that new properties have better governance provisions is not always the case; for example, some new flats in Dundee were recently sold with no provisions for effective decision-making to ensure on-going maintenance (Robertson and Rosenberry 2001).

So while certain tenements have a comprehensive set of title documents, others operate with the bare minimum, making the execution of even the most basic maintenance tasks something of a challenge. The vast majority of tenemental property lies somewhere between these two positions, with a set of title provisions that allow for some degree of decision-making and cost apportionment, but such provisions are variable. Even where comprehensive provisions exist, their actual practicality is dependent upon the drafting skills of the original developer's solicitor.

Differences in the historic patterns of property ownership, as well as regional variations in legal practices, have produced significantly different title deed provisions between one part of Scotland and another. Such patterns have, however, tended to decline in significance over time. In Edinburgh and the East of Scotland, it is common to have slight variations in the real burdens that apply to individual flats within the same block. This is a consequence of breakaway deeds being created at different times, as and when individual flats were sold. Solicitors when drafting deeds would add elements to improve governance practice, given that many years may have passed since the first flat was sold and title drafting practices would have altered. As a result, in order to ensure effective governance, all owners within the block would be required to read each and every title deed, because individual obligations could differ.

By contrast, in Glasgow and the West of Scotland, title deeds typically make reference to a subsidiary deed of condition. Although these documents vary in their detail, as was noted above, the basic provisions are relatively standard. Governance, as a result, is often easier to organize as a rudimentary system has always been in place. That said, problems with these deeds which may have arisen over time can mean that executing such work proves difficult.

The cause of this spatial variation is historic, arising out of distinct differences in nineteenth century property ownership and, in particular, between Scotland's two main cities, Glasgow and Edinburgh (see Elliot and McCrone 1989, Adams 1978). Edinburgh being the longer established administrative and commercial centre had a greater prevalence of large scale individual landlord holdings. Glasgow, by contrast, underwent a rapid but short-lived period of industrial expansion between 1860 and 1910. Finance for the city's massive associated tenement construction programme came largely from small individual investors and trusts who owned individual or small groups of properties. The original development and subsequent management of these properties was organized through 'factors', a term still used today for private property managers which emanates from rural Scotland, where the landowner of an estate would employ a factor to act as their steward of the entire property holding, undertaking the day-to-day management of the estate for the land owner (Sim 1996). The notion of property stewardship is still a prominent feature of Scottish property management interests.

So while the scale of individual property holdings in Edinburgh ensured that landlords themselves kept direct control of the management task, in Glasgow this had always been the remit of factors (Robertson and Bailey 1996, Sim 1996). Given the range of separate ownership interests they had to accommodate, factors imposed their own particular Deed of Condition to ensure the standardization of governance arrangements necessary in order for them to run their property businesses. Such an arrangement was not considered necessary within the Edinburgh context. With private rented property rapidly being sold into owner-occupation, largely during the 1950s, 1960s and 1970s, then these previous and different arrangements for governance merely carried across into the new titles for that property. Hence, property management in traditional tenement flats is common in the West of Scotland, but not so in the East. Property management is an intrinsic feature in modern apartment blocks being developed from the late 1980s onwards and thus this spatial pattern has started to break down.

So there has always been, and continues to be, a variety of arrangements in place that are specific to each property. This is in marked contrast with other legal jurisdictions where a standard statutory codified arrangement is in place (see for example Cassidy et al., Chapter 11; Christudason, Chapter 6; and Sherry, Chapter

10). What is peculiar is that Scotland has long had such a code, in the Law of the Tenement, but only as secondary background law.

Property Managers

The notion of the empowered manager, the 'steward', has long been favoured by property management interests. While this was beneficial for landlords, in that rents were collected and repairs carried out and their profits paid, this has been less well received by home owners. Owners, given their expectations when buying other services, assumed there would be some say in what they are paying for, yet this has not been the culture of Scottish property management.

West of Scotland property managers, given the core role they had previously played in relation to private rented property, saw their customer base switch over a protracted period to individual home owners and away from landlords. Due to strong resistance on the part of property managers, the demands of home owners to be more directly involved in the decision-making in respect of their property are only now starting to have an impact. The vast majority of property managers are still quite content to bill their annual fee without itemizing precisely what this invoice covers. Where major works are involved, given the financial outlay, property managers will not contract the work until all owners have contributed their share into a common fund held by the property manager. This can result in a very protracted timeframe while the problem for some owners persists. Again it is the manager and not the owners who effectively control the decision-making process.

There has also been much criticism of modern deed conditions because they effectively impose a property manager even before the owners have purchased their flats. Thus the specification of works and service quality has already been determined without any owner involvement. Sheltered housing for elderly people has been a growing niche within the private housing market, and this sector was also considered to be particularly prone to the marked lack of effective consumer choice, because of too close a relationship between the developers and the subsequent management company. This matter came to a head when a group of owners challenged the title provisions in relation to their sheltered housing development in Langside, Glasgow. The owners particularly objected to the cost of the warden service provided by the developer, Hanover Housing Association, which subsequently took on the role of property manager. The owners challenged the association's assumed right to control the management of the block through their position as superior owner, without proper consultation with the residents. After a number of legal attempts at dispute resolution had failed, the Court of Session ruled against the housing association (*Hanover (Scotland) Housing Association Limited and Others against John Reid and Margaret Reid*).[1] While the dispute was continuing, the owners gained a new right, under the Title Conditions

1 [2006] CSOH 56.

(Scotland) Act 2003, to dismiss their property manager, in this case the housing association, by a majority vote and to appoint another of their own choosing.

This notion of the 'empowered' property manager has also been prevalent within a public sector context. When tenants exercised their 'Right to Buy' and bought their council flat, under the title deeds drawn up by their previous public sector landlord, they were obliged to continue receiving their maintenance service from that landlord. Such owners also found themselves in a monopoly situation and even though the quality of the service provided was generally poor, and subject to a highly critical report by the Scottish Consumer Council (Welsh 1999), they could not dismiss the poorly performing manager. Owners, therefore, voted with their feet and refused to pay their contributions. The inability to dismiss the property manager, even where the private owners were in a majority within what had been previously a council block, was considered a major legal stumbling block to consumer choice being exercised.

It is interesting to note that the pattern of retaining the previous management arrangement, despite the change in the properties' ownership, was as much a feature of the public, as it had been in the private sector. The previous property manager, whether good or bad, could not be dislodged from providing governance services, because of title obligations.

Conveyancing Practice

Current conveyancing practice, in relation to private property transactions, is another major contributor to the problems associated with property governance. Flat purchasers are rarely properly advised as to the potential problems that could arise from having defective title provisions (O'Neill 2000, Welsh 1999, Randolph et al. 1998). Too often such problems only come to light much later, as a result of a serious fabric failure such as a leaking roof. Only then does it transpire that the title deeds fail to provide an adequate means of resolving the issue to the satisfaction of all affected parties. For many, purchasing a flat merely represents the first step on the home ownership ladder. The lack of clarity in respect of governance responsibilities thus has decided benefits for those with a strong motivation to save money for the deposit of their next purchase, rather than spending it on maintaining their current home.

Further, the vast majority of people buying flats rely solely on a building society or bank valuation survey, rather than a proper property condition survey (Housing Improvement Task Force 2003). This means that very few purchasers have any real idea of the general condition of the block they are purchasing into, or about who manages the property and what its actual maintenance history is.

Within property conveyancing the prime concern is to achieve the highest possible sales price, given that the key actors in this process, the solicitors and estate agents, operate on a percentage fee basis. Lenders, primarily interested in securing the loan business, also considered high valuations to be in their interest.

Given such overt commercial pressures there is little room for voicing concerns about the property's condition, or highlighting ineffective title deeds conditions as this would only act to deflate prices in Scotland's unique property market, in which sales are based on blind bidding. Solicitors justify such an approach by claiming that it is not possible to offer a comprehensive service which would alert their clients to possible problems with title, within the fee levels which the market can sustain.

These structural failings with the operation of the property market are not helped by a long held view within governmental and professional circles that those purchasing at the 'cheaper end' of the market, which is dominated by older flatted property, as well as those purchasing 'Right to Buy' properties, are not considered to be proper owners. Thus they are assumed to have a more limited appreciation of their actual responsibilities in respect of on-going management and maintenance of common property. Rather than try to protect the interests of consumers through legal remedies the focus has been on providing public information leaflets to fill these perceived knowledge gaps. So in the last decade, two government information leaflets on the topic of common property maintenance have been issued (Scottish Executive 2004 and 2001, amended 2006). The complacency and the patronizing nature of this approach was neatly revealed by Scottish Consumer Council research which showed that low income 'Right to Buy' home owners are well aware of their responsibilities, it is just that they are unwilling to pay for what they consider an inferior service (Welsh 1999).

House Conditions

Collectively these problems have a direct bearing on the condition of multi-owned property, especially where there is no active management arrangement in place. In such circumstances crisis management becomes the order of the day, activated by a leaking roof, or perhaps a structural collapse caused by a storm. When contractors are needed in a hurry they are randomly selected and are almost invariably of indeterminate quality. Not surprisingly, such contractors have no knowledge of the block's previous repairs history. Poor workmanship and bad working practices tend to ensure poor value for money. Again, due to a combination of speed and an overriding desire to save money, owners seldom make use of either an architect or surveyor to specify works. As a consequence, proper written tendering procedures are rarely initiated. Work procured in this way tends to alter once on site, with limited options to solve unforeseen problems being presented to owners as and when they arise. Inevitably costs rise, which further generates dissatisfaction and disagreement amongst fellow owners who realize they have no real control over the process.

Such problems also go some way to explain the unacceptably high levels of disrepair within older tenemental properties, as revealed by successive Scottish House Condition Surveys (Scottish Homes 1996, 2003). It should also be borne in mind that without recent and sustained high levels of public investment into large tracts of this stock, the overall scale of disrepair would be far worse. That said, given the lack of regular on-going maintenance following this public investment, disrepair is bound to re-emerge, but on this occasion public money will not be made available to help resolve this problem. The recent Housing (Scotland) Act, 2006 abandoned improvement and repair grants and what had proved to be the highly successful Housing Action Area interventions which had run for nearly 30 years (Robertson and Bailey 1996).

Overall, it is evident that the capacity to produce variable title provisions results in markedly different governance regimes. These, in turn, create a variety of problems – some minor, some major – for the majority of multi-owned property owners. Cooperation on the part of owners can often produce a satisfactory management arrangement which can be made to work around such difficulties. However, a simple change of ownership could bring about an abrupt end to such an arrangement, through the new owner's insistence that they be subject solely to title provisions, or where appropriate the common law if they consider that to be to their advantage.

So while certain problems can and do require to be worked around, typically to the disadvantage of some owners and the advantage of others, certain governance problems can never be properly resolved, which causes much frustration and resentment on the part of all owners. There are very few owners of flatted property who do not have to contend with such matters. Such feelings are intensified when it is clear they can do little or nothing to resolve the situation. Finally, it should be noted that, although it is not impossible to have a title deed altered, this does require the unanimous agreement of all the affected owners, as well as their creditors, which in most cases is either the bank or building society which has provided the home loan. Achieving unanimous agreement amongst such a large and diverse group, each of whom is separately legally represented, represents a challenging endeavour and is consequently something rarely pursued.

Recent Property Reforms

Given the nature of these problems and the consequences that fall from these failings, it could be assumed that the focus of reform would be primarily on trying to address them. Yet in reviewing the reform process it seems that while that ambition was evident, the means of achieving this was somewhat circumscribed.

As was noted earlier, the first part of the reform package was the Abolition of Feudal Tenure, etc. (Scotland) Act 2000. Extinguishing all existing feudal title conditions, to ensure only real burdens – those that are tied to the land, not to the person – was the prime objective of this Act. Feudal burdens were created by the original landowner to set down certain use conditions to which all future vassals were required to adhere. Real burdens, the more recent legal creation, allow servitudes to run with the title of the property, amounting to an early form of land use planning (RICS 1999). Under the Act, all existing non-feudal real burdens remain enforceable, should owners wish this to be the case. For all property the currently expressed rights will survive until 2010; the implication here is that as this is the average turnover period for any property, so the title burdens will be examined through the conveyancing process and if any are found wanting, they would not be re-registered.

This was then closely followed by the reform of real burdens, via the Title Conditions (Scotland) Act 2003. These reforms emanated directly from two Scottish Law Commission reports (Scottish Law Commission 1998b, 2000). Given the central significance of real burdens to multi-owned property ownership, this part of the reform package was fundamental. The designation of a distinct sub-set of real burdens – to be known as 'community burdens' – was intended to have a major bearing on the governance arrangements within multi-owned property. Community burdens are defined as real burdens which confer reciprocal obligations on all owners within a block of flats. This was a new name for an old concept, namely that owners who share facilities should be subjected to a common regulatory regime.

All existing real burdens which stipulate collective or shared responsibilities, automatically became community burdens, subject to the general proviso that these burdens are implied and thus can be enforced. The new Act also allows a majority that is in excess of 50 per cent of the affected owners, the power to vary or extinguish such burdens. So in future, title registration opens up the opportunity to create new community burdens, or to alter or extinguish existing ones. Where a real burden is inoperable, for whatever reason, the affected owners could choose not to register it. So owners who have no interest in enforcing an existing real burden could opt not to register such rights. Although this aspect of reform offers an opportunity to overcome many of the problems outlined earlier, as was noted, the process of altering title deeds is not straightforward. Objections from the minority might also demand a Land Tribunal judgement to get final acceptance of the majority decision.

In line with the Law Commission's recommendations, the Bill which preceded the Act proposed a Model Development Management Scheme as a means to govern facilities defined as community burdens. The basic model suggested was the creation of an association, a body corporate, whose membership would be composed of all owners who are subject to the specific community burdens. This association would be expected to meet at least once a year to approve a budget and accept the previous year's accounts for the ongoing management and maintenance of the facilities. The association would also be charged with making, or amending, regulations in respect of the facilities. Such regulations or obligations would be binding on owners and any tenants resident within the block. The scheme gives scope to establish a sinking fund to cover any future major repairs. Provisions were also outlined for the manager to invest these monies, although no guidelines were provided.

The annual meeting of the association would also be expected to appoint a manager, who would have responsibility for managing the necessary work and collecting the required monies in advance. The manager would also regularly inspect the property and advise the owners of any issues arising from these inspections. There is also an expectation that the manager would supervise any works that take place on the defined community facility. The owners would have the power to hold a special general meeting to dismiss the manager, should their performance fail to meet expectations.

However, because the Model Management Scheme would establish a body corporate structure, with a clear set of operating rules and specified responsibilities, this was deemed to be outwith the powers of the Scottish Parliament and would require Westminster legislation to enact. As a result it has been held up until a slot is found within UK legislation. It is also worth noting that the overall approach of this scheme remains firmly ensconced with the notion of the empowered manager and the opportunity to encourage greater owner control was ignored.

So the current position is that workable governance regimes can now be created, preserved or refined. Equally, they could also be abandoned, in that owners are now able to pick and choose the community burdens to which they wish to be subject. In such a context, however, the owners could find themselves more subject to the reformed common law default system, the Law of the Tenement.

Only after feudal title was abolished and real burdens reform was placed in statute, did the Law of the Tenement reforms come forward. The Scottish Law Commission had been asked in 1984 by the Westminster Parliament to come forward with proposals and eventually these were presented in 1998 (Reid 1998, Scottish Law Commission 1998a). These proposals were, in turn, incorporated into the new Tenements (Scotland) Act 2004 Act. Revisions to the common law now provide for a more robust default situation.

The new Law of the Tenement defines in some detail what is termed 'scheme property'. Scheme property includes roof and associated rainwater goods; the *solum*; foundations; external walls, any shared gables and any other load bearing walls; the close stairs, associated walls, windows and the external door. The Act also introduces a new 'mini' management system for the governance of scheme property.

The assumption here is that scheme property should be subject to a maintenance arrangement involving all owners within the block. Whereas in the past owners could hide behind the failings of their deeds to avoid their responsibilities, now the common law introduces a statutory duty to maintain scheme property given its significance in offering either support or shelter to the occupants of the building. So procedures for the appointment of a managing agent are outlined, as are the arrangements for the delegation of powers in relation to arranging and/or instructing works. Provisions are also made for the execution of emergency works. Owners can decide to collect the projected cost of the works in advance, with this cash being banked and paid to the contractor on completion of works. Title deed provisions, where these exist, will determine apportionment, otherwise the default position will be on the basis of equal shares. The only exception to this will be where there are unequal sizes of flats, in which case floor area would be adopted to define respective shares. The Act also states that both the seller and purchaser would be jointly liable for any such debts, but ultimately liability still lies with the purchaser.

Decision-making will be by majority, with all owners being bound by any majority decision. Decisions will also be binding on all future owners. Unless the property consists of three or fewer flats, each flat would receive one vote. Basic procedural provisions are laid out for decision-making, which are designed to be both informal and simple to operate. Decisions do not require a meeting to take place, as consents can be collected by going round the doors. Safeguards are built in for small tenements and where there is a serious discrepancy between voting powers and liability. The right of veto is available to owners whose group liability exceeds 75 per cent or more of costs as in the case of ground floor commercial premises. Oppression of such minorities, as they are described, is avoided by allowing owner(s) who did not support a decision, the right of appeal to the Sheriff Court within 21 days of the disputed decision being made.

This default 'mini-management scheme' also introduces certain requirements that are not within most titles. The most significant of these is the requirement for all owners to maintain adequate building insurance for fire and other standard risks. This was made an individual requirement, in that each individual owner within the block will be legally obliged to be properly insured. The suggestion that there would be major advantages in making this matter a scheme requirement, given the wide variation in insurance products, was dismissed being at variance with the principle of individual responsibility within tenement ownership.

The clarification of what constitutes scheme property, and having the governance responsibilities clearly laid down, represents a major advance on the previous common law. Where deeds are silent on particular matters then this should provide a solution. The introduction of a default management scheme is also a major advance. However, what these provisions failed to do was resolve the problem of deficient deeds through introducing an overriding statutory default system applicable to all existing tenemental property. Should not the new common law have been able to override poor or inoperable title conditions? Nervousness about the implications of the European Convention on Human Rights in respect of individual property rights ensured this was not to be the case. What the Law Commission brought forward and the Act encompassed, was a clever compromise, but a compromise nonetheless, in which existing ownership rights remain unchanged, although the background law affecting that property is subtly amended. But as a result only where title deeds are silent do the revised default provisions apply.

Critically, these legislative reforms, taken as a whole, still ensure a continuation of the infinite variety in deed provisions. So although the common law changes help to tidy up a number of loose ends, the reform package still fails to adequately address the basic and longstanding problems with this system. These reforms could have had a major impact on multi-owned private property, in both an ownership and governance sense. Abolition of feudal title and the reform of real burdens do ensure that the rights and responsibilities which are inseparable from ownership are now more transparent. There is also now an ability to reform existing title conditions, on a majority vote. Obsolete or unworkable burdens can now be extinguished and new community burdens introduced, thus creating a workable governance regime for the on-going management and maintenance of multi-owned property. Then if owners adopted the model management scheme, which is still in abeyance, an arrangement broadly similar to that which operates both in Australian and American common interest communities could be set in place (see for example the chapters by Cassidy et al. and McKenzie). But this would require a group of highly motivated and determined owners: owners who would not only need to be fully aware of the various legal possibilities but, in addition, able to convince their neighbours about the worth of pursuing such changes.

Access to the statutory default governance system is still subject to highly variable title provisions. Those most likely to benefit from the reformed common law are those whose title deeds in respect of governance arrangements are limited. Concerns about challenging individual property rights, in the light of European Convention on Human Rights considerations, ensured such arrangements could not be made to apply to all flat owners.

There was a strong case for insisting that the basic statutory system should be a legal requirement for the title deeds of all new multi-owned developments. Given the complexity of title conditions that currently prevail and the legal difficulties in implementing retrospective legislation to address these difficulties, this seemed an obvious reform. Having such a system in place for new flats would also have encouraged existing flat owners to adopt this system, through amending their present title provisions to those of the statutory system. But this suggestion failed to find favour amongst legal interests, who continued to support infinite developer flexibility in such matters.

So the real weakness, if not the fatal flaw of this entire reform exercise is that the power in relation to drawing up new title deeds still lies solely with the developer's solicitor. They can pick and choose from the proposed model management scheme, or the mini scheme in the reformed Law of the Tenement, to set in place workable governance provisions. Equally, they are able to simply ignore them, given that such title inclusions are not a statutory requirement, in favour of continuing to use their own standard title conditions. While this clearly suits both the developer and property manager interests, it takes absolutely no account of the consumer interests of owners.

Conclusion

Rather than introduce a common ownership arrangement, the norm in other legal jurisdictions, Scots law has stuck firmly with a system based upon individual ownership rights operating within the context of collective responsibilities. Further, solicitors still retain *carte blanche* when drafting the title deeds for a property, so no standard approach to the governance of multi-owned property yet exists. While the long established Law of the Tenement provisions were cleverly reformed, the value of this updating remains compromised because, as in the past, title provisions take precedence.

This legal reform was at variance with standard practice as operated in other jurisdictions. The reform agenda was dominated by a view that as there is no straightforward way of dealing with the future, opting for a standardized statutory system, which attempts to cover all situations was entirely the wrong approach. Rather, the best approach was to ensure that flexibility was retained. Van Der Merwe (1994: 6) noted, 'With the exception of Great Britain, it was recognised in most legal systems, that [flat ownership] cannot function properly or gain popularity without a firm statutory basis'. With England now having a statutory commonhold system (but see Blandy, Chapter 2), Scotland now stands alone. It would appear that while empowering home owners is an approach pursued in most other countries, this is not an approach favoured by Scottish legal interests.

Property law reform illustrates the long running and strong dominance of legal interests in Scottish policy-making. With the re-establishment of a Scottish Parliament it was thought that policy formulation would embrace other less politically articulate interests and thus become more inclusive. The establishment of the Housing Improvement Task Force in 2000, with its clear remit to examine private housing and the problem of on-going maintenance, could be considered as a move in this direction. The fact that the Task Force's work, on which the provisions of the Housing (Scotland) Act 2006 was based, has been overtaken and side-lined by the recent property law reform would suggest inclusive policy making has still some way to go in Scotland.

The failings of this reform process are ably illustrated by the fact that the Office of Fair Trading has just concluded an inquiry into property management services in Scotland (Office of Fair Trading 2009). This market investigation has been initiated as a result of sustained complaints over many years about the poor quality of property management/factoring services in Scotland (Welsh 1999). The recommendations were that the Scottish government should promote a self-regulatory scheme for factors, with an independent complaints redress mechanism, and should develop an advice and mediation service similar to that provided in England by the Leasehold Advisory Service (see Blandy, Chapter 2 for details). As this chapter illustrates, the issues involved here are both wide ranging and complex, but can be tied back to the inadequacy of the legal arrangements that underpin the governance of multi-owned property. This, more than anything else, contributes to the very poor quality and largely unaccountable property management services offered to home owners. Although as this book demonstrates, no system can ever hope to be perfect, current legal arrangements in Scotland continue to ensure a poor outcome for consumers of such services.

Two simple and basic reforms would make a major difference to this state of affairs. The first of these would be to insist that all future title deeds meet the requirements set down in the reformed common law. There is an irony that although there is a basic statutory system in place, it is not fully accessible to most flat owners. The second would be to insist that property management services for a block should be put out to competitive tender every five years. This would make the market more consumer focused and, in the process, encourage greater collective decision-making on the part of owners. An additional minor, but related, change would be to insist upon a collective insurance policy for all multi-owned blocks. The previous reform exercise made having insurance a legal requirement, but this was on an individual basis. Having this as a collective requirement would encourage the development of new insurance products and these, in turn, would provide a new income stream for property managers and thus make property management services more competitive. Such products would also help with the funding and organization of major repair works. With the demise of the improvement grant subsidy regime, heralded by the Housing (Scotland) Act 2006, there is no longer the public means to patch over the very obvious cracks in the current arrangements for privately owned housing. These proposals would start to change the balance of power by bringing consumer interests more to the fore.

References

Adams, I. 1978. *The Making of Urban Scotland*. London: Croom Helm.

Elliott, B. and McCrone, D. 1989. *Property and Power in a City: The Sociological Significance of Landlordism in Edinburgh*. Edinburgh: The University of Edinburgh.

Gretton, G. and Steven, A. 2009. *Property Trusts and Succession*. Edinburgh: Tottel.

Housing Improvement Task Force. 2003. *Housing in Scotland: The Final Report and Recommendations of the Housing Improvement Task Force*. Edinburgh: Scottish Executive.

Office of Fair Trading. 2009. *Property Managers in Scotland: A Market Study*. London: Office of Fair Trading.

O'Neill, S. 2000. *Home Truths: Research into Recent Experiences of House Buyers in Scotland*. Glasgow: Scottish Consumer Council.

Randolph, B., Wagstaff, M., Robertson, D. and Kendall, L. 1998. *Key Research on Easier Home Buying and Selling*. London: Department of the Environment, Transport and the Regions.

Reid, K. 1993. The Law of the Tenement, in *The Laws of Scotland: Stair Memorial Encyclopaedia*. Edinburgh: The Law Society/Butterworths, Volume 18: Property Law.

Reid, K. 1998. Reform of the Law of the Tenement. *Journal of Law Society of Scotland*, 43(4), 21–23.

Robertson, D. and Bailey, N. 1996. *Review of the Impact of Housing Action Areas*. Research Report, No 47. Edinburgh: Scottish Homes.

Robertson, D. and Rosenberry, K. 2001. *Home Ownership with Responsibility: Practical Governance Remedies for Britain's Flat Owners*. York: Joseph Rowntree Foundation and YPS.

Royal Incorporation of Charted Surveyors in Scotland. 1999. *Submission on the Scottish Law Commission's Discussion Paper No. 106 on Reform of Real Burden*. Edinburgh: RICS.

Scottish Executive. 2001 (last amended 2006). *We Are All Responsible: An Owner's Guide to the Management and Maintenance of Common Property*. Edinburgh: The Scottish Executive.

Scottish Executive. 2004. *Common Repair, Common Sense: A Homeowner's Guide to the Management and Maintenance of Common Property*. Edinburgh: Scottish Executive.

Scottish Homes. 1996. *Scottish House Condition Survey*. Edinburgh: Scottish Homes.

Scottish Homes. 2003. *House Condition Survey*. Edinburgh: Scottish Homes.

Scottish Law Commission 1998a. *Report on the Law of the Tenement*. Scottish Law Commission No 162. Edinburgh: Scottish Law Commission.

Scottish Law Commission. 1998b. *Reform of Real Burdens*. Scottish Law Commission Discussion Paper No. 106. Edinburgh: Scottish Law Commission.

Scottish Law Commission. 2000. *Report on Real Burdens*. Scottish Law Commission No. 181. Edinburgh: Scottish Law Commission.

Sim, D. 1996. *The Scottish House Factor*. Stirling: University of Stirling.

Van Der Merwe, C.G. 1994. Apartment Ownership, in *Volume VI: Property and Trust, International Encyclopaedia of Comparative Law, Instalment 29*, edited by A. Yiannopoulos. Leiden: Brill, 3–223.

Welsh, J. 1999. *In a Fix: The Views and Experiences of Owner Occupiers in Scotland Sharing Common Repairs Responsibilities with the Council*. Glasgow: Scottish Consumer Council.

Chapter 4
Emerging Regulatory Trends, Power and Competing Interests in US Common Interest Housing Developments

Evan McKenzie

Introduction

In the United States, the law of common interest housing, such as homeowner association-run planned communities, condominiums and housing cooperatives, has evolved rapidly in recent years. The pace of change is accelerating, with the stakes of state-level law reform in this area never having been higher. This chapter presents an overview of how this body of law has taken shape and focuses on recent reform efforts underway across the nation.

Common interest housing has become the predominant form of new housing construction in the US, yet early assessments that these developments would prove to be a more efficient alternative to municipalities are confronted by the fact of high levels of conflict and litigation, which are proving costly to residents as well as local governments. These disputes are largely the result of having unpaid, untrained volunteer directors carry out what were once municipal government functions. Cultural expectations of dominion and control over owner-occupied real estate fuel heated confrontations and litigation. Given that common interest developments (CIDs) form such a large share of the new housing stock, the stakes are enormous and it is important that the reforms succeed without over-reaching.

This chapter lays out the basics of the US legal framework for common interest housing, examines emerging regulatory trends, and offers an assessment of the political power dynamics that drive the competing law reform agendas.

A Quiet Revolution in Housing and Local Governance

Over the last four decades, there has been in the US a rapid, dramatic and probably irreversible transformation of the structure of local government, the nature of home ownership, and the organization of urban space. The new housing stock, once filled with detached single-family residences, has come to consist mainly of units in common interest housing developments; see Table 4.1. Since the early 1960s, an estimated 300,800 of these privately governed housing developments have been

Table 4.1 The Spread of Common Interest Housing in the US

	1970	1980	1990	2000	2008
CIDs	10,000	36,000	130,000	222,500	300,800
CID housing units	701,000	3,600,000	11,600,000	17,800,000	24,100,000
Total US housing units	67,699,000	86,759,000	102,264,000	115,905,000	127,901,934
CID units as % of total US units (%)	1.0	4.1	11.3	15.4	18.8
CID pop.	2,100,000	9,600,000	29,600,000	45,200,000	59,500,000
Total US pop.	203,211,926	226,545,805	248,709,873	281,421,906	304,059,724
CID pop. As % of total pop. (%)	1.0	4.2	11.9	16.1	19.6

Sources: Constructed by author from data published by the Community Associations Institute 2009 and the United States Census Bureau 2009.

constructed across the nation. These developments include 24.1 million housing units (Community Associations Institute 2009), representing 18.8 per cent of the American housing stock. Only 1 per cent of the nation's housing units were in CIDs in 1970 and the proportion rose rapidly to 4 per cent in 1980, over 11 per cent in 1990 and about 15 per cent in 2000. With an estimated 59.5 million residents (Community Associations Institute 2009), this housing sector now approaches 20 per cent of the American population (US Census Bureau 2009).

The Structure of Private Local Governments

In the US, the law of real property is almost entirely state law. Nonetheless, English common law doctrines lie at the foundation of US real property law, so it is possible to generalize about the law of common interest developments. The three main forms of CIDs are condominiums, planned developments of single-family homes with homeowners' associations, and housing cooperatives. They have certain common characteristics, as well as some differences. All types have some form of *common property ownership*; *private governing documents* that regulate what owners may do with and on their property; all come with automatic, mandatory membership in a *condominium* or *homeowners' association* of some sort, often known collectively as 'community associations'; and all have some form of *residential private government*. Common interest developments always involve some degree of *master planning*.

Common Property Ownership

The distinguishing characteristic of all forms of common interest housing is the bifurcated property interest that unit owners acquire with their deed. There is always a common interest and an individual interest. The common interest is a share in some or all of the real property that makes up the development. This interest takes different forms depending on the type of CID involved. The individual interest is that which the unit owner may call his or her own, which can range from a house and yard to an 'airspace' in a larger building that is basically a legal fiction.

In *condominium* developments, which are typically multi-family constructions resembling one or more apartment or townhouse buildings, each buyer acquires ownership of an individual unit consisting of just the airspace demarcated by the inner finished surface of the interior walls. This is coupled with a fractional interest in the ownership of the entire building. The condominium association has no ownership interest but manages and maintains the building on behalf of the owners.

Housing cooperatives give each owner a corporate share interest in the building or buildings, along with the exclusive right to occupy a particular unit secured through a lease. This form of housing is rare in the US and is found for the most part in New York City, Chicago and a few other cities. The cooperative association often has the right to approve the sale of units and may interview prospective owners before granting them the right to purchase.

Condominium and cooperative ownership is most often seen in the same types of multi-unit, multi-story buildings, but in the US condominiums are far more popular, so it is useful to consider the differences between these forms of ownership. It is debatable whether the literature on CID housing is even applicable to housing cooperatives, because they have a distinct history that is linked to that of other forms of cooperatives, and does not follow from the real estate developer and government initiatives that have shaped condominiums and planned communities. Consequently, the remainder of this chapter deals only with condominiums and planned communities with homeowners' associations. However, a few observations about cooperatives are instructive by way of comparison. Contemporary developers for the most part have no interest in creating new housing cooperatives, nor does any level of government encourage their development. The financial market is likewise not conducive to their creation, because they require one loan and mortgage for the entire building while condominium property is sold unit-by-unit with individual loans and mortgages. However, the relative lack of owner-board conflict in cooperatives as compared with condominiums of similar population density is worth noting. Cooperative boards routinely interview and screen prospective owners to ensure that they understand and accept the premises of shared ownership. Condominium sales, by contrast, typically are conducted as other private property sales between seller and buyer, with no intervention by the governing body representing the collectivity. That intervening step contributes to cooperatives being more animated by a spirit of voluntary collectivism than condominiums, where many owners seem to bring with them expectations of dominion and control more suitable to detached single-family ownership (see Blandy, Chapter 2).

Planned communities with homeowners' associations may include mixes of housing types but typically feature detached single-family homes with their own lawns and driveways, along with common areas such as private streets; recreation facilities such as golf courses, swimming pools, and lakes; and other facilities such as sewer and drainage systems, and parking areas. In such developments, the purchaser acquires individual ownership of one of the homes and perhaps a small yard. The owner's common interest is a voting right in the homeowners' association, an entity that has full ownership of the common areas. So, while a condominium association has only the right to manage the common area, in planned communities the homeowners' association actually has legal title to the common areas.

The differences among these three types of ownership give rise to different public policy issues. For example, many planned communities include such a wide range of what would otherwise be municipal facilities and services that they resemble private cities. They run parks, golf courses, swimming pools, and other leisure time activities, make decisions about street paving, ploughing and lighting, and even run private sewer and water systems. The need for such capabilities is related to location, because planned communities are often developed in newly developed suburban and rural areas where city or county government is relatively weak and lacks the capacity to provide services to large numbers of new residents. Legal arguments are being advanced that such associations are *de facto* local governments and should therefore be required to respect basic federal or state constitutional liberties (Askin 1998; Siegel 1998). Planned communities have been in existence under common law doctrines of restrictive covenants and equitable servitudes since the mid-nineteenth century.

Condominiums, by contrast, are often found in densely-populated urban areas, where general-purpose city governments provide most municipal services. These associations are more akin to apartment building managers than local governments, with functions such as maintaining lobbies, building security, and recreation rooms, and dealing with all the complex, inter-related components of a multi-family building. They also find themselves drawn into disputes among owners who run afoul of each other over noise, tobacco smoke, dripping water, and other opportunities for conflicting lifestyles generated by living in close proximity. Condominium ownership came to the US only in the early 1960s and must be specifically authorized by state enabling statute in order to qualify as real property.

Private Governing Documents

Common interest developments are created on paper before they take physical shape. They begin when a developer acquires a parcel of land and subdivides it into separate units. A Declaration of Covenants, Conditions and Restrictions (or similar title, generically referred to as 'CC&Rs') is drafted and recorded against all units so that it is permanently in the chain of title. A typical declaration will contain at least the following provisions: definition of the property and interests in it; stating that the covenants 'run with the land' and bind all subsequent purchasers; imposing numerous, detailed restrictions on the use of the property by all present and future owners; prescription of the rights, responsibilities and duties of the developer, unit owners, and the owners' association that will be established; allocation of voting rights in the association (typically giving the developer three votes for every unsold unit or another form of long-term control); description of how and when the turnover of control from developer to unit owners will happen; provision for automatic membership in the association for all purchasers of units; stating the duration of the covenants; vesting power in the corporate board of directors to administer the declaration for the benefit of the owners and to preserve the property; requiring owners to pay monthly and special assessments that become a lien on the unit if not paid, with foreclosure as the ultimate remedy for non-payment; and detailing how the covenants may be amended, which usually requires a two-thirds supermajority of all unit owners.

The developer also typically creates the owners' association as a not-for-profit corporation under the laws of the state where the development is located. This requires a set of articles of incorporation that authorize the association to conduct all necessary functions, and a set of corporate bylaws that should comply with the not-for-profit corporation act of that particular state. There may also be specific sets of operating rules and regulations which govern issues such as parking, use of common area recreation facilities, and review of owner proposals for architectural additions and modifications.

Although all these documents are typically drafted under the developer's auspices, the association is free to augment them after assuming control of the property, and it is common for them to do so. The most common amendment provisions require a two-thirds vote of all owners to change the declaration, which is very difficult to achieve because it is rare for two-thirds of the owners in most elections to vote at all. Other decisions, such as variances from the architectural standards or adoption of new operating rules, may be done by majority vote, and some changes can be made by majority vote of the board of directors. Illinois, for example, allows directors to make substantial changes in the rules on their own authority, including banning pets entirely (*Apple II Condominium Association v Worth Bank and Trust*)[1] and prohibiting the renting of units (*175 East Delaware Condominium Association v Hinojosa*).[2]

Community Associations

The not-for-profit corporate entity that represents the owners in their collective capacity goes by many different names, some reflecting differences in function and others simply different nomenclature. Condominium associations do, indeed, have special characteristics because they do not own property but have extensive building management duties. But a homeowners' association may be called a property owners' association, or even a neighbourhood association, with no implication

1 (1995) 277 Ill.App.3d 345.
2 (1997) 287 Ill.App.3d 886.

that its functions are any different. When people want to describe the entire range of associations, they sometimes use the generic term 'community associations', 'common interest communities', or 'residential private governments'.

The proliferation of these associations, and the fact that they are performing a wide range of the activities that previously were the purview of local governments, are perhaps the most transformative aspect of common interest housing. No longer can it be assumed that public local governments will provide a standard array of services and perform a typical set of functions for all residents. Neither can it be assumed that residents of an American community can count on being able to invoke familiar constitutional protections, such as expressive liberties, due process of law and the right to privacy, in their dealings with those who provide those services and perform those functions.

These associations are viewed by the law as voluntary membership organizations, but this is a legal fiction. Membership is mandatory and automatic upon taking the deed to the unit, and it cannot be resigned or revoked except by selling the unit, at which time membership automatically transfers to the new owner. The decision to purchase a home is certainly voluntary, but that rationale for describing membership of the community association as 'voluntary' is rapidly being undermined by the diminishing share of non-CID housing in new construction.

States typically require minimal reporting from the association within their borders. It is quite a task even to ascertain how many associations exist within any particular jurisdiction and researchers are often forced to pore laboriously through state corporate records and make individual judgments about the names of not-for-profit corporations to judge whether or not they are community associations. Data on the funds held in reserve by these associations and other matters are similarly difficult to obtain. This is why they have been referred to as 'shadow governments' that operate largely invisible to public scrutiny (Garreau 1988).

Residential Private Governments

All community associations have boards of directors who manage corporate affairs. This means making decisions on behalf of the members about how to maintain the common areas, raise and spend association funds and make and enforce the rules. The board of directors, then, is in essence a residential private government with jurisdiction over its members in many areas of their lives, including matters that would otherwise have been handled by a municipality and other matters that would have been beyond the reach of a municipality due to constitutional limits. For example, an association board may make decisions about how to maintain a storm water detention pond, just as a municipality would, but it may also decide to ban the display of political signs entirely, something a municipality cannot do under United States Supreme Court precedent: *City of Ladue v Gilleo.*[3]

3 (1994) 512 U.S. 43.

As common interest housing has come to predominate in new construction, so have the number of private governments increased. The model of community association governance that we see in the US is copied from the city manager model, which was in turn copied from business corporation governance (McKenzie 1994). While this model may lend itself to efficiency, it must be noted that business corporation governance is not intended to be democratic, in the sense that share owners are virtually powerless to control anything except by selling their shares if they are unhappy with the corporate direction. This may be a sensible arrangement for a business corporation because most share owners are not interested in any aspect of the enterprise except the share price. But for a community association, the 'shareholders' are living in the development and carrying out the most intimate and important activities of their lives there. In that context, their expectations of democratic control can, and often do, vastly exceed the amount of control they have over association affairs. This is the source of great discontent in many situations, so that disputes arise not just over substantive decisions of the association, such as over whether to re-roof the recreation centre, but over the monopoly of power held by the association directors. Consistent with the corporate model, these directors have the power to restrict access to records, control the meeting agenda, marginalize their critics, shield their decisions from scrutiny and even misuse corporate funds.

The entire institution of common interest housing rests on the volunteer directors, yet they are unpaid, untrained, often unqualified, and almost entirely unsupported by the governments whose work they are often doing. Those who run these private governments operate without institutional support from government at any level. To the extent that they have any support at all, it comes from contracting with property management firms that specialize in community association work, retaining legal counsel and hiring such other contractors as may be necessary for managing the property and financial affairs of the association. However, many states do not even require that community association managers have any professional license at all. Even where such licensing or certification is required, this remains an inchoate profession where there is enormous variation in the education, training, experience, wisdom and honesty of practitioners. In recent years, for example, there have been a number of scandals involving embezzlement of massive amounts of association funds by management firms.

These professionals are organized under the umbrella of a trade association, the Community Associations Institute, which offers training and education for its members and also is the single most involved and effective interest group in this issue area, being active in all relevant legislation and key appellate cases. The Community Associations Institute has an obvious interest in perpetuating the *status quo*. It advocates minimal governmental oversight of associations and the professionals who serve them, and to the extent that such oversight cannot be averted, it tries to put its organization in the role of certifying and training professionals to comply with any state licensing requirements. This is, of course, typical trade association behaviour, but the result is a relative lack of public support and public accountability for associations.

Because of the lack of public oversight over these residential private governments, the main check on their power is civil litigation between associations and owners. In these disputes, there are three different standards of care that can potentially be used to judge the actions of directors, depending upon which state's law applies and on the nature of the association activity that is at issue. These standards are the business judgment rule, the standard of reasonableness, and a quasi-governmental standard that might apply in certain rare situations.

The *business judgment rule* is derived from business corporation law that is invoked both to defend a corporate policy decision against challenge and to protect the directors who made it against personal liability. It is a judicial presumption that, if certain conditions are satisfied, a judge will not question the substance of a corporate decision, nor will the directors who made that decision be subject to personal liability. In essence, it is a policy decision that the judiciary should defer to the corporate board of directors and not re-evaluate the decision on its merits, as long as the decision was made in a detached, businesslike manner. The conditions for invoking the rule are that the decision was a business matter that was within the power of the board to make; that the board acted in a disinterested and independent manner in making it; that it was made in good faith and in an effort to promote the best interests of the corporation; that it was made after the directors undertook reasonable efforts to inform themselves on the matters in question, including obtaining advice from professionals if necessary; that there is no evidence of fraud, self-dealing, or waste; and in one formulation of the rule, that there is no evidence of an abuse of discretion. This standard is most often applied when members challenge action taken by directors, such as granting or denying applications for architectural modifications to units, deciding whether or not to file a lawsuit, entering into contracts, and other business-related matters.

The *reasonableness standard* is used most often for discretionary application of the behavioural rules, where the issues is how the directors balanced the various interests involved in light of the overall purpose of the rules and the board's mission to safeguard the property values and quality of life of all residents in the project. However, the standard can also be applied to the substance of a rule itself, with the question being whether the rule is reasonable in the abstract. For example, in one leading case, *Nahrstedt v Lakeside Village Condominium Association*,[4] a condominium resident had two cats in violation of a 'no pets' rule. She argued that the issue was whether it was reasonable for the board to expel her cats, under all the particular facts of her case. This view was consistent with two reported appellate cases that dealt with bans on satellite dishes and pickup trucks, where the courts had held that the issue was the reasonableness of the board's decision, given the facts of the situation to which the rule was being applied: *Bernardo*

4 (1994) 4 Cal. 4th 361.

Villas Management Corp. v Black,[5] and *Portola Hills Community Assn. v James*.[6] The resident claimed that her cats were always confined to her unit and generated no noise or odours that anybody else could perceive and that consequently they had no impact on anybody else's life. She claimed that the board had only become aware of them by surreptitiously peering through her windows. Thus, she argued, expelling them was an unreasonable application of the rule.

However, the California Supreme Court agreed with the board that the issue was whether the rule itself was reasonable in light of the type of property to which it was applied, not whether the application in her individual case was reasonable. The Court ruled that it was entirely reasonable for an urban condominium to have a blanket prohibition on pets and declined to commit the state's judicial resources to scrutinizing the minute details of feline behaviour. The *Narhstedt* decision represents a relatively deferential view toward the power of association boards of directors and seems to reflect a sense that with tens of thousands of associations in the state, the task of re-making board decisions on their individual merits would be an unwarranted burden on the courts. However, one justice, Armand Arabian, wrote a spirited dissent criticizing the majority's ruling and arguing that there must be judicial review of the substance of board decisions in order to protect the sanctity of the home.

It has been urged that boards should be subject to a third and higher, *quasi-governmental standard of review* when they infringe on fundamental constitutional liberties such as freedom of expression. For example, it has been argued that large, city-like planned communities should be held subject to state or federal limits on infringement of expressive liberties. This was most fully litigated in the case of *Committee for a Better Twin Rivers v Twin Rivers Homeowners' Association*,[7] where the plaintiffs argued that Twin Rivers was the functional equivalent of a municipality. The United States Supreme Court ruled in 1946 that the privately-owned town of Chickasaw, Alabama, although wholly owned by the Gulf Shipbuilding Corporation, had to respect the First Amendment rights of a Jehovah's Witness who had been arrested while distributing religious literature: *Marsh v Alabama*.[8] The Court ruled in *Marsh* that the town was 'the functional equivalent of a municipality', and that expressive liberties did not lose their power where a private corporation carried on all or nearly all the activities of a municipality. This ruling sounds on its face as though it would provide a solid precedent for applying constitutional standards of review to community associations. The Supreme Court has been unwilling to extend that US Constitutional ruling much beyond its own facts, but state constitutions provide a separate basis for civil liberties, so the *Twin Rivers* plaintiffs were proceeding under provisions of the New Jersey Constitution that had already been held to protect certain limited free speech rights on private

5 (1987) 190 Cal.App.3d 153.
6 (1992) 4 Cal.App.4th 289.
7 (2007) 192 N.J. 344.
8 (1946) 326 U.S. 501.

property. They advanced an argument based on the principles of the *Marsh* decision, but the New Jersey Supreme Court ruled that, in balancing the owners' rights against the association's policies, the Twin Rivers association had not violated the free speech and right of assembly clauses of the New Jersey Constitution. However, the Court's ruling did not eliminate the possibility that associations could violate those constitutional provisions under a different set of facts. There are numerous groups and individuals who continue to argue that some associations should be held subject to certain state or even federal constitutional protections and it is possible that this standard will at some point enter the jurisprudence governing community association board actions.

Master Planning

It is impossible to understand the nature of American common interest housing without some grasp of the role played by large institutions with an interest in turning housing into a mass-produced commodity consisting of fungible units, nested in a thoroughly predictable way within planned neighbourhoods or complexes. The origins of common interest housing lie in the works of pioneering nineteenth-century architects and visionaries such as Frederick Law Olmsted and Ebenezer Howard who believed that master planning of entire communities would produce a much higher quality of life than organic growth of neighbourhoods. In the US, developer Jesse Clyde Nichols planned many large private communities and founded the Urban Land Institute, the organization most responsible for standardizing building practices by large developers. The Urban Land Institute, the Federal Housing Administration, the Veteran's Administration, the Federal National Mortgage Association (Fannie Mae), the Federal National Mortgage Corporation (Freddie Mac), the General National Mortgage Association (Ginnie Mae), the Community Associations Institute and a number of private mortgage companies and insurers have all contributed to the standardization of nearly every aspect of community association life. That is why across the nation we see the same neighbourhood types geared to particular demographic slices of the population, along with the same housing styles, governance structures, and governing documents.

What Drives the Spread of Common Interest Developments?

The CID revolution is driven by the motivations of developers and local governments on the supply side and those of consumers on the demand side. CIDs are especially prevalent where land costs are high (McKenzie 1998). Developers seeking to mass-produce housing for the middle-class have found that CIDs allow them to build higher-density developments. If they can create commonly owned parks, swimming pools, and other amenities, they can put more people on less land and also provide these amenities to buyers to compensate for small lots. Private streets can be narrower than public ones, leaving more land for lots, and common utility lines further lower costs. For these reasons, CIDs enable developers to maintain profits and keep prices relatively affordable despite rising land prices.

Local governments seek growth and increased tax revenues with minimal public expenditure. It is no coincidence that CIDs became much more prevalent after the property tax revolt that began in 1978 in California (on this subject Sears and Citrin observed in 1985 that citizens appeared to want 'something for nothing'). Tax-sensitive property owners resist paying for the infrastructure and services needed for new residents, but want certain kinds of services for themselves nonetheless. CIDs privatize what would otherwise be government responsibilities. The cost of new infrastructure is added to the price of new homes and maintenance costs fall on new homeowners' association members, who pay them through monthly assessments. The associations arrange for garbage collection, plough snow in the winter and remove leaves in the autumn, repair and light streets, manage parks and do many other things that government would otherwise have to do. Thus cities can acquire new property tax payers without having to extend to them the full panoply of municipal services, thereby making CIDs 'cash cows' for local government. For this reason, many municipalities are now requiring that all new construction be in common interest housing developments (Siegel 2006).

These dynamics operating on developers and local governments produce a mutuality of interests that leads to a joint decision to build common interest housing. These two supply-side incentives are powerful, and a study of California shows that they explain about two-thirds of the variance in CID construction there (McKenzie 1998). That suggests that developers and local governments are primarily responsible for the rapid spread of CIDs.

In addition to these supply-side dynamics, there is a certain level of demand for the CID lifestyle. Some middle- and upper-class home buyers, concerned about crime and disenchanted with government, are searching for a privatized utopia offering a sense of neighbourhood control, enhanced security, a homogenous population and small-scale managerial private government that enforces high standards of property maintenance. Lang and Danielson (1997) suggest that the CID lifestyle appeals to corporate managerial employees who are very mobile and live in neighbourhoods where there is a high degree of transience and therefore an absence of relationship-based informal social controls to manage conflicts over routine neighborhood issues. In such 'corporate migrant communities', the formal social controls emanating from a homeowners' association are seen as a positive feature (Lang and Danielson 1997: 883).

Aside from those who are familiar with and eager to embrace common interest living, the vast majority of home buyers are not well informed about either the demands of common interest housing in general nor the terms of the particular set of governing documents to which they are subscribing by purchasing a home. Neither are they competent to understand how these terms would be applied, or anticipate what additional terms may be added by subsequent board action.

Problems and Law Reform

Municipalities may find the economic logic of actively promoting construction of privately governed communities compelling in the short-term. However, what is often lost sight of is that, in so doing, municipalities are abdicating some of their municipal functions to private corporations. It is this unacknowledged fact – that the rise of common interest housing is the most massive privatization of local government services ever undertaken in American history – that gives rise to the problems.

The most obvious set of problems arises from the conscription of owners into mandatory membership associations that must be run by directors elected from among them. Municipal dependency on private governance in high-growth areas also reduces housing choice. Lack of choice in the housing market draws unwilling owners into privately governed communities which contributes to a rising tide of owner resistance and activism (Siegel 2006, Sappenfield 2004).

There are also serious questions about whether this massive transfer of authority to unpaid and untrained volunteers can be made to work without a significantly increased investment of governmental resources. To date, the gap between the expertise needed to run a private residential government and the knowledge that owners actually have has been filled by hired lawyers and other professionals who serve as the main source of institutional support for boards. While this may serve for large associations who can afford the steep costs, small ones may lack the resources needed to bolster their volunteer government with trained professionals.

Additionally, many associations are underfunded, leading to massive special assessments that are imposed on owners when the time comes to replace streets or other major components. These events often produce negative press coverage that has the potential to adversely affect the market for this form of housing. Ultimate financial responsibility for deteriorating streets, roofs and other building components rests with the individual owners, as does potential liability for debts and civil judgments resulting from director mismanagement. This financial burden will increase year by year as these developments age (see also Alterman, Chapter 5). Municipalities are also accepting tax revenues from people to whom they are not delivering a full share of services, and who must in effect pay twice (property taxes and private assessments) for public services, which raises significant questions of tax fairness and charges of 'double taxation'.

Moreover, government has been turning a blind eye to the high level of conflict and litigation emanating from this privatized realm. The only recourse for owners and associations is the court system. Lawsuits over internal matters, nearly always filed by associations against owners, are commonplace in areas with large numbers of CIDs. Individual owners typically cannot afford the high cost of legal representation, while associations can, because they are able to tap the common resources of the development as a whole.

There are also many lawsuits filed by associations against developers over defects in original construction, with expensive problems such as water intrusion and mould becoming major problems in many developments. Issues also arise between associations and municipalities over maintenance and repair of association property that is adversely affecting the general welfare, such as bodies of water that are breeding mosquitoes. The public costs of resolving all these private disputes through expensive litigation are sufficient to trigger proposals for alternative dispute resolution.

Three states chosen here for examples of current reform trends, Florida, Arizona and California, have well-established interest groups representing professionals and institutions that have a stake in the success of common interest housing. The most prominent of these are the state Legislative Action Committees of the leading national trade association in this field, the Community Associations Institute, which represents the interests of attorneys, property managers, contractors and other professionals, and also has some associations as members.

Each of these three states also has its own network of homegrown activists who advocate for the rights of individual homeowners who find themselves in opposition to their association, its directors, or the lawyers and other professionals hired by the board. These activist groups use the internet to organize, setting up e-mail distribution lists, web sites, weblogs and discussion groups. They seek to counter the legislative efforts of established interest groups concerned with CIDs and their orientation varies from reformists who are mildly critical of the status quo to abolitionists who loathe everything about common interest housing and would, if possible, see it eradicated.

Historically, the Community Associations Institute and other established groups have been successful in marginalizing the owner activist organizations, who had acquired an image of disgruntled neighbourhood malcontents refusing to abide by the rules they agreed to at time of purchase, and that others comply with willingly. Yet for the last five years, in these three states and elsewhere, legislators have given more credence to the complaints of owner groups about homeowners' association board actions, including those of homeowners' association attorneys. These complaints concern alleged abuse of the foreclosure power; violation of procedural rules in meetings and elections; denial of member access to association records; inadequate disclosure of homeowners' association finances, such as inadequate reserves and pending special assessments, at time of purchase; mismanagement of association funds and undisclosed director conflicts of interest; denial of basic rights and liberties such as displaying the flag and political signs; and the absence of any governmental oversight, or any forum short of civil litigation where owners can assert their rights or adjudicate claims of association abuse.

Florida

Before the current round of reform began, Florida already had a regulatory agency for condominiums, called the Division of Florida Land Sales, Condominiums, and

Mobile Homes, located in the Department of Business and Professional Regulation. Continuing problems with the internal workings of condominiums and increased recognition of problems in non-condominium homeowner associations, led to the creation in 2003 of two special bodies tasked with proposing reforms. One group was a legislative committee established by the Florida House of Representatives, titled the Select Committee on Condominium Association Governance. The other initiative came from the executive branch and focused on homeowner associations. This was called the Homeowner Association Task Force, the members of which were appointed by Florida Governor Jeb Bush.

The two groups held hearings, took testimony, reviewed documents and produced reports. There followed a good deal of legislative manoeuvring that led to the eventual passage of two major reform Bills, SB (Senate Bill) 1184, which was signed by the Governor on June 23 2004, and SB 2984, signed into law on 30 June 2004.

SB 1184 made many changes in the law, but the most significant was the creation of the Office of Condominium Ombudsman, a gubernatorial appointee who would give aggrieved owners a governmental official to whom they could turn, rather than having to file a lawsuit. The Ombudsman also has the power to monitor disputes over condominium elections and meetings and recommend enforcement action by the Bureau of Condominiums. The Bill also created an Advisory Council on Condominiums, a seven-member board the function of which would be to receive public input concerning condominium-related matters, advise government on such issues and recommend improvements.

In addition to creating a vehicle for easy enforcement, SB 1184 greatly expanded owners' rights against associations. Among other provisions, the Bill prohibited associations from attaching liens to members' property for unpaid fines, so that foreclosure would not be allowed except for unpaid assessments. Residents are guaranteed the right to display flags. The law imposed detailed process requirements on associations regarding the conduct of meetings and elections, such as guaranteeing members the right to attend, to speak at meetings, and to have access to association records, and giving them the power to recall directors. Election disputes were sent to mandatory binding arbitration, and the right to alternative dispute resolution was expanded. Interestingly, the Bill empowers owners to challenge legal action taken against them by their homeowners' association board, by asserting a SLAPP (Strategic Lawsuits Against Public Participation) defence. Thus lawsuits are subject to dismissal if the defendant can show that the motivation for the suit is retaliation for asserting his or her rights against the association.

Many of the Homeowner Association Task Force's recommendations were incorporated into SB 2984. This Bill applies to all community associations, and most of the process regulation terms: elections, records, meetings, SLAPP lawsuits, alternative dispute resolution, recall of directors, flag display, and banning liens for fines – coincide with the provisions of SB 1184. However, the Ombudsman and Advisory Council on Condominiums would not have jurisdiction over non-condominium community associations.

Both these Bills made significant pro-homeowner changes in the law. However, some even more drastic proposals did not pass. For example, the House Select Committee considered but rejected a proposal to impose monetary fines on board members who abuse the foreclosure process, and even to file criminal charges against board members under certain circumstances (Select Committee 2004).

There was another significant round of property manager and condominium-only reform in the 2007–2008 legislative cycle. Florida law prior to 2008 required all community association property managers of developments with more than 50 units to be licensed and subject to the Regulatory Council of Community Association Managers. The new legislation, HB (House Bill) 995, lowered the threshold for licensing to ten units or a budget of $10,000 or more; expanded the responsibilities of the Regulatory Council to include public education and tightened licensing and regulatory requirements for property managers. HB 995 also made almost 40 process-type changes to the law governing condominiums, including a provision for monetary damages from association directors or agents for willful, malicious, or criminal violations of the law; civil penalties for destruction of accounting records; disclosure of information concerning reserve accounts; further specifications concerning who can serve on board of directors; hurricane protection; prohibition of SLAPP suits aimed at silencing critics; removal of board members by the regulatory agency for refusing to follow the law; and the establishment of a Community Association Living Study Council that would make recommendations for additional reform concerning all forms of common interest housing.

Arizona

In 2003–2004 there were at least 19 individual pieces of CID legislation introduced in the Arizona state legislature, nine of which were enacted. These included HB (House Bill) 2177, with a host of pro-homeowner operating procedure reforms dealing with access to records, open meetings and the right to speak; HB 2379, mandating annual audits of association finances; HB 2380, expanding association duties of written disclosure to prospective purchasers, including an explanation that association rules are a binding contract, and that the buyer is not protected against assessment liens by the state 'homestead exemption'; HB 2381, expanding rules governing conflicts of interest by members of association boards of directors; HB 2402, perhaps the most important from the standpoint of homeowner activists because it limited the power of associations to foreclose and required that the sale be for fair market value; HB 2478, guaranteeing owners limited rights to display political signs; HB 2492 mandating that associations must allow public safety vehicles to enter and drive on private streets; SB (Senate Bill) 1125, requiring counties to keep records of the addresses of condominium and planned communities in their jurisdiction; and SB 1137, granting any single member of an association legal standing to challenge in court the actions of an association, instead of 50, or 10 per cent of the voting members.

However, the owners did not get everything they hoped for. HB 2378 would have extended to associations the state's open meetings laws that apply to local governments. And the original foreclosure reform Bill would have allowed the delinquent owner seven years to pay the overdue assessments before foreclosure proceedings could be instituted. This provision would have seriously jeopardized the financial viability of associations by rendering them powerless to guarantee the stream of revenue essential to performing their functions.

Removal of this requirement from the Bill before passage underscores the limits of reform: legislatures are sympathetic to claims that owners are being abused, but they seem to stop short of enacting reform measures that seriously threaten the ability of associations to perform their quasi-municipal functions. As described below, something similar happened to foreclosure reform in California.

In 2005, proxy voting in condominiums was eliminated entirely, with absentee ballots still being allowed. This reflected a concern that proxy voting was conducive to corruption of the electoral process. In the 2007–2008 cycle, there was another round of some 20 single-issue Bills, of which only a few passed. HB 2440 prohibited associations from banning the gathering of signatures for political petitions such as referenda, and this was passed by both houses and signed by the Governor in May, 2008.

California

California, unlike Florida, deals with all forms of common interest housing under one rubric, which is the label 'common interest developments'. The main body of the legislation dealing with these entities is the Davis-Stirling Common Interest Development Act, which was passed in 1985. Foreclosure horror stories have become a staple of California media, and homeowner activism has focused on the issue of foreclosure for unpaid assessments. Owner groups had been arguing for years that the foreclosure power was being abused by homeowners' association boards and predatory attorneys who specialize in assessment collection. These claims were bolstered by the case of Tom and Anita Radcliff, who fell behind in assessments in the amount of $120, mistakenly paid all but $1.50 of it and had their $285,000 house taken from them in foreclosure and sold for $70,000. Faced with this horror story and others like it, state legislators began to seriously consider foreclosure reform (Yi 2004a, 2004b).

But there was also a more general sense that CID law in California was inadequate for the challenges facing associations, owners, and the public generally. The California Law Revision Commission, an influential state-funded law reform organization, began a project to reform CID law in January of 2001. It was preceded by a study by law professor Susan French, who characterized the Davis-Stirling Act as having four major flaws: first, it was 'too complicated and hard to understand … almost impossible to read, even for people with legal training. It is poorly written

– some parts are virtually incomprehensible; others are extremely difficult to wade through. The act lacks a logical organizational structure.' Second, 'The coverage is very uneven. The statute covers some areas in excruciating detail and pays little or no attention to others.' Third, 'Securing compliance with the law is difficult. There is no regulatory agency charged with overseeing CIDS once they have passed beyond [the California Department of Real Estate's] control over the initial sales stage. If association boards fail to carry out their responsibilities or fail to comply with the law, owners have little recourse except to the courts.' French also observed that 'Resort to legal proceedings is often very expensive and can be very risky for an owner because the association may have greater resources to spend on legal talent, and the owner who loses is often liable for the association's attorney fees'. Fourth, 'The protections for individual rights are weak' (French 2000: 3–6).

Based on French's study, the California Law Revision Committee focused on a number of specific CID issue areas, including rule-making, architectural review, elections, and alternative dispute resolution. In the 2002–2003 legislative session, the Revision Committee's recommendations were largely adopted in a new law, AB (Assembly Bill) 512, that reformed the procedures by which CID boards could make and amend rules. The Bill applied a quasi-legislative model to association rule-making. In AB 1836, the legislature adopted alternative dispute resolution provisions that followed the Law Revision Committee's recommendations, and, with AB 2376, the legislature followed their proposal that boards must follow the same due process guidelines in architectural review as they use for covenant enforcement.

The legislature also gave owner groups a major (but short-lived) victory by passing SB 1682 (fused with a companion Bill, AB 2598), that drastically reduced the power of homeowners' associations to foreclose for unpaid assessments. However, on the last day allowed by law, Governor Arnold Schwarzenegger vetoed the Bill on the grounds that, while reform was needed, this Bill would too severely reduce the power of associations to raise needed revenue and provide services to residents. This veto is extremely significant, because, combined with what happened in Arizona, it suggests limits to the potential for reform: where reforms would threaten the ability of homeowners' associations to perform their quasi-municipal functions, they are not likely to be enacted.

Despite the best efforts of the California Law Revision Commission and others, California law governing CIDs remained ultimately self-contradictory: on the one hand, the basic operating premise was the need for legislative micro-management of homeowners' associations, but on the other hand there was no government agency responsible for enforcing all these dictates, nor any convenient forum where individuals could seek to hold boards to the law. However, late in 2004 and after the 2003–2004 session had ended, the California Law Revision Commission issued a tentative recommendation to create a state regulatory agency. This recommendation remained subject to further public comment and revision. The proposal was to 'create the Common Interest Development Bureau within the Department of Consumer Affairs. The bureau would educate common interest development homeowners and board members as to their rights and obligations under the law, provide informal assistance in resolving disputes, and as a last resort, enforce the law governing common interest developments' (California Law Revision Commission 2004). The agency would have been funded by fees charged to all CIDs in the state. Given the CLRC's high success rate with the state legislature, it seemed likely that California would soon adopt a policy of direct state regulation of CIDs, as had already been done in Florida and Nevada. The Bill, AB 567, passed in both houses of the legislature but it too was vetoed by Governor Schwarzenegger, on the stated ground that creating another government agency would be costly and unnecessary.

The Commission was also successful in persuading the legislature to pass a law mandating that all CIDs in the state had to adopt, using the previously mandated rule-changing procedures, a set of election rules that complied with a set of public standards. This CID election statute is quite complicated and detailed, with standards concerning ballots and their preservation, voting procedures, secrecy and other matters, and even requires that all CID elections must be observed by a neutral election monitor. The statute makes no provision for how these monitors are to be compensated.

By 2008, the state of California had detailed process regulations in place for assessment collection, rule-making, architectural review, elections, and alternative dispute resolution. This was followed by the California Law Revision Commission's most ambitious undertaking: a complete recodification of the Davis-Stirling Act. In the 2007–2008 session, the Revision Committee delivered a Bill that would, they said, solve the confusion and duplication problems identified in 2001 by Professor French. The Bill, AB 1921, failed to pass in the 2008 session.

This episode underscores the incredible complexity of the law concerning CIDs, a body of law that, in California and elsewhere, is becoming more complex, ambiguous and spread out every year. The notion that this metastasizing body of law can be learned by volunteer CID directors in their spare time after job and family are attended to, is dubious at best. Yet the premise of California's process regulation paradigm is that the problems with CIDs can be solved by rules, rules and more rules.

Conclusion

In the US, the relationship between a CID and its residents has typically been viewed as a private matter governed by the laws of contract (McKenzie 1998). However, the production of CID housing is driven by the fiscal dynamics affecting developers and municipalities and over time the supply of new housing has become predominantly CID units. Consequently, the long-standing logic underpinning the rule of *caveat emptor* has been increasingly undermined as choice in the ability to choose non-CID housing diminished. Ironically, the market success of CID housing is producing a stronger rationale for subjecting the market-defined relationship between owner and association to greater regulation. Based on recent events in a number of states, there now seems to be an increased willingness among policy makers to view this relationship as one with some public aspects. At the very least, it is now seen as a private relationship that requires a considerable degree of public oversight and regulation. The elements of a new regulatory model may be emerging, consisting of an ombudsman's office, a standing study commission or regulatory agency and increasingly specific regulation of associations' internal processes.

However, the increased state role in regulation of association activities is not matched by a comparable governmental willingness to examine the larger issues. The dynamics of land costs and local taxation that fuel the rapid rise of common interest housing seem still to be viewed as conditions that are not proper subjects of state intervention at this juncture.

References

Askin, F. 1998. Free speech, private space, and the constitution. *Rutgers Law Journal*, 29(3), 947–61.

California Law Revision Commission. 2004. *Tentative Recommendation: State Assistance to Common Interest Developments. CLRC Document Number H-853*. Palo Alto: California Law Revision Commission.

Community Associations Institute. 2009. Data on US Community Associations, Alexandria, VA: Community Associations Institute. [Online]. Available at: http://www. caionline.org/info/research/Pages/default.aspx [accessed: 14 May 2009].

French, S. 2000. *Scope of Study of Laws Affecting Common Interest Developments: California Law Revision Commission Study H-850*. Palo Alto: California Law Revision Commission.

Garreu, J. 1988. *Edge City: Life on the New Frontier*. New York: Doubleday.

Lang, R. and Danielson, K. 1997. Gated communities in America: Walling out the world? *Housing Policy Debate*, 8(4), 867–99.

McKenzie, E. 1994. *Privatopia: Homeowner Associations and the Rise of Residential Private Government*. New Haven, CT: Yale University Press.

McKenzie, E. 1998. Homeowner associations and California politics: An exploratory analysis. *Urban Affairs Review*, 34(1), 52–74.

Sappenfield, M. 2004. The backlash against homeowners' groups. *Christian Science Monitor.* [Online]. Available at: http://csmonitor.com/2004/1014/p01s02-ussc.html [accessed: 14 October, 2004].

Sears, D. and Citrin, J. 1982. *Tax Revolt: Something for Nothing in California*. Cambridge: Harvard University Press.

Select Committee on Condominium Association Governance. 2004. First Report and Recommendations. [Online]. Available at: http://www.ccfj.net/condoHSCreport.html [accessed: 24 February 2004].

Siegel, S. 1998. The Constitution and private government: Toward the recognition of constitutional rights in private residential communities fifty years after Marsh v Alabama. *William & Mary Bill of Rights Journal*, 6(2), 461–563.

Siegel, S. 2006. The public role in establishing private residential communities. *Urban Lawyer*, 38(4), 859–948.

United States Census Bureau. 2009. *2009 Statistical Abstract*: *No. HS-27. Housing Units–Historical Trends for Selected Characteristics* [Online]. Available at: http://www.census.gov/statab/hist/HS-27.pdf [accessed: 14 May 2009].

Yi, D. 2004a. Panel hears home horror stories. *Los Angeles Times*, February 18, Part B, 6.

Yi, D. 2004b. Homeowner groups' power to foreclose is under attack. *Los Angeles Times*, 7 June, Part B, 1.

Chapter 5

The Maintenance of Residential Towers in Condominium Tenure: A Comparative Analysis of Two Extremes – Israel and Florida

Rachelle Alterman

Introduction

This chapter addresses an increasing problem caused by the intersection of two major trends in urban living. The first is the steep worldwide increase in the number of residential towers, defined here as buildings of 20 storeys or more. Although no official data are available, some estimates indicate this trend (Council on Tall Buildings and Urban Habitat 2008). The second trend is the dramatic rise in condominium ownership and other forms of homeowners' associations. Not all the residents who belong to condominiums or other forms of homeowners' association live in residential towers, but the combination of these two trends harbours problems. A fast-rising proportion of the world's population is already or is expected to be living in this category of housing. An extremely challenging question concerning residential condominium towers has so far received very limited attention, namely: is there a sustainable legal-financial mechanism that can ensure their long-term maintenance so as to prevent their deterioration?

In addressing that question, the chapter focuses on two dichotomized types of condominium law, referred to here as 'simple' and 'enhanced'. The first type is represented by a Mediterranean country, Israel; the second by the US state of Florida. The main part of this chapter compares the degree of suitability of these two types of laws to tower housing. It concludes with a discussion of some public policy and legal instruments that may be required in order to bridge the gaps. The current financial crisis casts an additional shadow over the desirability, as a matter of public policy, of relying on tower condominiums as a mainstream part of the housing market.

The Cost of Long-term Maintenance

Contrary to conventional wisdom, tall buildings often entail *higher* rather than lower maintenance costs per unit despite the large number of owners; the taller, the more complex, although not quite in a linear relationship (for details see Alterman 2009). A further problem is related to the structural attributes of tower buildings, which operate like complex, closed machines that are not amenable to structural changes. Unlike regular buildings, in towers it will not be possible to grant additional development rights in the future as an incentive to finance the necessary updating costs. Tower buildings are less amenable to structural modifications, so there is a greater danger that their relative value will eventually diminish, causing them to lose their position in the housing market, and thus to deteriorate faster than smaller apartment buildings. In addition to current expenditures for routine maintenance, comparatively larger investments are required for periodic repair and replacement of expensive machinery, large scale upgrading and renovation of the whole building and so on, than applies to regular buildings.

The problem of finding a mechanism for financing the long-term maintenance of tall buildings is complicated by the fact that the costs are not consistent over time. Four levels of maintenance may be distinguished schematically by the frequency of action required:

- *Level 1 Ongoing Maintenance*: Day-to-day or weekly activities, such as cleaning of the foyer, staircases, elevators, gardening, security (where provided).
- *Level 2 Preventative Upkeep*: Periodic upkeep needed every few years to prevent deterioration of structures and machines.
- *Level 3 Periodic Replacements*: Structures, machines and elevators, may need replacement approximately every decade, alongside external walls.
- *Level 4 Renovation and Updating*: After approximately 20 years even well-maintained buildings will likely need renovation and upgrading to reflect higher housing standards in the marketplace, in order to prevent the otherwise natural process whereby the building would move down the ladder of housing quality, and price.

In terms of visibility, if Level 1 maintenance is neglected it quickly becomes obvious to the residents. In regular condominiums with a small number of owners, collection of funds for this level of maintenance should be less difficult than for the other levels because owners are able to see what their payment has financed close to the collection date, and the periodic payment is relatively small each time. For the other levels of maintenance, as the time periods grow longer, the connection between the date of collection of the maintenance fees and the maintenance activity becomes less direct. The visible benefits of Levels 2 and 3 maintenance activities are likely to be less obvious to the owners. By contrast, Level 4 maintenance refers to renovating the building as a whole, and is therefore likely to be highly visible. However, it is rarely undertaken and, in any case, is not usually budgeted for beforehand. In order to pay for maintenance activities of types Levels 2 to 4, a condominium should have a pool of financial resources over and above what is collected on a regular basis. As the time range expands, it becomes increasingly likely that many of the original owners will have moved out. An 'intergenerational' problem then arises, whereby upon sale, the current owners have an interest in passing on the onus of financing maintenance to the new purchasers.

The problem of financing maintenance is much more severe in tower buildings than low or middle-rise ones because they inevitably house a very large number of owners and are thus more susceptible to market failure than low-rise buildings. The costs also increase with the age of the building. Owners' willingness to pay higher one-off costs when the time comes is very susceptible to the 'free-rider syndrome' (Olson 1965). Where so many owners are involved, and where many apartments have changed hands, unwillingness to pay even relatively modest sums may well be anticipated.

Two Types of Condominium Law: Simple and Enhanced

Condominium laws differ from country to country. For the purposes of this chapter, prototype laws have been chosen from two jurisdictions, in both of which the author has contextual knowledge and has conducted fieldwork. These two types of law have emerged from different housing traditions and socio-economic contexts, but share a similar definition of condominium property. However, they represent two sides of the spectrum (although not necessarily the extreme edges): the basic type of condominium law on one hand and the more sophisticated type on the other hand. The differences between these 'simple' and 'enhanced' condominium laws are most apparent when considering management and maintenance aspects.

Enhanced condominium laws prevalent in the US and Canada are here exemplified by Florida. Although there are differences among legal provisions in the states in the US and among the provinces in Canada, they have enough in common as a group to be labelled 'enhanced' condominium laws. In contrast, the condominium laws prevalent in the Mediterranean region and in some other parts of the world may be termed 'simple', and are here typified by the Israeli law. In Israel, condominium living encompasses a broad spectrum of households in urban areas, with housing units and apartment blocks varying greatly in economic value, size, the level of services provided, physical design, and levels of maintenance. Some are simply constructed and offer minimal services. Others offer luxury and prestige. A high proportion of all socio-economic groups apart from the very poorest owns condominium property. In Mediterranean countries, most of the existing stock of condominium buildings is not in towers but rather in 'walk up' buildings or in moderately high-rise buildings.

The laws and jurisdictions of Florida and Israel[1] are comparable because they are both democratic regimes and both belong to the same legal family: the common

1 Note that the discussion here applies to Israel in its international borders. A different set of laws and practices applies to the occupied areas, both those areas held by Israel and those administered by the Palestinian Authority.

law tradition (Glendon, Carozza and Picker 2007: 23–49). More precisely, Israel is regarded as a mixed-system jurisdiction, with the influence of civil law being more apparent in less traditional areas such as the series of quasi-constitutional 'Basic Laws'. Israeli property law dates back to legislation enacted during the British Mandate over Palestine 1921–1948, which drew heavily on English common law as exported to the colonies. Once the State of Israel was established in 1948, it adopted almost all the pre-existing legislation along with its common law foundations.

Although there are differences in gross domestic product per person between the US and Israel (Florida's is considerably higher), both jurisdictions belong to the group of advanced economies. The socio-economic differences between them in fact permit conclusions from this comparative study to be applied to a wider range of jurisdictions.

The Simple Type of Condominium Law: The Example of Israel

As in many countries in the Mediterranean regions, the Israeli law was first enacted when most condominium buildings were middle-rise (2–5 floors), providing housing for many sections of the population. The prevalent building heights across Israeli cities until the late 1990s were three to five stories. Until the early 1990s, most high-rise residential buildings reached only to eight to 12 stories. The steep leap in the height of residential towers developed in steps from the late 1990s onwards; first came towers of 20-plus floors, then 30-plus floors, and, more recently, even 40-plus floors have been gaining popularity. All but a few of these buildings are condominiums, with the few exceptions being institutional buildings that cater to special groups, such as the elderly, which are built either with government support or on a commercial basis. The same condominium law applies to all shapes and sizes of condominiums buildings. The question is, to what extent are the tower condominiums likely to be able to cope with the exacerbated market failures embedded in them?

The Israeli Law Governing Condominiums

The 1969 Real Property Law establishes the basic rules of property rights as well as of condominium law. There is no other national legal mechanism that generally regulates maintenance in condominiums and in other forms of ownership of buildings. The 1965 Planning and Building Law, and its many subsequent incremental amendments, do not directly empower government to impose maintenance responsibilities on house owners, and nor do the laws that regulate construction quality and contracts between developers and residents. The Real Property Law 1969, which incorporated an earlier statute concerning condominiums dating back to British rule in the 1940s, sets out only two simple conditions to define a condominium: the building must have at least two separate units designed to serve for housing, business or the like; and the building must be registered with the State Registry of Condominiums. This legislation defines 'common property' in a way similar to condominium laws elsewhere, as comprising the ground areas, roofs, external walls, foundations, staircases outside private units, elevators, utility rooms and the like. The owner of each unit is assigned a non-specific part of the common property and any transaction in a unit also applies to the common property. The statute's criterion is that the proportion of common property is calculated according to the relative portion of each unit's floor area out of the cumulative floor areas. Under some conditions, the law permits a specific part of the common property, for example, the ground areas adjoining ground-floor units or parts of the roof directly above the top-floor unit, to be designated as attached to a particular unit.

Regarding cost sharing, all that the law specifies is that each unit owner must pay the due share of maintenance and management costs necessary for the 'proper maintenance' of the building. Proper maintenance is defined as activities necessary to keep the building in its original condition, plus any improvements made with time. The cost share is proportionate to the unit's floor area out of the total floor area, unless the regulations adopted by the co-owners specify otherwise. The law devotes a single clause to authorizing the condominium to hire a professional maintenance company. The underlying assumption (and the practice, as discussed below) is that condominiums will be largely self-managed.

The Israeli law makes the management of condominium buildings as simple and easy as could be imagined. There is no obligation to form a separate legal entity such as a corporation or association; the law itself grants the elected representatives of the condominium legal authority to represent the condominium wherever necessary, for example to sign and enforce contracts for the necessary maintenance activities and to take legal action against unit owners who have defaulted in payment of maintenance fees. The elected representatives are also authorized to open a bank account in order to manage the money collected and to carry out the necessary expenditures for maintenance. However, they are unlikely to have legal authority to carry out ancillary economic activities such as purchasing real estate.

Rules of governance are set by default regulations, the Common Condominium Regulations, which are annexed to the Real Property Law 1969. These apply until or unless the owners in a specific condominium adopt a different set of regulations and register them with the State Registry of Condominiums. In practice, the majority of condominiums in Israel – which means the majority of households in the country – choose to remain with the default regulations. The Common Regulations specify that a general assembly of all unit owners must be convened at least once a year to set the maintenance fees and to elect a body of representatives of between one and five members for one year, irrespective of building size or number of units. The Regulations empower the general assembly to approve expenditures and make similar decisions 'entailed by life as neighbours[2] in a condominium'. The representatives may convene more frequent meetings, and in fact must do so if a third of the owners so demand. One of the representatives should act as treasurer and must prepare six-monthly financial accounts to bring to the annual general assembly.

Most important is what the statute does *not* include. Unlike the 'enhanced' type of law, it does not oblige the condominium to establish a reserve fund for future maintenance expenditures (Levels 3 or 4). Indeed, the word 'fund' is not mentioned, though the condominium is fully empowered to create such a fund, whether on its own or by means of a management corporation. As discussed in the next part of this chapter, many condominium buildings encounter problems when they need to collect periodic lump sums for Levels 3 and 4 maintenance activities.

The Israeli law is also weak on enforcement powers. While the law obliges every unit owner to pay their share of the maintenance fees, whether for current or anticipated future costs, it does not grant the condominium special enforcement powers beyond those available as remedy in civil action for regular debts (see also Blandy, Chapter 2, for the similar provision relating to English commonholds). Neither the condominium entity nor a maintenance company has authority to place a lien on the privately owned unit as security for the maintenance fees owed. If, as frequently happens, a unit owner defaults in payments of the maintenance fees the condominium may submit a claim to an office of the State Inspector of Condominiums. This national statutory officer is empowered to hear both sides and request professional appraisals. Inspectors usually try to resolve conflicts in alternative ways but if necessary, they can also serve as a tribunal. Their judicial decisions have the powers of a magistrate court, with streamlined procedures. The Inspector's powers encompass the regular civil means of enforcement of civil contractual obligations. These do not usually include direct powers over real property unless other means have been exhausted, especially if the unit is the owners' residence.

The Knesset (Israeli Parliament) has revised the condominium legislation many times, but their amendments have focused on issues other than maintenance and upkeep. The basic structure and powers of condominium organizations, and the issue of collection of fees, have not been altered for decades. Concern for other urban and social issues have prompted the amendments, which each represent a particular need to update buildings on one specific issue. For example, Amendment 19 (1966) substituted a two-thirds majority for the unanimous consent of all unit owners which was previously required, before an elevator may be installed to update an older walk-up building. The growing social awareness of the Knesset is expressed, for example, in Amendments from 1987 and 2001. These empower apartment owners to alter the staircases and similar common

2 The Hebrew term used is *ha-shhenut* which could be translated dryly as 'living in proximity' and, more emotively, as 'neighbourliness'. There is no official English translation of these Regulations.

property leading to a given apartment to make them accessible to disabled persons, without the consent of other condominium owners. Amendment 23 (2001) applies a similar rule to the introduction of solar energy heating and for disconnection from collective oil or gas heating.

These examples show that the Knesset's responses to these needs have all been ad hoc, and have each adopted the solution of providing for a special majority of owners to permit adaptations for newly emerging needs. To date, there has not been any attempt to establish a general rule requiring less than full consent of all owners before building renovation can take place. Nor has the Knesset revised the condominium legislation to address financial mechanisms for maintenance, the reserve fund, and the issue of enforcement. These issues will be further discussed in the concluding section of the chapter.

Condominium Maintenance in Practice in Israel

As may be expected, conflicts among condominium unit owners are not rare. However, in practice most are either resolved at the social level, without the Inspector's help, or are left unresolved. On this issue there are probably major differences both internationally, from one society to another, as well as within Israel's social mosaic. Although there is no empirical research to rely on, it is clear that in Israel, a highly urbanized condominium-based country, the capacity for self-resolution of conflicts in condominium buildings is an extremely important resource with many wider implications for city life.

Where the Inspector does take enforcement action for default on condominium maintenance payments, he or she is likely to take social needs into consideration. This is because in Israeli society and law, housing is regarded as a primary need. Israeli courts are unlikely to approve an action that deprives people of their home (which in Israel usually means a condominium unit). The courts will not usually order that a unit is to be sold to pay the fees owed to the condominium, unless all other means have been exhausted and the unit is not the person's primary residence. The court may also view the value of the apartment unit and the very act of ordering its sale as highly disproportionate to the sum owed for maintenance. Therefore, Israeli courts rarely issue such an order except in very extreme situations.

Despite their modest enforcement powers, the hundreds of thousands of middle-rise condominiums in Israel have somehow been operating for decades in a tolerable way with regard to ongoing activities such as cleaning. The amount needed for Level 2 urgent maintenance works is also usually collected, sooner or later. At times, condominium owners put up with some free-riders, who do not pay their share, although not necessarily without any conflict. However, the deterioration of condominiums in lower income neighbourhoods is becoming an insoluble problem. While Level 1 type maintenance is often carried out in these communities by the owners themselves, such buildings do encounter problems in raising money for any additional actions such as roof maintenance. There is no general public mechanism for investment in the maintenance of condominiums owned by low income households, except for occasional area-based government regeneration programmes.

The mechanism that compensates, somehow, for the weaknesses in legal mechanisms depends on the informal social norms that prevail in Israel and some other societies along the Mediterranean. Where the number of owners is not exceedingly high – say, up to 30 so that residents may know each other personally – the social expectation to pay one's share of the maintenance fees is the major mechanism which mitigates the free-riding phenomenon and unblocks some of the inhibitors to information flow. In these circumstances, free-riding cannot enjoy the social protection of anonymity.

However, where the number of owners is very large, such as in condominium towers, this social mechanism cannot operate. Furthermore, as explained above, the costs of long-term maintenance are much higher in towers than in middle-rise buildings. While the architecture of the middle-income towers may not be distinguishable from that of high-income towers, the location and socio-economic characteristics of the residents determine their future. Such towers are springing up not only in areas of high demand, but also in cities such as Beer Sheva, where there is no ostensible justification in terms of real estate prices or open space preservation.

In an attempt to find a solution to the management problem, an increasing number of new tower condominiums have recently hired the services of maintenance companies. These companies were recently granted the same legal powers over defaulting individual owners as the condominium representatives. Field interviews conducted in 2005–2006 with several leading companies showed that none has discovered a method to solve the free-rider conundrum (see Alterman 2009). When the condominium representatives compare offers by competing managers, they tend to select the least expensive package of services, rather than considering the proposals for long-term maintenance programmes. Most management companies do not even try to establish a fund to cover long-term expenses, probably because the chances of collecting the contributions from owners are small.

Where towers are designed for and sold to middle-income households, their quick deterioration seems inevitable. The real costs of long-term management (and even ongoing management) are high, relative to the paying capacity of such households which are usually also making high mortgage repayments on the same apartment. The extreme signs of decline may not be as strikingly visible on the exterior because current architectural design does not expose the external signs of deterioration, as buildings of the 1970s and 1980s do. However, the effects on property values caused by deterioration of elevators, staircases, or gardens are likely to be just as dramatic. The decline in the relative place held by such towers on the ladder of housing price and prestige may be quick to follow.

This scenario is ominous for Israeli cities, and for their counterparts in other countries with similar characteristics of condominium law and practice. Unlike mid-rise condominiums, towers are like sealed machines, making it difficult for future urban regeneration programs to offer additional development rights on the roofs or side wings of the towers as incentives to upgrade the buildings. And, of course, demolitions are so unfriendly to the social and physical environments!

The Search for Surrogate Legal Mechanisms by Local Governments

The shortcomings of the Israeli condominium law for managing tower condominiums has gradually become apparent to some Israeli planners, especially since the early 2000s and the sharp increase in numbers of tall residential buildings. In addition to the maintenance issues, developers and residents have occasionally also found it difficult to cope with the apportionment of special common facilities such as swimming pools, sports facilities, and concierge services. The law offers only one basis for allocation of common ownership and costs (by floor area), which sometimes seems inappropriate or unjust (see also Christudason, Chapter 6).

The main emerging concern about tower condominiums revolves around the issue of long-term maintenance. The author's research found that some individual local Planning and Building Commissions and local authorities around the country had already begun the search for legal mechanisms which might ensure that a newly approved residential tower would be well maintained. Some local governments had indeed foreseen the emerging problem, although, in general, they underestimated its magnitude. Most of the local planners looked for a solution along the same path as had already emerged voluntarily in practice: the employment of maintenance companies. The planners believed that if a legal mechanism could be found that would oblige condominium owners to contract with a management company, sustainable maintenance would ensue. Without any national legal platform to guide them, the local Planning Commission and other local government agencies began to experiment with alternative legal instruments.

Field research conducted in 2005–2006 indicated that three different measures, which nonetheless all tend in the same direction, were being adopted or considered by some local governments in an uncoordinated experiment:

a. Condition inserted directly into the *building permit*, stipulating that the building may not receive a completion certificate (and so may not be transferred to the buyers) until the developer or the condominium representatives sign a contract with a management company;
b. Condition inserted into the *detailed plan* (equivalent to planning permission in the UK, and zoning or planning unit development in the US) stipulating that the developer or the condominium representatives must sign a contract with a management company;
c. Agreement made between the local Planning Commission, or the municipality, and the developer *outside* the statutory planning process (where it has discretion to do so). This agreement stipulates as an external condition that the developer must show a signed maintenance contract as above before the Planning Commission will exercise its powers and approve a plan and building permit.

All these solutions fall short of providing a sustainable solution to the problem. All orbit around the 'panacea' of a maintenance corporation, solving neither the free-rider problem in willingness to pay, nor the asymmetric information problem with respect to past and future costs. None of these three ideas tackles the problems of the expenditures needed in the future for maintenance Levels 3 or 4.

The first suggested remedy – relying on the building permit – is attractive to local governments because under Israeli law permitting development is almost totally within their control. At the permit stage, the developer is 'ripe' financially and eager to obtain the authorization to start building. Although this solution is the most flexible and can address potential problems with each new tower before it is too late, the building permit itself is a short-term, self-terminating certificate. Further, the legality of the condition itself is problematic, an issue discussed together with the next item.

The second instrument relies on a more permanent legal instrument – a statutory plan. However, approval of statutory plans for major projects takes years and cannot be 'retrofitted' to approved plans without great financial consequences to the municipalities. Thus, many tower projects would be able to escape the new proposed rules, if these were adopted. Furthermore, in current Israeli law there is some uncertainty about the legality of conditions of this type in statutory plans. There are no statutory guidelines specifically authorizing such a condition to be inserted, so this issue can only be resolved through case law.

The third instrument – an agreement outside the statutory instruments – is legally somewhat more robust since it is based on contract law. However, it may or may not be a better instrument for ensuring long-term maintenance. This depends on how enforceable such a contract would prove to be in the future. If the developer defaults, how will this affect the long-term maintenance of the condominium building? Furthermore, the legal status of developer agreements in the planning laws of most countries is often problematic. Unless they are specifically authorized by statute (and that is rare in comparative terms, and does not hold in Israel), their legality must be determined case by case (Alterman 1988, 1990). However, even if such a condition were to be legal, its wisdom is dubious.

Beyond the unresolved legal questions, all three instruments proposed by local governments are based on weak ground. Even if the contract that the developer is required to sign with a management company were to be ruled legal, the management company itself may not survive more than a few years. There is nothing in Israeli law to oblige maintenance corporations to stay in business or to protect the buildings they serve against the company's bankruptcy. The very fact that many local planning agencies around the country continue to fall for this illusion merely emphasizes the degree of their desperation to find some regulatory tool.

Little Help from Central Government and the Knesset

Local governments on their own cannot be expected to tackle a major national problem such as the one outlined here, at the scale encountered in Israel. The national government has not yet stepped in. There have, however, been two pre-legislative initiatives containing modest suggested steps in the right direction. In summer 2005 a then Member of the Knesset prepared a rough draft of a bill that would have revised the Law of Sales (Apartments) 1973, to oblige any developer of a condominium with over 40 units to state in the sales contract that the maintenance will be carried out by a management company, and to specify what services the company would be committed to undertake, and at what price. The bill would also have required each condominium regulation to insert an equivalent clause, but the draft bill did not go any further. This initiative is too rudimentary to be assessed, yet its grounding in the Law of Sales (Apartments) opens up an interesting possibility for future reform.

In 2008 there was a more serious attempt at legislative reform, this time from the then chair of the Knesset Finance Committee, M.K. Stas Misezhnikov (now Minister of Tourism). While this initiative also focuses on the management company concept, it anchors the obligation to contract with such a company in condominium law, rather than in sales law, which seems a more straightforward way of tackling the issue. It also begins to address the problem of how to oblige condominiums to establish a long-term fund. This more recent initiative is backed by a report prepared by the Knesset Research and Information Unit (2007).

However, both of these initiatives are still a long way from being submitted to the Knesset for enactment. The first legislative initiative outlined above makes the important distinction between regular condominiums and those with large numbers of units, while the second is unclear on this point. This distinction makes good sense: too many regulatory and financial burdens should not be imposed on the vast majority of regular condominiums serving all population groups.

'Enhanced' Condominium Laws: The Example of Florida

Among the US States Florida has been chosen as exemplar because, as the ultimate 'sunbelt state', it has attracted an especially high demand for condominium apartments for a relatively long time. In recent years, more and more Florida condominiums have taken the form of tower buildings. Many of these cater mostly to small households with no children, at upper-middle and upper-level income levels. Florida's condominium law falls among the 'enhanced' group, although there may very well be jurisdictions that have yet more stringent rules in order to reduce as far as possible the various free-rider tendencies amongst owners.

Florida Law Governing Condominiums

The Florida Condominium Statute 2008 is 92 single-spaced pages long – much longer than its Israeli counterpart – and is indeed much more sophisticated. It is clear that in the legislators' minds were not only the rudimentary objectives of establishing a special form of joint tenure and an organizational framework to operate it effectively. The intricate rules of governance indicate that the legislators also sought to curtail, or at least reduce, the major types of market failures inherent in condominiums.

The Florida condominium law requires that residents take positive action to form an association, as a Florida corporation for profit or not-for-profit. Unlike its Israeli counterpart, the Florida law empowers the condominium association to carry out real estate transactions including buying, leasing, and selling apartment units in the building. The Florida legislation tackles the issue of the inherent incentives for sellers to withhold information about prospective maintenance costs by obliging the initial developer to provide the buyer with a detailed calculation of the projected maintenance costs for the forthcoming years, prepared by qualified and regulated experts. All this information must be included along with the usual legal, structural, and mechanical information as part of the declarations that developers are required by law to provide to prospective buyers. The developer must supply the new owner with the initial bylaws of the condominium association, which must be read and signed by the buyers; new bylaws can later be adopted by the association. The entire package of information is usually scores of pages long and usually requires the help of a lawyer. The bylaws are overseen by a state authority.

It is clear that the Florida legislators, unlike their Israeli counterparts, sought to make a clear distinction between the ongoing maintenance tasks of Levels 1 and 2, and those that require larger periodic investments. In addition to quarterly estimates of income and expenditures, the Florida law obliges the condominium association to make a full estimate of future expenditures for the sort of repair actions that we have classified as Levels 2 and 3. It specifies that the budget shall incorporate reserve accounts which:

> include, but are not limited to, roof replacement, building painting, and pavement resurfacing, regardless of the amount of deferred maintenance expense or replacement cost, and for any other item for which the deferred maintenance expense or replacement cost exceeds $10,000 (Section 718.112.1(f)2, Florida Condominium Statute 2008).

The state's regulatory authority must approve each condominium association's annual budget and estimates of future expenses. For capital expenditures, the Florida Act requires that the budget includes 'reserve accounts'. The rationale behind the legislation is clear: if money is not reserved in advance over a span of time, its collection in a lump sum is likely to encounter the free-rider syndrome in enhanced dosage. Yet at the same time, the statute authorizes a simple majority of the unit owners to waive the requirement to set up a reserve fund; thus the statute's ostensible wisdom in seeking to quell the free-rider effect regarding long-term expenses remains in part a paper tiger. The condominium association also has extensive authority to impose additional fees as needed and to enforce their collection, as discussed below. The legislation in Florida does not provide a default set of condominium regulations, but requires that each association set up its own bylaws (see McKenzie, Chapter 4, for the recent consumer protection measures which regulate these bylaws). The statute makes it mandatory for the association to assess each owner for *at least* the amount required in advance for payment of all of the anticipated *current* operating expenses and for all of the unpaid operating expenses *previously* incurred. This means that the condominium association is legally obliged to make assessments at a level that would prevent free-riders, but not necessarily for the full cost.

Perhaps the most important difference between the Florida and the Israeli laws lies in associations' powers of enforcement. The Florida statute specifically authorizes condominium associations to place a lien on each apartment unit and to sell it if necessary in order to secure the funds owed by the owners for the maintenance of the building. The associations are third in line of priority for securing their debt, after the local authority and the bank. The association's powers to claim the unpaid fees are extensive, including the powers to impose fines. In exercising most of these powers, the associations are independent; they do not need the authorization of a government agency nor a court order (see discussion by McKenzie, Chapter 4, on the wider implications of these foreclosure powers). Under normal circumstances when real estate prices are high, this linkage of the payment of maintenance fees to the apartment units themselves, which characterizes the 'enhanced' type of condominium laws, does provide an effective means of enforcement. It acts as a deterrent against failure to pay, since the owner is likely to lose a lot of money in the process of foreclosure, and at the same time provides adequate security to the condominium association's interests. However, can the degree of deterrence withstand an economic crisis?

Condominium Maintenance in Practice in Florida

As in Israel, research was undertaken to investigate the extent to which the Florida law indeed fulfills its objectives of preventing free-riders and other forms of market failure in maintenance. Interviews were held with several knowledgeable professionals in the Southern Florida area, including the president of the property management division of a leading property management group in Florida and his staff, a condominium developer, two lawyers who specialize in condominium transactions, and several real estate agents. The author also participated as an observer in the meetings of the condominium representatives of the building in the Miami area where she resided during 2006.

These expert informants were asked the degree to which, in their view, the statutory instruction to set up a reserve fund was in fact being observed; in other words, to what extent Florida condominium associations rely on the escape clause that leaves the establishment of a reserve fund to their discretion. The picture we obtained was mixed: the president of the maintenance company and his staff converged in their estimates that approximately 10 per cent of the condominiums entirely forego the establishment of a reserve fund. Our informants conjectured that these are largely condominiums with a majority of elderly households. At the same time, the interviewees estimated that only 40 per cent of the condominiums did set aside a reserve fund of adequate size for the full long-range needs of maintenance at Levels 3 and 4. It is debatable whether 40 per cent constitutes a reasonable degree of fulfillment of the law's objective, but there is no doubt that for the tower condominiums included in the other 60 per cent, this finding bodes bad news.

The research also found that there is a very high degree of professionalization of condominium management in Florida, with professionals from a variety of disciplines providing various specific services related to long-term maintenance. The legal requirement for each condominium association to prepare a forecast of its long-term maintenance expenditures, even if it decides not to set aside a reserve fund, has created the demand for such professionals. The fact that this task is overseen by government has further boosted this trend. Some of the professionals who must be consulted are specified in the statute; other specializations have evolved with time as market demand for better maintenance has become more sophisticated.

Even though the Florida statute does not require the engagement of a management company (unlike some of the surrogate solutions with which local authorities in Israel have been experimenting), a high proportion of high-rise condominiums in Florida do engage the services of such corporations. According to our interviewees, the competition in the marketplace among management companies does not revolve around the price of short-term maintenance services. This probably reflects the Florida requirement, absent in the Israeli statute, that each condominium association prepares and approves an annual long-term estimate of prospective maintenance costs. The performance of management companies can thus be assessed against preset benchmarks that encompass preventive maintenance actions from Level 1 to Level 4. Another factor may be that some of the companies in Florida – unlike their Israeli counterparts – have been on the scene for a long time. All these factors together contribute to reducing the asymmetric information failure in the market of tower condominiums, especially regarding maintenance operations of Levels 3 and 4, which are particularly complex and costly.

Finally, the enforcement issue is key to the capacity of any regulation to curtail the free-rider phenomenon. Our interviewees all testified that in Florida the condominium associations routinely exercise their powers against delinquent owners after about a month's grace. They do not (or at least did not, until the current economic crisis) hesitate to exercise liens and take possession of apartment units. If necessary, the association will offer the unit for sale, deduct the amount owed plus the legal and administrative costs and return the balance to the owner.

Now that both types of condominium laws have been analysed, we come to the concluding sections, where we compare the two laws in order to tease out their broader implications for public policy. The Florida type of enhanced law appears to be the clear 'winner'. However, a closer, multi-faceted look reveals a mixed picture and some challenges for urban policymakers worldwide.

Comparative Analysis

How well do the two types of condominium law – the simple and the enhanced types – perform as instruments to ensure sustainable, long-range maintenance of tower residential buildings? How well does each of them work to minimize free-riding among the condominium co-owners as well as asymmetric information between buyers and sellers? The conclusions are far from simple.

The Capacity to Ensure Sustainable Maintenance

Under normal economic circumstances, there is no doubt that the enhanced type of condominium law, as exemplified by Florida, is immensely more suited to tackling the long-term maintenance problems of tower condominiums than the simple type laws. It is clear that the Florida legislators methodically thought through the various types of market failure and attempted to address most of them by closing loopholes. But the legislators did not manage to close all the holes hermetically. They left the creation of a reserve fund and its level to the discretion of the condominium associations. Furthermore, even if such a fund is created, nothing in the law obliges the associations in the future to undertake actions beyond those that arise from Level 3 maintenance. Who will finance the costs of updating the building to the higher standards that are likely to apply in the future? Without such Level 4 upgrading, condominiums towers are likely to lose their ranking on the housing ladder in terms of price and prestige.

Yet even these unequivocal advantages apparently hold only under economic circumstances in which real estate prices and the general economy are more or less stable in the long run. The 2008 sub-prime loans crisis and the ensuing financial 'meltdown' provide a rare laboratory to test the enhanced type of condominium laws. Both banks and condominium associations now own many apartments in condominiums. A January 2009 respondents' survey conducted by the Florida Community Association reports estimates of dramatic increases in the number of foreclosures and, as a result, in non-payments of maintenance assessments (Community Association Leadership Lobby 2009). The survey indicates that the foreclosure crisis has resulted in postponements of major capital investments in upkeep or repair of buildings and other property, and that, in order to sustain their finances, many condominium associations are now finding it necessary to impose higher assessments on the non-delinquent owners.

Thousands of condominium owners are now offering their units for rent in order to pay the maintenance fees and avoid takeover by the condominium association. Other owners sell their units. A large percentage of renters and frequent turnover of owners tend to increase the prevalence of the intergenerational asymmetric information problem, and a large number of renters further increases the probability of free-riding compared with owner occupation. These trends inevitably imply a further plunge in the market price of the condominium units, and this, in turn, means that the new buyers may be a rung lower on the income ladder. Since the tendency to free-ride is also related to the capacity to pay, the decline in relative prices of the Florida condominium towers due to the economic crisis accelerates market failure. The situation is so grave in some parts of the US, including Southern Florida, that a Miami Beach city commissioner has called it the 'condos' "death spiral"' (Loney 2009). One may argue that the economic crisis accelerates the life trajectory of tower condominiums. It has made clear that even an enhanced condominium law such as Florida's cannot withstand the extraneous social and economic factors that a crisis of the current magnitude brings with it.

While the 'simple' type of condominiums laws takes a rather old-fashioned approach to maintenance issues, it has some advantage in time of crisis, being inherently more flexible than the enhanced type of laws. In a simple type jurisdiction, condominium owners are better able to meet the economic crisis because they do not have major overhead costs arising from the heavy regulation entailed by the Florida law. They are also free to change the maintenance fee level because they are not legally bound to a certain fee threshold as in Florida. Under the simple Israeli regime, owners are not legally bound to set aside money for future maintenance, and may therefore choose to reduce the fees during an economic crisis. While this is bad news for long-term maintenance in normal times, in a stressful period this flexibility may reduce the number of owners who would otherwise have to sell or rent out their unit in order to pay the maintenance fees. The ability to avoid an abnormally high turnover of condominium units may have significant economic value, and thus may provide a better interim solution than the Florida law. Crisis-driven decisions may not be very good for ensuring long-term maintenance, but their flexibility may balance out the weaknesses of the simple regulatory frameworks.

Conclusions and Policy Implications

Whether or not to permit, or even encourage, tower condominiums is one of the most important urban policy questions facing decision-makers in cities and national governments around the world. Not enough policymakers are as yet aware of this question's importance, and this chapter's aim is to raise its profile. It has been shown that when it comes to condominium towers, rather than low or mid-rise condominium buildings, neither of the two types of law provides an adequate answer that ensures financing of long-term maintenance. While the enhanced type of laws offers a distinctly better legal framework when economic conditions are stable, they are less flexible when facing an economic crisis.

Given the higher maintenance cost in tall buildings, the higher probabilities for free-riding and the fact that essential investments increase with time, acceptable maintenance levels are less likely to continue over time in tower condominiums than in middle or low-rise condominiums. Once tall buildings deteriorate, they are difficult to rehabilitate and wasteful to replace, creating negative effects for the whole neighbourhood.

Policy Recommendations

The major recommendation is that policymakers should regard all proposals for tower condominiums with suspicion. There should be extremely weighty public planning goals to justify their approval. For example, if the overriding urban goal is greater density, it is often possible to consider alternative urban design formats that achieve similar densities through middle-rise buildings. Calculations conducted by Alterman and Churchman (1998) show that mid-rise apartment buildings or moderately high-rise development can achieve adequately high densities and efficient use of scarce land resources. Towers do not necessarily achieve a more efficient use of land (see also Churchman 1999).

Unless there is public subsidy to finance maintenance for the long-term, policymakers should approve condominium towers only in prime real estate locations where property values are initially high. Tower projects should be aimed only at upper-income households. The probabilities of free-riding and foreclosures will be lower amongst wealthy residents than in towers oriented to middle or even upper-middle-income households.

If policymakers feel that condominium towers are nevertheless desirable, then the legal and financial mechanism that regulates their maintenance should be of the enhanced type. It should be mandatory to establish a full reserve fund adequate for Levels 1 to 4 of maintenance and renovation into the future. The range and extent of the reserve fund should be defined, and it should be directly monitored and regulated by a public body.

References

Alterman, R. (ed.) 1988. *Private Supply of Public Services: Evaluation of Real Estate Exactions, Linkage and Alternative Land Policies*. New York: New York University Press.

Alterman, R. 1990. From Expropriations to Development Agreements: Developer Obligations for Public Services in Israel. *Israel Law Review*, 24(1), 28–81.

Alterman, R. 2009. *Failed Towers: The Problem of Long-term Maintenance in High-rise Condominiums in Israel*. Haifa: Center for Urban and Regional Studies, Technion [available only in Hebrew].

Alterman, R. and Churchman, A. with Garon, M. 1998. *Density of Housing Areas: A Guidebook for Increasing the Efficiency in Utilizing Urban Land.* Haifa: Center for Urban and Regional Studies, Technion [available only in Hebrew].

Churchman, A. 1999. Disentangling the Concept of Density. *Journal of Planning Literature*, 13(4), 389–411.

Community Association Leadership Lobby. 2009. *State of Distress: The Mortgage Foreclosure Crisis within Florida's Condominium and Homeowner Association Population: Results of the 2009 Florida Community Association Mortgage Foreclosure Survey.* [Online]. Available at: http://www.callbp.com/

publication_pdfs/State_of_Distress__Final_Report_20090224134555.pdf [accessed: 26 May 2009].

Council on Tall Buildings and Urban Habitat. 2008. The Tallest Buildings in the World: Past, Present & Future. *CTBUH Journal* 2, 40–41. [Online]. Available at: http://www.ctbuh.org/Portals/0/Tallest/InNumbers/InNumbers_Issue2_2008.pdf [accessed: 5 April 2009].

Glendon, M.A., Carozza, G.P. and Picker, C.B. 2007. *Comparative Legal Traditions: Text, Materials and Cases on Western Law*. 3rd Edition. St Paul, MN: West Group.

Knesset Research and Information Unit. 2007. *Difficulties in Managing Condominium Buildings*. [Online]. Available (in Hebrew) at: http://www.knesset.gov.il/mmm/data/docs/m01771.doc [accessed 20 May 2009].

Loney, J. 2009. US Property Bust Threatens Condo 'Death Spiral'. *Reuters* [Online, 2 April]. Available at: http://www.reuters.com/article/domesticNews/idUSTRE53200O20090403?sp=true [accessed: 20 May 2009].

McKenzie, E. 1996. *Privatopia: Homeowner Associations and the Rise of Residential Private Governments*. New Haven, CT: Yale University Press.

Olson, M. 1965. *The Logic of Collective Action*. Cambridge, MA: Harvard University Press.

Chapter 6
Share Value as Determinant of Strata Owners' Bundle of Rights in Collective Sales in Singapore

Alice Christudason

Introduction

This chapter deals with some of the issues arising from the use of share value as the single determinant of discrete matters affecting the rights of strata owners, with a particular focus on its impact in the context of collective sales of mixed-use strata developments. The chapter commences with a background to Singapore's planning framework and discusses the implications of share value and its application to strata property. The chapter then considers how the way was paved for the collective sale phenomenon and urban rejuvenation in land-scarce Singapore through radical amendments to strata legislation. 'Radical', because the new laws replaced the previous requirement for unanimous consent in collective sales with a requirement for just *majority* consent. This shift in the balance of power among strata unit owners resulted in the derogation of the property rights of minority owners who had no desire to sell their units which often carried freehold titles.

The chapter then proceeds to examine the role of the Strata Titles Board. While the Strata Titles Board is the watchdog of minority rights in collective sales, it is also tasked to ensure that collective sales (and urban rejuvenation) are facilitated, while simultaneously assisting the majority to realize the value of *their* property rights. The chapter uses a case study to illustrate the anomalies caused by a 'one-size fits all' share value allocation and concludes with a discussion of the measures taken by the Singapore Parliament and the courts to attain a finer balance between the majority and minority's property rights.

Background

Singapore is a small, heavily urbanized island city-state in Southeast Asia, located at the southern tip of the Malayan Peninsula between Malaysia and Indonesia. Comprising one main island and a number of islets scattered off its northeast and southern coast, Singapore presently accommodates 4.8 million people within its total land area of 699 square kilometres (Economic Development

Board 2008), less than half the size of Greater London. Reclamation has been actively pursued for decades to meet the infrastructural demands of Singapore's burgeoning economy. Between 1960 and 1990, 51.5 square kilometres of land was reclaimed, accounting for almost 10 per cent of Singapore's total land area at the time. By 2030, it is estimated that another 100 square kilometres will have been added. However, there is only so much that land reclamation can do and then again, not all the land area can be developed. For example, water catchment areas already take up 40 per cent of the land area and land also has to be set aside for business, port activities, housing, recreation, military and industrial uses.

With its intractable land scarcity problem, Singapore's land planners are constantly seeking new ways of creating space to accommodate a possible 40 per cent population increase to 6.5 million over the next 40 to 50 years. The population density is presently second highest in the world with 6,208 persons per square kilometre (Economic Development Board 2008). This provides some perspective of the challenges faced by Singapore's national land-use planning agency, the Urban Redevelopment Authority, in the judicious allocation of precious land resources. One of the Urban Redevelopment Authority's objectives is 'to create a vibrant, sustainable and cosmopolitan city of distinction' (Urban Redevelopment Authority: Introduction n.d.) and provide quality high-rise housing. The latter reflects certain architectural influences including the 'vertical garden cities' of Le Corbusier (1946, 1947), renowned for designs which are noted for freeing up land, and Soleri's concept of high-density, self-sufficient and multi-level communities in cities which expand vertically into space, rather than horizontally along the ground (Lima 2003). Thus, in such a densely populated and compact city-state, it seems that the only way to go is up. Already 87 per cent of the population reside in high-rise *public* housing – the tallest being that at Duxton Plain, which is 50 storeys high and comprises 1,848 units built on 25,600 square metres of land. The *private* residential sector is characterized largely by high-rise condominiums and apartments (also known as strata-titled properties), rather than landed housing. Yet there are constraints on building heights; for example, residential developments in certain areas like Tampines, Simei and Changi cannot exceed 12 storeys, due to the flight paths of planes from Singapore's Changi International Airport.

Singapore's Planning Framework

While it is widely acknowledged that the general purpose of government intervention in the use and development of land is 'to guide developers collectively to make the best use of national resources in the interests of the community as a whole' (Stone 1988: 210), this assertion has even more force given Singapore's scarce land resource. Singapore's planning framework is primarily statutory, being governed by the Planning Act 1998 which is based on the English Town and

Country Planning Act 1947. As in England, the planning framework in Singapore addresses the twin concerns of the making of plans, as well as the control of development. In this regard, it is Singapore's Concept Plan and Master Plan that set out its land use policy. The Concept Plan is a broad visionary plan, reviewed every ten years, intended to guide Singapore's physical growth over a long term of 40 to 50 years. The Master Plan is the statutory land use plan which guides Singapore's development in the medium term, over the next ten to 15 years. It is reviewed once every five years and translates the broad long-term strategies as set out in the Concept Plan into detailed implementable plans for Singapore. It shows the permissible land use and density for every parcel of land in Singapore. Those who are required to seek planning permission are directly affected through the statutory control of development, implemented through Development Control Guidelines, in the form of regulations, guidelines and circulars. In the 1990s, the Urban Redevelopment Authority introduced a two-tier planning system comprising the Revised Concept Plan at the upper tier and detailed plans called Development Guide Plans at the lower tier.

Prior to the implementation of the new Development Guide Plans system, the primary means of urban redevelopment had been State-led, through compulsory acquisition under the Land Acquisition Act 1985 for 'public benefit'. The Government could compulsorily acquire land for public development and the legislation facilitated the acquisition and combination of fragmented lots. Such land could subsequently be sold by public tender to private developers through the Government Land Sales programme. In the late 1980s, in accordance with the governmental stance towards capital sovereignty, Singapore's planners adopted free market principles to achieve planning goals. Rather than leaving land assembly to be completely State-led, the private sector was offered incentives to amalgamate diverse interests in land under the new planning system (Lum, Sim and Malone-Lee 2004).

The 1991 Revised Concept Plan set out the overall strategy for maximizing land use in Singapore (Urban Redevelopment Authority 1991a) with one of the key objectives being to increase the overall provision of housing land (Urban Redevelopment Authority 1991b). Under this system, the Development Guide Plans would further the Concept Plan by providing new channels for growth with more land being rezoned for residential use (Urban Redevelopment Authority 1993). Development Guide Plans are essentially statutory local plans that contain details such as land-use zones, development intensity, transportation networks, open space and recreational areas and conservation designations that guide land development in a demarcated area. For each of the 55 areas into which Singapore was divided, a Development Guide Plan was prepared where the broad strategies contained in the Concept Plan were translated into operational details at the local level. As each Development Guide Plan was completed, it became the reference for development control, and provided guidelines to landowners and developers on the type of use to which their land could be put (Urban Redevelopment Authority 1991a).

One of the key features of the Development Guide Plans was that various sites (including residential) were assigned higher development intensity or plot ratios. As a result of this strategy for maximizing land use, many areas, particularly parcels in locations with enhanced public infrastructure such as improved road or rail systems and other community amenities, would enjoy enhanced development intensity. Given these higher intensities, sites in the affected urban areas stood to enjoy positive market gains in terms of higher redevelopment potential (Lum et al. 2004). Thus, private developers were able to realize the gains from betterment potential accorded by the planning measures articulated in the Development Guide Plans and thereby engender redevelopment.

The second revision of the Concept Plan in 2001 continued to reflect the importance of providing a variety of housing, from low to medium and high-density housing. 'Low'-density housing includes both low-rise housing that is five storeys or less and landed housing. 'Medium'-density housing has a gross plot ratio of 1.4 to 2.1, with heights varying up to 24 storeys. 'High'-density housing has a plot ratio above 2.1. Building Height Plans depict areas with special height controls, while other areas are subject to prevalent development control guidelines. For example, residential developments follow the Gross Plot Ratio/Storey Height Typology for flats and condominiums. The Gross Plot Ratio for a residential parcel is as stipulated in the Master Plan. In 2000, the Urban Redevelopment Authority relaxed the storey heights of these areas with a view to allowing architects more flexibility in building design to enhance the quality of their developments. For example, if the Gross Plot Ratio were 1.4, the existing height control of four storeys would be relaxed to allow five storeys; if 1.6, from ten to 12 storeys; if 2.1, from 20 to 24 storeys; and if 2.8, from 30 to 36 storeys. By building higher, architects would be able to create more innovative designs and buildings would also have a smaller 'footprint', thus freeing more ground space for better facilities (Urban Redevelopment Authority 2008).

Strata-titled Properties

Strata developments are the main form of housing in Singapore, given its physical context and the focus of its planning framework. Any parcel of land which is intended for strata subdivision must first be registered under the current Land Titles Act, based on the Torrens system of title registration from Australia, which was first adapted for use in Singapore in 1959. The subdivision of land into strata under the Land Titles (Strata) Act 1999 (again, modelled on Australian, or more specifically, on New South Wales' legislation; see Sherry, Chapter 10) covers the subdivisions of any parcel of airspace above the ground and any subterranean space. Any part of land consisting of a space of any shape below, on or above the surface of the land, or partly below and partly above the surface of the land, may be created and owned. Once built, strata-titled properties are governed by the Building Maintenance and Strata Management Act 2008.

Strata Title Plans

The rules on subdivision of land under the Land Titles (Strata) Act 1999 are prescribed in the Planning Act 1998 where it is noted that no subdivision may be carried out unless permission is first obtained from the Chief Planner of the Urban Redevelopment Authority. In addition to obtaining building plan approval, the registered proprietor of the land must file a schedule of strata units with the Commissioner of Buildings. The Building Maintenance and Strata Management Act 2008 provides that the schedule of strata units must have been accepted prior to sale. Importantly, this schedule indicates the proposed share values to be allotted to all the units in the development. The Commissioner of Buildings must consult with the Registrar of Titles and will not accept the proposed share values unless they are allocated in a just and equitable manner. The Commissioner is required to notify the registered proprietor of his acceptance or rejection of the schedule.

Where a schedule of strata units has been accepted by the Commissioner of Buildings, no changes may be made to the share values in the schedule without approval. If any changes are sought, an amended schedule of strata units must be filed with the Commissioner of Buildings. Changes may be made to the areas of flats that have not been sold, provided that the aggregate share value of the development is not changed. Where a flat in a development has been sold, the share value assigned thereto cannot be changed without the purchaser's consent. However, the purchaser's consent is not required for any minor adjustment to the share value which is necessitated by an increase or shortfall in the area of the flat after it has been surveyed on its completion.

Share Value: Concept and Implications

'The share value of a property is a figure that represents the proportionate share entitlement assigned to each strata unit in the same development. The purpose of the share value is to determine the amount of shares each owner has in relation to the other owners in the development' (Building and Construction Authority 2005: 3). So for example, if the share value of an apartment unit in a condominium is represented by the figure 5/350, then 350 represents the share value of all the units in the condominium and 5 is the share value allotted to that unit (Building and Construction Authority 2005). Though there are various methods of determining share value including equal share basis, usage basis and judgment basis, it is not possible for a single method to be fair to *all* strata owners. The two most acceptable methods are the floor area basis and the capital value basis, although it is rare that both these are used together.

In Singapore the floor area approach is the most commonly used method, though it is subject to certain weightage factors. These vary according to the type of use, rather than the extent of usage (Khublall 1995). It will be recalled that the schedule of share values is filed by the developer and must be accepted by the Commissioner of Buildings before the sale of any strata lot in a development.

The Commissioner of Buildings issues Guidelines on the filing of the schedule of share values. In the latest Guidelines, share values of condominium units are assigned on the basis of floor-area groupings of 50 square metre intervals (Building and Construction Authority 2008).

The importance of share value lies in the fact that it is the *single and only* determinant of the powers (and obligations) of strata owners for the following three critical (and discrete) matters, set out in the Building Maintenance and Strata Management Act 2008. First, the share value determines the maintenance contributions that an owner has to pay to the Management Corporation of the estate. The Management Corporation is statutorily tasked with the responsibility of maintaining the common areas in the development. For practical purposes, the most significant function of share value is that it determines proprietors' contributions towards maintenance and administrative expenses, as well as their proportional liability for the debts of the Management Corporation. As noted by Lai J. in *Management Corporation Strata Title Plan No 980 v Yat Yuen Hong Co Pte Ltd & Anor*,[1] 'It is the cornerstone of the Act that subsidiary proprietors are co-owners of the common property and for their maintenance and repairs and so on, they also share the financial burden in the proportion of their share units'.

Second, the share value of a strata lot determines the voting rights of unit owners. The higher the share value, the greater the owner's voting rights. By regulating the voting rights of a proprietor, the share value determines the extent of a proprietor's power and role in the administration of the strata scheme. In practice, the voting rights of proprietors can be material not only in matters requiring a special resolution and where a poll is demanded, but also in relation to achieving the requisite majority percentages for a collective sale to proceed.

Third, the share value determines the share that each owner has in the common property, which is jointly owned by all the owners in a development as tenants in common. Generally, the fact that each proprietor's undivided share in the common property is determined by the share value has little significance in relation to their use and enjoyment of the common property, as long as they do not interfere with the reasonable use and enjoyment thereof by other proprietors. However, the share value becomes critically important when profits resulting from transactions involving the common property are distributed; for example, where part of the common property is leased out to a third party. Another instance is when the strata scheme is terminated, as in the case of a collective sale, and the proceeds of sale have to be apportioned (see below).

Determination of Share Value

A developer engages a professional surveyor to prepare a proposal indicating the share value that has been allocated by the developer to all the units in the development. The share value proposal for each unit must be accepted by the

1 [1993] 1 SLR 555, at 560.

Commissioner of Buildings before any sale of property can take place. However, despite the obvious significance of share value, it is neither defined in the legislation, nor is mention made as to exactly how share value is to be determined. Nevertheless, as mentioned previously, the Commissioner of Buildings has provided a set of Guidelines to assist developers to determine share value allotment (discussed further below).

The general underlying principle in the allocation of share value is the perceived degree of usage of common facilities. A unit that uses more of the common facilities is allotted a higher share value and consequently, has to make a higher maintenance contribution. The following explanations of how share values should be calculated in different building types are taken from Guidelines issued by the Building and Construction Authority (2008).

Share Value in Single-user Residential Properties In the case of residential properties, an important consideration for the determination of share value is occupancy, as this directly reflects usage. Floor area groupings are used to take into account the number of occupants who are likely to occupy a unit. It is assumed that units within a larger floor area grouping have more occupants and therefore incur a higher proportion of maintenance costs of the common property. In a wholly residential development, the share value allotted to strata units is based on floor area groupings of 50 square metre intervals in ascending order: the share value increasing by one for every 50 square metres of floor area. Hence, if the floor area is 50 (or smaller) the share value is 5; with a floor area of 51 to 100 square metres the share value is 6; with a floor area of 101 to 150 square metres the share value is 7 and so on.

Share Value in Single-use Non-residential Development For single-use non-residential developments comprising wholly of shops or offices or factories and so on, the share value is allotted on the basis of floor area. The share value allotted to the building(s) in the development is in multiples of 10, for example, 100, 1,000, 10,000 and so on, while the share value allotted to each strata unit is determined as follows:

$$\text{Share value of strata unit} = \frac{\text{Floor area of strata unit}}{\text{Floor area of all strata units}} \times \text{Share value allotted to the building}$$

Share Value in Mixed-use Developments A mixed-use development may comprise residential units, offices and shops in one development. As at November 2008, there were 373 simple mixed-use (comprising commercial and residential users) and 63 complex mixed-use (comprising commercial, retail and residential users) strata developments in Singapore (personal communication to author from officer of the Building and Construction Authority, 27 November 2008). Allotment of share value in mixed-use developments is based on the floor area of the strata units, and weight factors are used for each type of strata unit. The computation of weight factors for each user group is based on the share of the maintenance costs proportionate to the expected use or benefit each user group will derive from, or the risk it will contribute to, the common property. If there is income to be derived from the common property, for example car park fees, they could be shared in a similar manner, just as expenses are shared. Shops, which incur a higher percentage of maintenance expenses because they use more air-conditioning and other facilities like escalators, are allotted a proportionately larger share value. Shop owners therefore pay higher maintenance charges than owners of offices or residential units. Any of the following factors may be considered in determining the weight factors: gross floor area; common area; strata area; frequency of usage; human traffic; and risk factor. The developer should consult a registered surveyor, an architect, a mechanical and electrical consultant and a managing agent in computing the weight factors. The developer may also consult the Commissioner of Buildings before filing the schedule of share values for mixed developments.

Finality of Share Value Generally the share value of a strata lot cannot be changed once the strata title application is registered. However, the Registrar of Titles may allow changes to be made to the share value in the following cases: where there is an error in the entry; where the value has been fraudulently assigned to a lot; or where there is a subdivision of a lot or an amalgamation of two or more lots.

Collective Sales in Singapore

As discussed above, the measures taken by the Urban Redevelopment Authority to alleviate Singapore's land scarcity problem included the lifting of building height restrictions and assigning higher development intensity (or plot ratios) for various sites in 1994. The planning measures coalesced to transform such sites into highly prized assets overnight. This triggered the collective sale phenomenon, especially of strata developments holding freehold titles. Collective sale is a form of collective action whereby all owners of separate units within a development sell their properties collectively and at the same time, to a single party or to a consortium/joint venture, which has the intention to redevelop the site into a new development. It is viable when there is development potential, that is, where the land value is greater than the individual units' aggregate value. It is also viable when land is not optimally utilized, for example where the existing plot ratio (that is, the ratio of the floor area of a building to its site area) is less than the permitted plot ratio, or when the existing use is inferior to the allowable use.

In such a situation, multiple property owners motivated by monetary gain act together to sell their combined sites for redevelopment collectively to one buyer who, in turn, is prepared to pay a premium for the site. Property owners reap hefty profits as where plot ratios have been enhanced, the value of the land exceeds the accrued value of the individual units (Christudason 2005a).

'Marriage Value' for Collective Sale Sites, but Obstacles to Collective Sales

Thus there was a predictable response from multiple owners of fragmented interests in land, who saw the opportunity of making private gains by amalgamating their combined interests for sale and eventual redevelopment. 'By pooling multiple interests to form a more attractive redevelopment configuration, an en bloc [collective] sale allowed real estate owners to capitalize on the "marriage value" of the en bloc site' (Lum et al. 2004: 3). However, such efforts have often encountered difficulties, particularly in developments where numerous owners with differing interests were involved. Thus, for example, many owners resisted attempts at collective sale because comparable substitute homes in the same areas could not be obtained with the proceeds they could receive under the collective sale transaction. Even if unanimous in-principle consensus could be secured for a joint sale, disagreements arose with regard to the selling price, the valuation method used, apportionment of the sales proceeds, the mode of disposal and the timing of events and composition of the collective sale committee (Christudason 2005b, Lum et al. 2004). As a result, many collective sales stalled.

The sites that experienced the greatest betterment potential were often in areas where the State had made, or was scheduled to contribute heavy infrastructural investments (Lum et al. 2004). In these circumstances, if opportunities for comprehensive redevelopment were abortive on account of the problems involved in acquiring properties held under multiple ownership, the Government stood to lose the ability to leverage on its investments for an optimal level of urban renewal (Boyle 1985). This led to far-reaching amendments being effected to the Land Titles (Strata) Act in 1999.

Transfer of Power and Rights to the Majority

The controversial amendments were made to the Land Titles (Strata) Act with the professed objective of 'facilitating collective sales'. The amendments were considered radical because the legal requirement of decision-making through *unanimous* agreement among strata owners (on whether a collective sale of their development should proceed) was removed. The amendments now shifted the power to place property rights squarely in the hands of just a *majority* to make that decision, in true democratic form. The requisite majority thus empowered is determined by the age of the building and the percentage of votes that they could garner in favour of the collective sale. If the development is less than ten years old, consent had to be obtained from owners with at least 90 per cent of the share values. If the development is more than ten years old, consent had to be obtained from owners with at least 80 per cent of the share values. Thus, upon just a majority obtaining an order from the Strata Titles Board, minority owners would now be *compelled* to sell. Not unexpectedly, this led to great discontent and a slew of cases were brought before the Strata Titles Board and the courts by minority owners.

The Strata Titles Board as a Watchdog of the Exercise of Powers by the Majority

The Strata Titles Board is empowered to make orders for collective sales, and to decide certain types of disputes arising in respect of the strata development. It is an administrative tribunal comprising lawyers, architects, surveyors and other property professionals. Its duty, under the Building Maintenance and Strata Management Act 2008, is to ensure that for all collective sales, the requisite consent percentages are met, procedures followed and that the sale is in good faith and at arm's length. The Land Titles (Strata) Act 1999 requires the Board to consider the interests of *all* owners and evaluate the minority's objections. Once the Board is convinced that the sale is genuine, it will approve the application. No data are available on the number of collective sales rejected by the Board, but from January 2005 to September 2007 the Board issued 3,700 private residential units with orders for collective sale (Singapore Parliament Reports 2007); and as at 3 March 2008, the Strata Titles Board had approved the collective sale of 142 developments (personal communication to author from Senior Manager, Registration Services, Regulatory Division, Singapore Land Authority, 7 March 2008).

Objections to be Considered by the Strata Titles Board

A subsidiary proprietor (in other words, any strata owner) of any lot in the strata title plan, who has not agreed in writing to the collective sale, may file an objection with the Board, stating the grounds for the objection. It seems that the Strata Titles Board will approve the majority's application and order the sale of the development except in the following situations. First, where it appears that the objector will incur a financial loss; and second, where the proceeds of sale for any lot to be received by any subsidiary proprietor, mortgagee or chargee, is not sufficient to redeem any mortgage or charge in respect of the lot. On the other hand, the Board must not approve an application for a collective sale if it is satisfied that the transaction is not in good faith. The Strata Titles Board, when assessing whether a transaction is in good faith, must consider *only* the following factors: the sale price for the lots and the common property in the strata title plan; the method of distributing the proceeds of sale; and the relationship of the purchaser to any of the subsidiary proprietors.

Cases have revealed a variety of objections raised by minority proprietors: these have ranged from monetary issues, more specifically pertaining to apportionment methods and lack of good faith, to sentimental reasons (Ter 2008). The Board provides mediation sessions whereby some proprietors may be persuaded to withdraw their objections. It appears that in most cases, the collective sale is approved unless the owner would suffer financial loss; where, for example, the sale proceeds would be less than the purchase price, or insufficient to redeem the outstanding mortgage. The Strata Titles Board's decision is final and binding on all the owners, though appeals may be made to the High Court on points of law and/or non-compliance with prescribed procedures.

Share Value Allocation and Anomalies in Exercise of Powers

It is curious that a single share value allocation is relied upon to determine three very disparate matters. These three matters are obviously not following the same trajectory. So for example, a high share value is a disadvantage in that the maintenance contribution obligations are higher. Yet it is an advantage in terms of voting rights and entitlement to shares in the common property upon the dissolution of the strata scheme as is the case in the collective sale of the development. It is therefore not surprising that the share value of a lot is the single most common factor that has given rise to disputes among strata unit owners. This is particularly evident in cases where: there are both high-rise and low-rise buildings within a residential development; and the development comprises mixed-use and large space users such as hotels and anchor tenant stores in a strata development. Many of the problems centred on the quantum of maintenance charge contributions (see for example, *Sumitri M Menon v MCST Plan No 335*;[2] *Leong Siew Cheng v Subsidiary Proprietors and MCST Plan No 647*;[3] *Cortina Development Store Pte Ltd v MCST Plan No 557*),[4] and on the management of mixed developments (Select Committee Report 2004).

Case Study: The Kim Tian Plaza

In the context of this chapter, the case of the Kim Tian Plaza (*Tan Jui Meng v Hoong See Chye and Tan Lem Yee*)[5] illustrates the problems arising from share value allocations in the particular context of collective sale. Kim Tian Plaza is a mixed-use development in Kim Tian Road which comprises five shops on the first storey, 11 offices on the second storey, one office on the third storey and 28 residential lots on the fourth to the tenth storeys. As discussed earlier, mixed developments are unique in that 'weighted' share values are allocated. For the same floor area, the share values of residential, office and retail units in a development are generally allocated in the ratios of 1:4:5. Thus, a shop unit will have five times the share value of a residential unit with the same floor area (Building and Construction Authority 2008). Residential units may make up 30 or 40 per cent of the number of units or total floor area in a mixed development, but their share value can be as low as 10 to 15 per cent. As a result, when it comes to deciding on a collective sale, voting rights would be skewed in favour of the owners of shop and office units. At Kim Tian Plaza, this resulted in the majority proprietors having 91.4 per cent of the vote.

There were two main objections from the minority owners, who were residential proprietors. First, they alleged that the 'wrong' timing of the sale had led to a

2 Unreported, STB No. 8 of 1989.

3 Unreported, STB No. 28 of 1989.

4 STB No. 17 of 1991.

5 [2005] SGSTB 1.

'low' price being obtained for the site. The second was the inequitable method of apportionment which was not 'fair and reasonable'. With regard to this point, the Strata Titles Board stated that a sale is considered to be transacted in good faith if the majority of the subsidiary proprietors have adopted a method of distribution of the sale proceeds which can be justified as being rational and is designed to be as fair as possible in the circumstances to all the subsidiary proprietors. The method of distribution adopted is part of the good faith requirement which can be satisfied only if it is equitable. The objection was that the lots comprising shops and offices had been given too large an allocation and the residential lots too small an allocation. However, it is important to note there was no complaint that there had been an inequitable distribution as between the residential lots.

The Strata Titles Board acknowledged that while there is no best method of distribution, the method chosen should be defensible by the majority (that is at least 80 per cent, as in this case) and must be not be unreasonable. The method advised in Kim Tian Plaza for sale proceeds distribution was 50 per cent strata area, and 50 per cent valuation method. The Board found that this method of allocation was not unreasonable for the following reasons: (a) the allocation of share values in the common property for shop and office units was higher than that of the apartment units (thus unit owners would be unduly disadvantaged if only the share value method was adopted); (b) unit sizes varied widely from 34 square metres to 1,165 square metres (thus smaller unit owners would be unduly disadvantaged if strata area method alone was adopted); and (c) the valuation method adopted enabled all unit owners to enjoy the same percentage gain from the sale proceeds, consistent with their existing values. Accordingly, the Strata Titles Board granted its approval for the collective sale to proceed.

It is important to note that here, the minority owners were *residential* users objecting against the *commercial* users (see also Cassidy et al., Chapter 11, for divergent interests amongst owners). The inherent discrepancy in share values had led to the imbalance in the respective powers of the residential and commercial users through their voting rights entitlements. This is characteristic of difficulties faced by residential users in mixed-developments who wish to object to a collective sale. However, this problem has to some extent been alleviated by amendments in 2007 to the Land Titles (Strata) Act 1999, which introduced an additional consent requirement in terms of floor area, and which will now be discussed.

Balancing Power and Rights through Further Amendments to the Land Titles (Strata) Act 1999

In March 2007, in response to the groundswell of discontent over the collective sale phenomenon and its associated procedures, the Ministry of Law conducted public consultations on proposed changes to the Land Titles (Strata) Act 1999. Over 400 suggestions from more than 100 respondents were received, with the vast majority suggesting that the collective sale process be clearer, fairer and more transparent. After consulting with about 40 industry players including lawyers, property consultants, developers, academics and representatives of the Singapore Institute of Surveyors and Valuers experienced in handling collective sales, and with further inputs from the Strata Titles Board, important amendments were made; the one considered below is directly relevant in the context of share value and collective sales.

Additional Consent Requirement and Consent Levels

The earlier discussion of the Kim Tian Plaza case revealed how the 'weighted share value' concept had created an inherent bias against residential unit owners in mixed-use developments. To mitigate this kind of bias, an additional consent requirement based on the area of lots was introduced as an amendment to the Land Titles (Strata) Act 1999. This now constitutes the second consent requirement (that is, in addition to the requisite percentage of consent based on share value). It was said that such a requirement would mitigate the existing bias against residential unit owners in a mixed-use development, though not to the extent of causing bias against owners of commercial units with much larger areas. The requisite percentage of consent levels was maintained at the existing 80–90 per cent consent level for all owners. Calls to introduce a higher consent level were dismissed on the ground that a higher consent level, especially unanimous consent, would make it unduly onerous to bring about a sale, which would in turn affect rejuvenation and redevelopment.

Other Solutions to the Problem of Divergent Uses of Single Share Value Allocation

As noted above, the share value of a proprietor's unit regulates three discrete matters namely; their voting rights, share in the common areas, and the quantum of maintenance contributions. However, it is clear that these matters do not necessarily operate in the same direction.

De-linking Share Values for the Different Purposes

As the previous discussion has shown, high share value is an advantage as far as voting at General Meetings is concerned and for participation in a distribution of assets on termination of the strata scheme. However, it is a disadvantage during the life of the strata scheme because of the increased contributions to common expenses and these can lead to inequitable outcomes. In this regard, it is noted that the United States' Uniform Condominium Act 1977, as amended in 1980, provides for a separate basis of allocation for each interest. In other words, one strata owner's maintenance contributions, voting rights and share of common property may each have different determinants arrived at through different formulas.

In addition, several suggestions have been made on how a different set of criteria could be applied for the three divergent matters affecting a strata owner (Teo 2001, Khublall 1995). These include: (a) a weightage factor for each type of user; (b) three separate share values for each lot, one for the undivided share of common property, one for the maintenance contribution, and another for voting rights (as in the Uniform Condominium Act); and (c) greater flexibility with regard to share value calculation for different types of development or mixed-used developments. In essence, the idea is to move away from a single share value for the very differing matters affecting strata owners' powers, rights (and obligations). To some extent, this has already been implemented by the Building Maintenance and Strata Management Act 2008 with regard to the maintenance of common areas within a mixed development. This has been achieved through the implementation of a 'two-tier Management Corporation' scheme, whereby a main Management Corporation is responsible for the maintenance of common areas used by *all* subsidiary proprietors, while sub-Management Corporations are responsible for the maintenance of 'limited common property', meaning common areas that are used only by a limited user group (Christudason 2008).

Summary and Conclusion

This chapter has focused on the importance of share value and its impact on the power and rights of strata owners in the context of collective sales in Singapore. A total of 308 strata developments have undergone collective sale in Singapore between 1999 and 2007, generating more than 35,000 new high-rise dwelling units (personal communication to author from Executive Director of Credo Real Estate Pte Ltd., Singapore, 29 May 2008). Since 1999, almost 70 per cent of developments sold collectively exceeded 20 years in age; and between January 2005 and August 2007, the average age of developments applying for collective sale was 25.9 years (Singapore Parliament Reports 2007). Thus it seems that the Government's planning objective of urban rejuvenation has been achieved through the redevelopment of older estates. This welcome phenomenon in land-scarce Singapore was made possible through the Government's two-pronged approach to incentivize private sector led redevelopment. The approach involved on the one hand, the revision of planning measures, in particular the lifting of building height restrictions and enhancement of plot ratios. On the other hand, it involved the removal of supply-side constraints through the elimination of the legal requirement of unanimous consensus for a collective sale to proceed. The latter has been unabashedly acknowledged by the judiciary as a 'derogation of fundamental property rights' (*Tan Siew Tian v Lee Khek Ern Ken*)[6] as it marked the shift of power to the majority unit owners and in the process, derogated the value of the minority's property rights (Christudason

6 [2008] 3 SLR 64 at paragraph 19.

2005a). The Strata Title Board's position as watchdog of the minority's rights was also discussed, although its power does seem constrained by the provisions of the Land Titles (Strata) Act.

It is puzzling that three disparate matters including voting rights and the owners' share of common areas are regulated by the single determinant of share value. While this has given rise to several anomalies, this chapter has focused on its impact in the particular context of collective sale of mixed-use developments. The problem of inherent bias against residential strata owners has to some extent been mitigated through amendments to the Land Titles (Strata) Act 1999 and Building Maintenance and Strata Management Act 2008, which imposed an additional consent requirement. Thus now the requisite percentage of strata area, in addition to the requisite consent percentages, must be achieved in order for collective sales to proceed. Since 2005, the Building Maintenance and Strata Management Act 2008 has allowed the flexibility of creating multiple management corporations for the maintenance of common areas. In other words, Parliament's response has been dynamic and reactive.

Nonetheless, judging from the numerous cases that have been brought before the Board and the Courts (Ter 2008) there is a continuing groundswell of protests against majority-powered collective sales of strata developments in Singapore (Cheam 2008, Cheong 2007). This reveals that there remain crucial issues that still need to be addressed, to mitigate the predicament of the minority who feel that their property rights have been sacrificed at the altar of urban rejuvenation and land optimization. Minority strata owners may not have envisaged that their share values could be the single and ultimate factor to eventually strip them of their property rights.

References

Boyle, R. 1985. UDAG: The urban development action grant. *Policy and Politics*, 13(2), 179–90.

Building and Construction Authority. 2005. *Strata Living in Singapore: A General Guide.* [Online]. Available at: http://www.bca.gov.sg/BMSM/others/strata_living.pdf [accessed: 10 November 2008].

Building and Construction Authority. 2008. *Guidelines for Filing Schedule of Share Values under the Building Maintenance and Strata Management Act.* [Online]. Available at: http://www.bca.gov.sg/BMSM/others/Share_Value_Guidelines.pdf [accessed: 10 November 2008].

Cheam, J. 2008. En bloc uproar at Bayshore Park, Mandarin Gardens. *The Straits Times*, 7 May.

Cheong, Y. 2007. En Bloc Sales Boosting Housing Rentals in Singapore: Analysts. *Channelnewsasia* [Online, 21 September]. Available at: http:/www.channelnewsasia.com/stories/singaporebusinessnews/view/301299/1/.html [accessed: 10 November 2008].

Christudason, A. 2005a. *Optimisation of Land Use through Innovative Legislation in Singapore*. Paper to the Pacific Rim Real Estate Conference, Brisbane, 2005. [Online]. Available at: http://www.prres.net/Papers/Christudason_Optimisation_of_land_use_through_Innovative_leglation%E2%80%A6.pdf [accessed: 10 November 2008].

Christudason, A. 2005b. Impediments to the success of collective sales in Singapore: Lessons for the property consultant. *Property Management*, 24(3), 271–85.

Christudason A. 2008. Legislation affecting common property management in Singapore: Confusion or solution through fragmentation? *Property Management*, 26(3), 207–19.

Economic Development Board. 2008. *Singapore Facts and Figures*. [Online]. Available at: http://www.sedb.com/edb/sg/en_uk/index/why_singapore/singapore_facts_and_figures.html [accessed: 10 November 2008].

Khublall, N. 1995. *Strata Titles*. Singapore: Butterworths Asia.

Le Corbusier. 1946. *Towards a New Architecture* (translated by Etchells, F.). London: Architectural Press.

Le Corbusier. 1947. *The City of Tomorrow and its Planning* (translated by Etchells, F.). London: Architectural Press.

Lima, A.I. 2003. *Soleri: Architecture as Human Ecology*. New York, NY: Monacelli Press.

Lum, S., Sim, L. and Malone-Lee, L.C. 2004. Market-led policy measures for urban redevelopment in Singapore. *Land Use Policy*, 21(1), 1–19.

Select Committee on the Building Maintenance and Management Bill. 2004. *Report of the Select Committee to the Tenth Parliament of Singapore on the Building Maintenance and Management Bill [Bill No. 6/2004]*. [Online]. Available at: http://www.parliament.gov.sg/Publications/Report%20and%20Appendix%20I%20(Homepage).pdf [accessed: 25 April 2009].

Singapore Parliament Reports. 2007. *Written Answers to Questions: Strata Titles Board (Application for Collective Sales)*. Volume No. 83, Sitting No. 10, 2007-09-17, Column No. 1645. [Online]. Available at: http://www.parliament.gov.sg:80/reports/public/hansard/full/20070917/20070917_HR.html [accessed: 11 May 2009].

Stone, P. 1988. *Development and Planning Economy*. London: E and FN Spon.

Teo, K.S. 2001. *Strata Title in Singapore and Malaysia.* Singapore: Butterworths Asia.

Ter, K.L. 2008. A man's home is [not] his castle – en bloc collective sales in Singapore. *Singapore Academy of Law Journal*, 20 (March), 49–98.

Urban Redevelopment Authority. 1991a. Living the next lap. *Skyline*, March/April. Singapore: Urban Redevelopment Authority.

Urban Redevelopment Authority. 1991b. The DGP process: URA's new planning approach. *Skyline*, May/June. Singapore: Urban Redevelopment Authority.

Urban Redevelopment Authority. 1993. Rezoning to increase the supply of prime residential land. *Skyline*, March/April. Singapore: Urban Redevelopment Authority.

Urban Redevelopment Authority. Not dated. *Introduction.* [Online]. Available at: http://www.ura.gov.sg/about/ura-intro.htm [accessed: 10 November 2008].

Chapter 7
Management Rights in Multi-owned Properties in Hong Kong

Ngai Ming Yip

Introduction

Rapid urbanization has compelled countries in East Asia to adopt a high density development approach in cities in which the construction of multi-owned residential properties has become almost inevitable. Yet the management of multi-owned properties has never been straightforward. Even in western countries where the legal framework for multi-ownership is more established and the scale of such development is often much smaller, problems in multi-owned housing management still attract wide concern (e.g. Cole and Robinson 2000, Barton and Silverman 1994, McKenzie 1994, Wekerie et al. 1980). Such problems are often worse in an East Asian context, given the growth of large scale residential projects within the context of an inadequate legal infrastructure for multiple ownership. The management of multi-owned housing does not involve merely technical matters of finance and maintenance but is embedded in complex problems of common pool resources and communal governance, which are made even more complicated when entangled with issues around collective action. In East Asia where civic society is still relatively underdeveloped, communal governance is more difficult to take root. A highly concentrated power structure that skews towards the state and the bias of the state towards economic development (and hence towards developers), often puts the rights of small owners in multi-ownership properties in an unfavourable position.

It is within such a context that owners' rights to manage in Hong Kong are discussed. Hong Kong offers an interesting case study in East Asia, particularly when viewed in relation to China. Extensive and rapid property development, which began in the 1960s, has compelled Hong Kong to adapt a system that suits local needs, resulting in high density, high-rise, multi-owned residential developments becoming widespread. Yet no attempt was made to establish a condominium ownership system. Instead, a co-ownership system was employed, based on shared ownership rights to the piece of land on which the resident development sits. How management responsibilities are shouldered is a matter of private arrangement; the formation of an owner organization, which forms an integral part of condominium ownership in many countries (Van Der Merwe

1996), is purely a voluntary endeavour, arguably to ensure consistency with the constitutional right of freedom of organization (or not being forced to join any organization). Without proper legal facilitation and a legitimate platform for representing their rights, the protection of flat owners from exploitation by developers is under-developed. The imbalance of power is further exacerbated within the specific political economy of Hong Kong in which the oligarchic real estate market is controlled by a few, very powerful property developers, whose influence penetrates not just to the political centre of Hong Kong but also is directly linked to Beijing.

Flat owners are even more vulnerable in Mainland China. With flat owners' property rights to common areas only being properly recognized for the first time in 2007, when the Property Rights Law of the People's Republic of China was enacted, exploitation by property developers and their property management agents is extensive. Highly constrained by the inadequate legal infrastructure, legitimate and formal channels of resolution are extremely limited. Some owners who were desperate in their struggle against their powerful developers or management agents, took the issue outside the 'proper' arena tolerated by the current power regime. A few such actions were hostile and violent. Under the 'one country two systems' policy, both the legal system which is based on the Soviet and Continental legal systems, and the socio-economic context in Mainland China are rather different from those of Hong Kong, yet the organization of the Chinese real estate market, particularly the property management system, has mirrored heavily that of Hong Kong. Within this context research on management rights of property owners in Hong Kong can also shed light on the development of similar rights in Mainland China (see Wang, Chapter 8).

This chapter explores issues around the right to manage in Hong Kong within the 'critical legal events' framework – the catalyst for this book. It will focus on the transfer of power and the problems associated with such transfer, between property developers and residential owners in multi-owned property. The role of the management agent is also a central concern. The analysis in this chapter is drawn from legal and policy documents as well as from interviews the author conducted in 2006 with owner organizations in multi-owned apartments. The chapter begins with a description of Hong Kong's approach to high density development. Following this is a brief consideration of the 'bundle of rights' concept which offers a theoretical foundation to the 'critical legal events' approach in the subsequent section through which the rights to manage is analysed. The next section discusses how the embedded power of the developers in Hong Kong can have a negative impact on the exercise of owners' rights to manage. Silence and murkiness of the law in relation to multi-owned properties, which is discussed in the subsequent section, has exacerbated such an imbalance of power. The chapter will offer some short concluding remarks on the situation for multi-owned properties in Hong Kong.

High Density Development in Hong Kong

In a small city of 1,000 square kilometres, the rugged terrain and the competition for land use for economic and public development have constrained the availability of land for residential development. With only one tenth of the total area of the city being allocated for housing, a high-density approach is arguably the only choice for Hong Kong to accommodate its population of 7 million. All land in Hong Kong is owned by the state and leased out, either by public auction, land application or private agreement, for residential and other development under government land grants. As the freehold system of multi-ownership makes it difficult to pass on obligations for upkeep and repair to subsequent owners by the burden of positive covenants (Christudason 1996; also see Blandy Chapter 2), the leasehold system is used to provide the legal foundation for the introduction of multi-ownership of homes.

In the 1960s and 1970s when the expansion of both the population and the economy was at its fastest, the old city areas were already too congested for new development. Thus new residential developments had to be moved to either land newly reclaimed from the sea or abandoned agricultural lands in the New Territories which had become economically sub-optimal with the pace of urbanization. Limited by the capacity of the government at the time, bottlenecks in the construction of infrastructure (roads, community facilities and sometimes even land formation or reclamation) constrained the momentum for new residential development. In order to speed up development, plots of 'raw' land (with only very minimal infrastructure and sometimes none), were leased to developers who had to shoulder the responsibility for the construction of infrastructure. In return developers received concessions in the form of a reduced land premium or extra floor space beyond the limits set by the plot ratio. Such a practice continues in the planning system, even when the construction of infrastructure is no longer a burden for government. Private developers are asked, as a condition of the land grant, to provide community facilities, such as bus terminals, parks, foot bridges and public open space, with the assumption that private developers will employ better design principles and invest more in such facilities to enhance the value of their own developments.

Hence, it was deemed to be in the best interests of both the government (to save on the cost of infrastructure development) and developers (to achieve economy of scale) to develop large plots of land, the size of which were perhaps constrained only by the financial risk the developers were willing to bear. As a consequence, parcels of land granted to developers for residential developments in the 1970s and 1980s were usually very large, requiring extensive capital to develop. The high threshold would have filtered off all but the most resourceful developers (Renaud, Pretorius and Pasadilla 1997) and explains why the property market in Hong Kong in the recent two decades has been largely oligarchic (Consumer Council 1996).

This background offers an explanation for the massive scale of Hong Kong's multi-owned residential projects. For example, the largest residential development of Kingswood Villa in the New Territories comprises more than 15,000 households. On average, over half of the households in Hong Kong live in residential projects of over 1,000 households.[1] Under a high density development strategy in which the population density in the old city areas can reach 40,000 to 50,000 inhabitants per square kilometre (even the new towns in formal rural areas have to accommodate 7,000 to 8,000 people per square kilometre) (Census and Statistics Department 2006) it makes economic and social sense to adopt a high-rise development strategy in order to maximize the profit for the residential land, as well as to squeeze more land for community and leisure facilities. Whilst the average residential block in Hong Kong is eight storeys high with 42 flats, such figures are, in fact, distorted by the existence of a large number of old and small blocks built before the 1970s in the inner city areas, as well as by small blocks for 'indigenous' settlers in the New Territories. In fact, two thirds of the flats in Hong Kong are located in buildings which are over 20 storeys and nearly one in 10 flats in Hong Kong are in buildings which are taller than 40 storeys (see Table 7.1). While these data exclude public tenants who constitute around one third of the population, development density of public rental blocks is at least as high as private sector development. The Hong Kong Housing Authority began to build public rental blocks of 30 storeys as early as the 1970s and the height of standard public rental blocks after the 1990s usually exceeded 40 storeys (also see Alterman, Chapter 5).

Table 7.1 Building Height in Hong Kong

Height of Building	As % of Flats	As % of Buildings
Below 3 Storeys		47
• Urban area	3	41
• New Territories		6
4-5 Storeys	3	12
6-9 Storeys	6	14
10-19 Storeys	21	14
20-39 Storeys	59	13
Over 40 Storeys	9	1
Total	N=1,492,766	N=34,786

Source: Author's calculation based on a Home Affairs Department (2005) database of Buildings.

1 Author's calculation, based on building data supplied by Hong Kong's Department of Home Affairs.

The System of Multi-ownership in Hong Kong

About 70 per cent of households in Hong Kong are in private sector housing which contains a mix of owners and renters in multi-owned, high-rise apartment buildings. Only a very tiny minority of households live in detached houses. Unfortunately there are no statistics which differentiate houses from flats, nor any information on the profile of households who live in houses. Some indirect statistics may help to give some clues though. For instance, 5,700 building blocks[2] have only one building unit. These are believed to be houses, most of which are bungalows in the New Territories (some are in planned gated communities) and the remaining one thousand or so are located in the traditional elite area of Victoria Peak and along the scenic beaches in the south of Hong Kong Island. There are another 16,363 building blocks which are three storeys high, the majority of them (nearly 90 per cent) are believed to be 'Exempted Houses' under the Small Houses Scheme, a policy which allows self-built houses for male descendents of the clan who had settled in the New Territories before the British occupation (Nissim 2008). Yet many such exempted individual houses have already changed hands to become part of larger multi-owned sites. In the last two decades, a number of large residential projects have developed houses in gated communities on converted agricultural lands. For instance, the biggest gated community, Fairview Park, accommodates over 5,000 semi-detached and detached houses in Unlong and each of the adjacent gated projects of Palm Springs and Hong Lok Yuen in Taipo has enclosed about 1,000 detached houses.

It is believed that residents in houses roughly belong to three types. Houses on Victoria Peak, the scenic beaches on the south side of Hong Kong Island, as well as in central Kowloon Peninsula (Kowloon Tong and Kadori Hill) accommodate the very rich, the political elites as well as top executives from multinational companies, whereas residents in gated communities in the New Territories (Palm Springs, Discovery Bay, etc.) are mostly middle-class professionals and proprietors of small and medium businesses. Profiles of residents in small houses in the New Territories are more diverse. 'Indigenous' clan members who live in such houses are mostly old people, whereas small houses which are close to main public transport lines are mostly sold off to owners outside the clan. Such patterns largely match the analysis of spatial segregation by Forrest, La Grange and Yip (2004). However, it should be noted that gated communities, even some new luxury developments in traditional elite areas, are being organized as multi-owned sites, although they remain detached houses.

In Hong Kong the share of multi-owned apartments is overwhelming and is equated with residential developments *per se*, whereas houses are in a very small minority and deemed to suit very wealthy people or those with special tastes or

2 The statistics as to what constitutes a 'building block' are not very clear – it is believed that only small houses which have been converted into multi-owned properties are included.

backgrounds. Multi-owned apartments are also spread across a very wide spectrum, from dilapidated, dysfunctional low-rise buildings, to large scale 'estates' as big as a small town, with comprehensive community and commercial facilities in the 'town centre'. Restrictions on multi-owned apartments are a non-issue in Hong Kong and instead, this type of residential building is strongly encouraged by both the town planning and land policies.

Despite the extent of multi-owned residential developments in Hong Kong, there is no equivalent of a Strata Title Act as is found in many common law countries (for example, Singapore, Australia, New Zealand) (also see Christudason, Chapter 6, Bounds, Chapter 9 and Dupuis and Dixon, Chapter 12). Hence, it is not mandatory to form an owners' corporation (as homeowners' associations are known in Hong Kong), to realize the collective property rights to the common areas and to take over the responsibilities of management from the developer. Nevertheless, the formation of such associations is strongly encouraged by the government. Because of the absence of a Strata Title Act, such organizations are governed by a dedicated piece of legislation, the Building Management Ordinance 1993, most recently amended in 2007, which regulates the formation, organization, operations and power of the corporation, as well as how it should interact with its members and the management agent it appoints. The owners' corporation, once it is formed, is coercive in terms of its automatic inclusion of all flat owners, as well as its power in executing the Deed of Mutual Covenant.

The Deed of Mutual Covenant is the contract binding all owners (current and future) of multi-owned or multi-storeyed properties; it sets out the rules for the management and regulation of these properties. In fact, under the leasehold system in Hong Kong, conditions in each land grant are unique. Thus, it is in the interest of the government to ensure that such obligations can be enforced for subsequent owners through legally binding documents. It is common practice under common law to create such rules in the form of a covenant, a contract between the developers and the first batch of purchasers, which is passed on when the first purchasers sell their properties to subsequent purchasers. In Hong Kong, since the Deed of Mutual Covenant is a private contract, by convention the government would not interfere with the process. Yet, in order to protect the interests of individual purchasers, terms in the Deed of Mutual Covenant (which are usually drafted by the developers and are non-negotiable for individual purchasers) are regulated by directives from the legal profession to ensure that equitable practice is upheld. However, under the law of contract, the terms of the Deed of Mutual Covenant can be changed only with the unanimous consent of all owners. In practice, getting an absolute consensus of all owners is prohibitively difficult. Yet, there is no alternative provision to change clauses in the Deed of Mutual Covenant.

Land grants also play an important role in the formation of owners' corporations. As the land grant is referenced in the transferral of obligations, owners bound by the same land grant can only form one owners' corporation, however large the residential site. As forming owners' corporations is not mandatory, theories of collection action (see Olson 1971) would have predicted that the size of the residential development alone would be the major impediment in the formation of owners' corporation (Yip 2005, Lai and Chan 2004). In fact, in 2003, only 39 per cent of residential projects in the private sector had successfully formed their owners' corporations, albeit those projects with owners' corporations tend to be bigger and hence the coverage of population for projects with owners' corporation is much higher at 60 per cent (Yip 2005). Forming the owners' corporation, as a legal entity representing flat owners in management issues, signifies an important step in exercising owners' rights to manage. Without the owners' corporation, there is no other legal alternative to oust the management agent of the project who is often imposed upon owners by the developer.

The Bundle of Rights

Ownership, under the common law system, can be conceptualized as a bundle of rights (Blandy, Dixon and Dupuis 2006). In practice however, shaped by cultural norms and customs, as well as historic events and legislation, the bundle of rights may vary in substance and be allocated differently across tenures (Ruonavaara 1993) both spatially and temporally. Nevertheless, its expression is conditional on both the institutional and organizational arrangements of both ownership and management.

First, Ruonavaara (1993: 14) identifies three different sub-types of ownership 'on the basis of the range or extent of the consumer's ownership rights': individual (exclusive rights of individual households); shared equity (individual households who own their own housing units and collectively own some common elements of the properties); and collective (where the community holds the collective ownership rights). Ownership arrangements have implications for how the right to manage is discharged. Such a right is straightforward for individual ownership where the proprietary right to manage is the simplest in terms of the decision-making process as well as the allocation of benefits and costs. In collective and shared equity ownership, further complications of the right to manage are caused by the necessary extension of such rights 'to the right to enforce obligations against individual owners and the right to collect service charges and to determined how they should be spent' (Blandy et al. 2006: 2371). Yet comparatively, collective ownership, in which the collective (usually a co-operative) owns the right, is more efficient than shared equity ownership (which is the system of Hong Kong) in decision-making and allocation of costs and benefits. The quality of management of the former ownership type was also found to be higher (Yip and Dalholm 2006). The inefficiency of the latter type is perhaps further complicated by difficulties in discerning and defining individual and collective ownership in the buildings and their associated rights and obligations (Blandy et al. 2006).

Second, the organizational arrangement of management is also significant in influencing how the right to manage is discharged. Honore (1987) interprets the right to manage to include also the power of control and the power to contract. Yet the organizational platform on which the powers to control is exercised is pivotal. In theory, under the current legal framework in Hong Kong, owners in multi-owned properties can exercise such powers in different ways. An owners' corporation is a formal and permanent legal entity. A more informal way is to set up a pseudo-representative organization, the owners' committee, to create consensus among flat owners and to advise the management agent. Such a committee can be set up if there is provision for this in the Deed of Mutual Covenant, yet the committee has neither the legal status to enforce their resolutions, nor to represent the collective interest of flat owners. The other alternative is for the owners to exercise such powers in an extemporary manner by holding *ad hoc* meetings to resolve specified issues. The most common examples of such issues in Hong Kong are incidents of mandatory repair orders issued by the government. At the same time, whether such a right to manage is further contracted out is also significant. Blandy et al. (2006) found in their research that the common interests shared by the developers and the management agents they continually co-operated with, has motivated many developers to draw up contractual arrangements in such a way as to ensure the management agent would be employed by the new owners even after the developer has left. This is also an issue in Hong Kong which will be elaborated further in the subsequent section.

Critical Legal Events

Blandy et al. (2006: 2371) argue that the interaction of actors (owners, developers and management agents) cannot be fully understood without considering the notion of power, and particularly important are the 'instances of legal silence and murkiness (which) facilitate the exercise of power'. Inspired by Callon's (1986) concept of obligatory passage points, they created a theoretical framework of critical legal events to analyse the process in which the right to manage is transferred from the developer to individual owners. Such critical legal events hold the key in tracking 'how the law shapes the distribution of rights in the process of development, sale and management of multi-owned residential sites' (Blandy et al. 2006: 2372). Based on the critical events framework three critical legal events are identified in the process of the development of multi-owned residential properties in Hong Kong (see Table 7.2). The power relationships embedded in the legal process can then be revealed in light of the actors that are involved, what aspects of (and how) the right to manage is being transferred and the silence or murkiness of the legal process in such shifts of power.

The first critical legal event is the drafting of the Deed of Mutual Covenant. This is done unilaterally by the developer during the construction stage. Until 1987 the content of the Deed of Mutual Covenant was unregulated. Via the Consent Scheme,

Table 7.2 Critical Legal Events in Hong Kong

Critical Legal Events	Actors	Comments
• Contract for management of the site – Deed of Mutual Covenant Manager	• Developer • Management agent	• Drafting of the Deed of Mutual Covenant • Appointment of Deed of Mutual Covenant Manager
• Transferring management to Deed of Mutual Covenant Manager	• Developer • Deed of Mutual Covenant Manager • First Purchasers • First batch of owners	• Developer withdraws from the project (may hold minority share) • Deed of Mutual Covenant manager holds the right to manage
• Transferring management right to Owners' Corporation	• Deed of Mutual Covenant Manager • Owners' Corporation • Majority of owners	• 30% of share to form owners' corporation • Resolution supported by majority of share to oust the Deed of Mutual Covenant Manager

Source: Constructed by the author.

established in the mid 1950s for the regulation of the pre-sale of uncompleted properties (Kent, Meery and Walters 2001), guidelines for drafting the Deed of Mutual Covenant were issued and have since been amended periodically. Once signed by the first purchaser, the Deed of Mutual Covenant is binding to all subsequent purchasers. The appointment of a manager is often included in the Deed of Mutual Covenant, particularly for bigger developments. Often this position is referred to as 'the Deed of Mutual Covenant manager' to differentiate it from other management agents who are subsequently appointed. It is not surprising to find that the Deed of Mutual Covenant manager is unilaterally appointed by the developer. Big developers in Hong Kong, who enjoy a large market share in new residential developments, are usually engaged in vertically integrated enterprises. All of them run their own property management companies, and some of them even run more than one type of company to capture different segments of the housing market. The role of Deed of Mutual Covenant manager is inevitably taken by one of their subsidiary companies. Medium size developers, without their own subsidiary companies, will usually team up with partners with whom they have long-standing relations.

The second critical event is when the site is being occupied and management responsibilities are transferred to the Deed of Mutual Covenant manager who, as executive director, holds unopposed power during the first stage of occupation. It is also not uncommon for the parent company to reward the subsidiary company handsomely (with the residential owners' money). Most residential developments charge a fixed percentage of the total management outgoings as management remuneration, and a higher than market level manager remuneration is fixed in the Deed of Mutual Covenant (10–15 per cent were not uncommon until directives for Deed of Mutual Covenant drafting introduced a sliding scale of charges). Under current provisions of the Building Management Ordinance, when an owners' corporation is formed, it can resume the right to manage, which includes the right to contract out this right. However, even before the owners' corporation is formed, both the Deed of Mutual Covenant manager's appointment and the level of management remuneration are secured. Yet, forming the owners' corporation remains voluntary and, in practice, not easy to establish, albeit the threshold of forming an owners' corporation has been moved downward to 30 per cent of all shares in the development (even 10 per cent with a court ruling). Even if an owners' corporation can be formed, the Deed of Mutual Covenant manager is guaranteed an initial contract of two years by Deed of Mutual Covenant drafting guidelines.

The third critical event is when the owners' corporation is formed and the management right is formally assumed. Owners can then exercise their collective right of contracting and oust the Deed of Mutual Covenant manager or negotiate a new charge for the management service. Before 1987, Deed of Mutual Covenant managers were often appointed for periods as long as ten or 15 years, with the option of reappointment for the same period (some even had unspecified periods of appointment). Although after 1987, the directives for drafting Deed of Mutual Covenants allowed for an initial appointment period of no more than two years, there is still no provision in the statutes or guidelines for an extension or renewal of the appointment of Deed of Mutual Covenant managers (Kent et al. 2002). Nevertheless, under the current Building Management Ordinance, it is extremely difficult to oust Deed of Mutual Covenant managers as to do so requires majority consent (i.e. over 50 per cent) of all shares in the development to terminate the contract of the Deed of Mutual Covenant manager.

The Embedded Power of Developers

Blandy et al. (2006: 2374) describe the power of developers as 'power by proxy' which 'is embedded within legal contracts and passed from developer to managing agent at a critical point'. The developers in Hong Kong also have nearly absolute power in framing the governance regulations for the management of the development, which includes setting the in-house rules (in the form of the Deed of Mutual Covenants) and protecting their interests (setting the formula in allocating the shares and the associated benefits), as well as appointing a management agent with whom they have an ongoing connection.

First, the developers have the unchallenged power in setting up the Deed of Mutual Covenant which went largely unchecked before 1987 in Hong Kong.

With such powers, it is not difficult for developers to exploit individual owners by inserting inequitable terms in the Deed of Mutual Covenant. This is exemplified by litigation filed by flat owners of Sea View Estate (*Uniland Investment Enterprises Limited v The Incorporated Owners of Sea View Estate & Ors*).[3] In this case the residents objected to sharing of maintenance charges for the outside walls when the income from use of the walls (advertisements, etc.) went exclusively to the developer. Although abuse as serious as this is not common, it is believed lesser exploitation may be commonplace.

Second, in the absence of strata title or condominium legislation, multi-ownership in Hong Kong is, in practice, a co-ownership system. Individual owners are allocated notional undivided shares of the land on which the building sits in order to realize their ownership interest. Hence, right of ownership is attached to the shares but not to the flat itself (Kent et al. 2002). Yet, until 1999, there was no statutory regulation regarding how shares were allocated. There are examples where developers assigned owners' shares to the common parts only and retained the ownership themselves (Kent et al. 2002). However, after 1999 common areas were assigned shares and allocated to the manager as trustee on behalf of all owners without any voting rights. At the same time, it is extremely strategic for the developers to hold even a very small number of shares in the development. It is a cheap yet powerful instrument for blocking any future amendments of the Deed of Mutual Covenant. As one chairman of an owners' corporation remarked:

> We all have to follow the Deed of Mutual Covenant ... They [the Housing Authority as the developer] also said they are following the Deed of Mutual Covenant. Yet, there are inequitable clauses, just like an unfair treaty, we want to rewrite [such clauses] but it needs the consent of 100 per cent of the owners. They [the Housing Authority] just hold two shares (a flat in their development usually holds 20 shares and the total shares of 640 flats are about 12,800) and they can block all proposals of amendments.

In some cases, the developer can even assign the majority of shares to the commercial premises of the development which they own and thus block the formation of the owners' corporation. An owners' committee chairman from the New Territories commented:

> There are 430 flats in four 27-storeyed buildings which sit on a base of a 3 storey shopping centre which is owned by the developer. Yet 50 per cent of the undivided shares are assigned to the shopping centre and hence even if an owners' corporation can be formed [an owners' corporation can be formed by as few as 30 per cent of the shares], it would not be meaningful as it would be controlled by the developer.

---

3 [1999] 4 HKC 141.

Third, the law in Hong Kong empowers the developer to draft the Deed of Mutual Covenant which includes the appointment of a Deed of Mutual Covenant manager at the time of the first critical event. It is only when both the second critical event (transferring management rights to the owners' corporation once it is successfully formed) and the third critical event (passing a resolution to oust the Deed of Mutual Covenant manager) can be consequently reached, that the owners can gain the full power of their right to manage. Yet, the right of owners to form owners' corporations was only extended to all residential developments when the Building Management Ordinance was passed in 1993. Under the infamous clause 2a of the old legislation enacted in 1970, the Multi-Storey Buildings (Owners Incorporation) Act, developers of large residential projects could object to the formation of an owners' corporation in the project (by inserting a clause in the Deed of Mutual Covenant preventing the formation of an owners' corporation) and hence, retain their subsidiary as the Deed of Mutual Covenant manager forever. Although the Building Management Ordinance 1993 removed the ability of developers to block the assumption of full right to manage of multi-owned property owners and the 1987 directives further limited the Deed of Mutual Covenant managers' initial appointment to two years, issues of respective power are still not resolved. The law still requires an absolute majority of shares to oust the Deed of Mutual Covenant manager. As there is no provision in the law and directive for extending and renewing Deed of Mutual Covenant managers' appointments, it is not uncommon for Deed of Mutual Covenant managers to stay after the initial period expires and until their services are terminated by the owners' corporation (HAD 2003). To counteract this skewed power structure which puts individual owners in an unfavourable position, an owners' committee can be formed in cases where an owners' corporation cannot be established. Yet, although most owners' committees are similarly structured and operate in similar ways to their close equivalent the owners' corporation, they are not recognized as a legal entity representing the interests of the owners.

Silence and Murkiness of Law

Blandy et al. (2006: 2371) described the silence and murkiness of law in multi-ownership of housing which 'facilitate the exercise of power [of the developers and their agents]' in the context of the legal systems of England and New Zealand. Similar silence, gaps and confusions are also found in Hong Kong. The law in Hong Kong has remained silent on how the Deed of Mutual Covenant can be drafted, regardless of the extensive existence of inequitable clauses which are biased towards the interests of the developers and the management agents they appoint, often at the expenses of home owners' interests. Some Deed of Mutual Covenants contained clauses which prevented the right of owners to form an owners' corporation, and this was perhaps the most serious abuse arising from the silence of the law. It was not until the late 1980s that some minimal action began to circumscribe the abuse of developers in Deed of Mutual Covenant drafting, and not until 1993 that provisions in the Multi-storey (Owners Incorporation) Act that allowed developers to bar the formation of owners' corporations were repealed, representing a bold move in establishing the right of owners to manage multi-owned properties.

Yet, despite subsequent amendments of the law, as well as directives in drafting Deed of Mutual Covenants, usually with the intention to rectify unjustifiable clauses, murkiness of the law in such aspects still persists. For instance, directives on Deed of Mutual Covenant drafting have explicitly specified the maximum period of Deed of Mutual Covenant managers' first appointment to two years; yet legal provisions regarding reappointment and renewal are still murky. This opens up possibilities of manipulating the Deed of Mutual Covenant so that more stringent procedures to terminate the Deed of Mutual Covenant managers' service (which requires consent of an absolute majority of shares) have to be evoked. Since developers and agents have access to specialists in the juridical field to draw up something to their advantage, it is extremely difficult for flat owners to mobilize comparable resources to protect their interests.

Even if flat owners are ready to devote such resources, their attempt to challenge the inequitable clauses in Deed of Mutual Covenants is an uphill battle that only has the slimmest chance of success. A Deed of Mutual Covenant, under the current legal system, has been viewed as a private contract whose modification demands unanimous consent of all parties concerned. In fact, the law has been extremely silent on the other possible implications of a Deed of Mutual Covenant, given how it is being enacted and the parties that are involved in the covenant. The law simply does not take into account the balance of interests, and the public nature of such contracts as well as the social rights of owners.

In fact, the Hong Kong government has realized the legal shortcomings regarding the termination of the appointment of Deed of Mutual Covenant managers. In a proposal to amend the Building Management Ordinance in 2004, it was proposed to reduce the threshold to terminate the Deed of Mutual Covenant manager from an absolute majority, to a resolution in a meeting attended by not less than 20 per cent of the shareholders. This would greatly empower owners in attaining their full rights to manage. Yet, this also triggered vigorous reactions from the property management industry. With the support of their powerful parent companies of property developers which have the biggest shares in residential developments, intensive lobbying forced the government to drop the proposal in the 2007 Building Management Ordinance amendment. This is in the interests of many subsidiary property management companies of big developers which have been acting as Deed of Mutual Covenant managers since the inception of their projects. Retaining such management rights is also instrumental to some developers in protecting their business interests besides the guaranteed profits they gain from their property management business. Without any anti-trust or fair trading laws, Deed of Mutual Covenant managers have the power to influence the provision of service in big residential projects. For instance, it is not uncommon to find supermarkets in residential projects to be part of a chain of stores that are owned by the same developer. There have also been complaints about the monopoly of paid television services provided by subsidiaries of the same developers, or even worse was a case in which the internet service for a whole development, supplied by a subsidiary of the same developer, was paid from the management fee, regardless of whether the residents used such services or not.

In addition, the discourse of documents associated with multi-owned properties also largely deters all but the most determined owners. Written in language associated with legal documents, the Deed of Mutual Covenant is almost unintelligible to most lay people without proper legal training. It is also a document which is not normally attached to the sale and purchase contracts in property transactions. Hence, all but a small minority of owners who have a particular interest (for instance, because of a particular conflict with their Deed of Mutual Covenant managers) will have never read the Deed of Mutual Covenant, not to mention understood it. Although upon request and payment of a fee, the Deed of Mutual Covenant can be recalled from the Land Registry and the management office is also obliged to keep one copy, very few owners would request a copy themselves.

Concluding Remarks

Conflicts in multi-owned properties can be a potential threat to the perpetuation of a harmonious community. Whilst protecting the possession of individually owned portions of the property is necessary, it is not sufficient to stress only individual ownership. Identification of the bundle of rights that are associated with the ownership of both the individual and collective portions is also essential. It appears that most of these rights are not difficult to establish, yet, the right to manage seems to be among the most complicated of issues relating to multi-ownership of residential properties. While statutes or common law may help to construct a framework on which such rights can be based, they are inadequate to deal with the conflicts that arise in the process of competing for the right to manage.

The right to manage among multi-owned, shared equity properties is particularly complex as it involves also the right to compel others to abide by some agreed upon or enforced regulations, as well as the right to collect charges and the right to contract. How such rights to manage can be implemented in practice is also contingent on the institutional and power arrangements in such multi-owned properties. The framework of critical legal events used in this chapter offers an analytical tool through which power relationships between the major stakeholders, as well as the silence and murkiness of the legal system, can be identified.

Similar to the findings of Blandy et al. (2006: 2381) in which 'the seemingly neutral instruments of property, contract and company law can be manipulated to favour the long-term interests of developers and of the professional managing agents whom they appoint', our findings in Hong Kong uncover an even more serious abuse of the right of flat owners to manage which is generated by the silence of law in this aspect, as well as by the skewed power balance between the developers (and their management agents) and the individual residential owners. Although the legal (and administrative) system appears to be ostensibly moving towards a rationalization of power distribution in favour of the protection of flat owners' rights, there is no action to fundamentally rectify the power imbalances discussed in this chapter. Powerful lobbying by the property management industry, backed by their big developer parent companies, has delayed any move in this direction. In this aspect, property owners are powerless, unorganized and unable to counteract such resistance.

In fact, most owners do not feel the burning need for reform. This is partly because serious abuse is not common, and if abuse does occur then losses to owners are perhaps not great. Mostly however, it is because the standards of property management in Hong Kong are quite high and most owners are satisfied with the management service their agent delivers. Forming an owners' corporation to take over the full right to manage may not be in the interests of owners who do not want to devote time to this activity. The imbalance in the power distribution between owners and their management agents appears to be an academic rather than a practical concern which is remote from most ordinary owners who, instead, would prefer to spend more time in pushing the management agent to deliver a better service. Efforts in mobilizing owners' corporations for collective lobbying in changing the Building Management Ordinance have therefore been mostly unsuccessful.

References

Barton, S. and Silverman, C. 1994. *Common Interest Communities: Private Governments and the Public Interest*. Berkeley: Institute of Governmental Studies Press, University of California.

Blandy, S., Dixon, J. and Dupuis, A. 2006. Theorising power relationships in multi-owned residential developments: Unpacking the bundle of rights. *Urban Studies*, 43(13), 2365–85.

Census and Statistics Department. 2006. *Hong Kong 2006 Population By-census Summary Results*. Hong Kong: Government Bookstore.

Christudason, A. 1996. Subdivided buildings: Development in Australia, Singapore and England. *International and Comparative Law Quarterly*, 45(2), 343–63.

Cole, I. and Robinson, D. 2000. Owners yet tenants: The position of leaseholders in flats in England and Wales. *Housing Studies*, 15(4), 582–95.

Consumer Council. 1996. *How Competitive is the Private Residential Property Market?* Hong Kong: Consumer Council.

Forrest, R., La Grange, A. and Yip, N.M. 2004. Hong Kong as a global city? Social distance and spatial differentiation. *Urban Studies*, 41(1), 207–27.

Home Affairs Department. 2003. *Proposed Amendments to the Building Management Ordinance, Consultation Paper*. Hong Kong: Home Affairs Department.

Honoré, A. 1987. *Making Law Bind: Essays Legal and Philosophical*. London: Clarendon Press.

Kent, P., Meery, M. and Walters, M. 2002. *Building Management in Hong Kong*. Hong Kong: LexisNexis.

Lai, L. and Chan, P. 2004. The formation of owners' corporations in Hong Kong's private housing estates: A probit evaluation of Mancur Olson's group theory. *Property Management*, 22(1), 55–68.

McKenzie, E. 1994. *Privatopia: Homeowner Associations and the Rise of Residential Private Government*. New Haven: Yale University Press.

Nissim, R. 2008. *Land Administration and Practice in Hong Kong*. Hong Kong: Hong Kong University Press.

Olson, M. 1971. *The Logic of Collective Action: Public Goods and the Theory of Group*. Cambridge, MA: Harvard University Press.

Renaud, B., Pretorius, F. and Pasadilla, B. 1997. *Markets at Work: Dynamics of the Residential Real Estate Market in Hong Kong*. Hong Kong: Hong Kong University Press.

Ruonavaara, H. 1993. Types and form of housing tenure: Towards solving the comparison/translation problem. *Scandinavian Housing & Planning Research*, 10(1), 3–20.

Van Der Merwe, C. 1996. The comparative law of apartment ownership. *Scottish Law and Practice Quarterly*, 1(3), 205–15.

Wekerie, G., Dragicevic, R., Jordon, R., Kszyk, I. and Sorenson, M. 1980. Contradictions in ownership, participation and control: The case of condominium housing, in *Consumers' Experience in Housing*, edited by C. Ungerson and V. Karn. London: Gower.

Yip, N.M. and Dalholm, E. 2006. *Comparing Housing Co-operatives in Sweden and Condominiums in Hong Kong*. Paper presented at the European Network of Housing Research Conference 2006, 'Housing in an Expanding Europe: Theory, Policy, Implementation and Participation', Ljubljana, Slovenia, 2–5 July.

Yip, N.M. 2005. *The Institutionalisation of Residents Involvement in the Private Housing Sector in a High Rise High Density Environment*. Paper presented at the APNHR Conference 2005, 'Housing and Globalization', Kobe, Japan, 6–8 September.

Chapter 8

Regulations and the Imbalance of Power Relationships in Newly Developed Residential Neighbourhoods in Urban China

Feng Wang

Introduction

Newly developed residential neighbourhoods ('new neighbourhoods') are a very recent phenomenon in China. In the past, the Chinese government and state-owned enterprises took charge of housing investment, construction, management, maintenance and social service delivery to urban residential neighbourhoods. Since the 1998 urban housing reforms, the Chinese government has encouraged private homeownership and has also set up rules for managing new neighbourhoods. Private property rights were not institutionalized in China until 2007, when the Property Rights Law of the People's Republic of China was enacted. The encouragement of private homeownership, in the absence of private property rights, produced much concern among homeowners. Developers and property management firms have significant power and more often than not deal with neighbourhood issues in ways that conflict with owners' common interests. In order to protect their property rights, homeowners are organizing associations and taking various forms of legal, political and social action.

This chapter discusses the regulatory environment for the management of newly developed neighbourhoods and analyses the imbalance of power relationships among developers, property management firms, residents' committees and homeowner associations (HOAs). The chapter is based on documentary analysis and data from interviews with HOA committee directors of 92 registered HOAs in Beijing undertaken during 2006–2007. The remainder of this chapter is divided into seven sections. The first section describes the newly developed residential neighbourhoods in urban China. The second introduces the organizations that are influential in the new neighbourhoods. Next, is a description of the regulatory system governing HOAs in China. Sections four and five present the author's research on the topic. The sixth section examines how regulations and local governments' attitudes toward HOAs have affected the imbalance of power relationship between HOAs and other actors. The chapter concludes that to facilitate the development of HOAs, a favourable legal and institutional environment must be created in China.

Newly Developed Residential Neighbourhoods in Urban China

In China, commercial housing and property management first appeared in the late 1980s in coastal cities, the frontiers of Chinese economic reforms. However, their development was limited until the 1998 urban housing reform. By the end of 1998, welfare housing distribution was completely replaced by pecuniary subsidies nation-wide (for detailed documentation of China urban housing reform see Lee 2000, Wang and Murie 1996, Wang and Murie 1999a, Wang and Murie 1999b). Since those reforms, the government has encouraged the development of private homeownership, as a result of which newly developed residential neighbourhoods have burgeoned in many large and medium sized cities. Currently, therefore, two types of residential neighbourhoods exist in urban China: old residential neighbourhoods established before the urban housing reforms, and newly developed residential neighbourhoods.

Before the reforms, various work units (*danwei*), including government agencies, state-owned enterprises and quasi-public organizations like hospitals and schools, provided public housing at no cost to their employees and thus created what have now become 'old residential neighbourhoods' (*jiu juzhu xiaoqu*). After the housing reforms, public housing units were assessed and sold, in most cases, to the current occupants at low prices. However, the new owners can only claim property rights on their building units. The common spaces, such as stairways, open spaces around the building and other public areas, still belong to the original work units. These neighbourhoods are not mandated to hire professional property management firms to provide services to the community. The work units can choose whether or not to provide services and how to provide services to the new owners (Guo and Pan 2008).

The newly developed residential neighbourhoods (*xinjian zhuzhai xiaoqu*) include commercial housing (*shangpin fang*) and economically affordable housing (*jingji shiyong fang*). After 1994, real estate developers began building houses and apartments which were sold on the free market (Chen 1996, Ding and Song 2005, Wang and Murie 1999b). These dwellings are commonly called 'commercial housing' and include: high-rise apartment towers; multi-storey buildings; condominiums; townhouses; and villas. Normally these neighbourhoods are gated. To ensure that families on low or medium-incomes also have a place to live, the government builds some subsidized houses and apartments and sells them at a lower price than the commercial housing (Quan 2006). This 'affordable housing' (*jingji shiyong fang*) is cheaper, but correspondingly is located in less desirable places and has inadequate common facilities.

In the new neighbourhoods, real estate developers are now responsible for providing the community infrastructure and common facilities that had traditionally been provided by local governments or work units. These include water, heating and electricity facilities, public toilets, parking lots and so on, and in large neighbourhoods such facilities as daycare centres, supermarkets, health centres, banks, post offices and schools. Moreover, responsibility for providing community services such as cultural and social activities, public lighting, green space maintenance and waste management, has been shifted from local governments to neighbourhoods (Leung and Wong 1999). Because they are not associated with any work unit, new neighbourhoods lack a traditional administrative presence. To manage these neighbourhoods and facilitate the provision of the community services mentioned above, the Chinese government has promoted the professional property management model, asking developers or homeowners to hire property management firms to deliver property management services. These services include, but are not limited to: the provision of water, heating and electricity services; public area maintenance and repairs; neighbourhood security; neighbourhood transportation and parking management; common area cleaning including snow and trash removal; environmental improvements; neighbourhood road maintenance; fire prevention and fighting; and the collection of property management fees.

New neighbourhoods include a variety of developments, but are relatively young, having been in existence for no more than ten years. They also accommodate residents of differing socio-economic status, and range in size from neighbourhoods with more than 100,000 residents, to 100 residents. These neighbourhoods have grown very quickly and already outnumber old residential neighbourhoods in urban China. In most cities, old residential neighbourhoods now account for only one third of urban residential neighbourhoods (Guo and Pan 2008). For example, of Beijing's 6,000 neighbourhoods, nearly 4,000 are newly developed neighbourhoods (Qin 2007).

Centres of Power in Newly Developed Residential Neighbourhoods in China

In new neighbourhoods, there are four centres of power that play an important role in neighbourhood governance: homeowner associations; property management firms; the developer; and the residents' committee. Figure 8.1 shows the power relationship among these actors. The solid line denotes a direct and formal relationship, while the dotted line indicates an informal but influential relationship.

Homeowner Associations (HOAs)

Chinese HOAs are citizen-initiated and self-governing neighbourhood organizations that set goals freely and maintain autonomy from governmental agencies. They emerged in the mid-1990s and burgeoned after China's 1998 housing reform as a grassroots response to severe infringements upon private property and other related rights by local governments, developers and property management firms. They take a variety of political and legal action to protect property rights, such as engaging in demonstrations against the government and developers, initiating petitions, advocating for legislation, supporting candidates

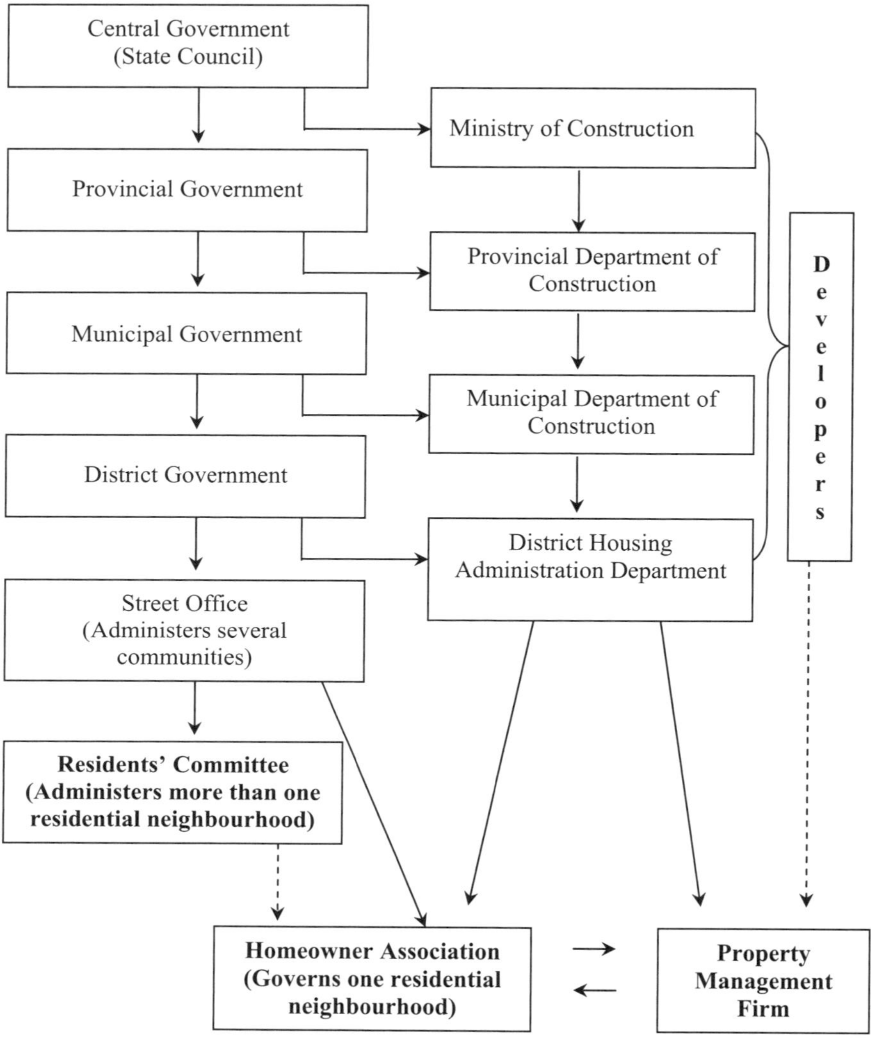

Figure 8.1 Power Relationship Structure amongst Actors in Chinese Multi-owned Developments

to run for Local People's Congress and residents' committees in competition with Communist Party-nominated candidates, and litigating against government and property management firms. They are thus seen as an important social force in urban governance and 'the pioneer of Chinese civil society' (Chen 2007: 90).

Neighbourhood management committees (*guanweihui*) were the precursors to HOA Committees. The composition of a Neighbourhood Management

Committee was complex, including representatives of owners, renters, the real estate developer, the property management firm, the residents' committee and the local police. Homeowners normally played only a marginal role in the neighbourhood management committees, which were in most cases initiated and controlled by developers. Without a regulated property management market in the late 1990s, developers usually set up their own management firms to deliver neighbourhood services, which normally brought them monopoly profits. To ensure that Neighbourhood Management Committees do not replace the property management firms which they have designated, developers tend to initiate and secure control over the committee, and often successfully do so. With developers dominating Neighbourhood Management Committees, owners would have little say in neighbourhood governance. Because homeowners' interests more often conflicted rather than aligned with those of developers and government agencies, owners felt the need to establish an independent organization to protect their common interests.

In response to the rapid growth of new neighbourhoods and widespread homeowner complaints, the State Council of the People's Republic of China promulgated the Regulations on Real Property Management 2003. Under these regulations, homeowners can organize a formal assembly (the HOA) in their neighbourhood once half of the housing units are sold, or after two years from the time the first homeowner moved into the development. Unlike in neighbourhood management committees, homeowners are the only organizers and members of these HOAs. Representatives from local government agencies and property management firms cannot join HOAs. Furthermore, owners can elect their own HOA Committee through a democratic voting procedure. HOAs then have become the major grassroots organizations through which homeowners independently govern neighbourhood issues. So far, most HOAs are established in the new neighbourhoods (Liu 2007) and have only recently emerged in old residential neighbourhoods.

Residents' Committees (jumin weiyuanhui)

The Chinese government set up residents' committees in the early 1950s to liaise between street offices and residents, thus ensuring effective control over urban residents and maintaining reasonable responsiveness to their needs. On average, around ten to 30 residents' committees representing more than 10,000 residents are set up in the jurisdiction of one street office (*jiedao banshichu*). For example, in Beijing, each street office in urban districts administers about 70,000 residents and each residents' committee represents about 4,000 residents (Beijing Municipal Bureau of Statistics 2007). Residents' committees primarily facilitate government administrative tasks at the neighbourhood level and manage residents who do not belong to any work unit. Although the mission of residents' committees is to enable urban residents to administer their own affairs and to promote a socialist democracy in cities, in practice they serve more as an administrative branch rather than a self-governing organization. The Organizational Law of Urban Residents' Committees 1989 provides that, as municipal governments initiate residents' committees, they are also responsible for providing them with financial support, materials (office, supplies, etc.) and salaries as well as operational guidance. Moreover, the street office traditionally appoints the directors of residents' committees. As a result, most residents view residents' committees as a part of, or an extension of, urban government, although residents' committees remain outside the formal hierarchical administrative system.

Property Management Firms

Professional property management has emerged as a new industry in China since the early 1980s, beginning in some coastal cities (Zhou et al. 2005). Property management firms are now a major player in neighbourhood governance, more latterly replacing the traditional property management services which were provided by governments or state-owned enterprises nationwide.

The Regulations on Real Property Management 2003 provide that a residential neighbourhood can have only one property management firm that manages all housing in the neighbourhood and provides all the services needed. The Regulations also vest property management firms with many functions beyond simply property management, such as assisting local governments in maintaining public security and stopping homeowners from violating rules regarding housing decoration and use of their property.

In reality, property management firms, in particular those preliminary management firms designated by developers prior to the establishment of HOAs, have substantial power in managing neighbourhood issues. They have powers transferred from developers, including managing and using common property and facilities (on this issue see also Blandy, Chapter 2; Sherry, Chapter 10; Cassidy et al., Chapter 11; and Dupuis and Dixon, Chapter 12). Local government agencies entrust property management firms with managing infrastructure services, such as water, electricity and heating. Consequently, property management firms have considerable power which can significantly impact on residents' lives.

Real Estate Developers

In terms of their administrative relationship with government agencies, developers can be classified into two types: central and local. The majority of developers have administrative relationships with local governments. For example, in Beijing, the central government administered only 8 per cent (89) of the 1,142 developers, while local governments administered the other 92 per cent (Beijing Municipal Bureau of Statistics 2002). Normally, developers have close relationships with local governments and, in some cases, development companies are even owned by local government. Developers have significant influence on local government policy-making because of their financial contributions, including land-use fees and land taxes (see McKenzie, Chapter 4).

Developers are required to build neighbourhood infrastructure and facilities, including civil air defence, schools, neighbourhood streets and lighting, and electrical and heating facilities previously provided exclusively by local governments. As they control the use and management of these public facilities, developers play an important role in neighbourhood governance. In fact, many neighbourhood problems, such as construction defects, changes in development plans and infringement upon common property, stem from developers (Wang 2008).

Management Regulations in Newly Developed Residential Neighbourhoods

This section is devoted to describing the regulation of new neighbourhoods at both central and local government levels. Central government regulations have the most impact on neighbourhood governance for two reasons. First, formal state laws and rules are important sources of authority in guiding neighbourhood governance. China's legal system follows the continental tradition, whereby the central government sets up laws and rules to guide social activities which people are supposed to follow. Second, the Chinese governmental system emphasizes central control. With few exceptions local governments tend to follow the regulations from central government. Therefore, how the regulations from central government define different actors' rights, roles, functions and activities in new neighbourhoods has a pivotal impact on neighbourhood governance.

The Regulations on Real Property Management 2003 are the main central government regulations of HOAs. These were amended in August 2007 by the State Council of People's Republic of China, to take account of the newly passed Property Rights Law of China. The 2003 Regulations are the source of the rules governing preliminary property management firms and subsequent property management services and all aspects of HOAs.

Government at both central and local levels also has a role in these rules, apart from providing a planning framework which facilitates the commercial development of new neighbourhoods. The Chinese central government requires local governments to set up detailed provisions to manage new neighbourhoods and regulate HOAs, in consideration of local political, economic and cultural conditions. While they must follow the main principles of the 2003 Regulations, rules published by local governments may differ in the detailed guidance for HOAs, such as voting procedures, the calculation of voting weights, the procedures for replacing committee members and so on. Some provinces or cities pass their own rules for HOAs, while many others directly use central government rules in their jurisdictions. For example, in Beijing the municipal government has not passed local regulatory rules but adopted central government rules with little customization.

The 2003 Regulations appear to give homeowners considerable rights to self-government, such as monitoring the performance of the property management service and the use of common spaces and facilities, but must be read in context to gain a true picture. A key issue to examine is the way the new neighbourhood has been organized by the developer and what happens at the point when the owners take over control. According to the Regulations, before developers sell housing units they must prepare temporary homeowners' covenants (*yezhu linshi gongyue*) which cover the use, maintenance and management of property; the common interests of homeowners; and the duties of homeowners and liabilities for breaching the covenants. While a model is provided by the Ministry of Construction, developers have full autonomy to design their own temporary covenants, to which individual buyers commit themselves when they sign purchase contracts with developers. The 2003 Regulations require HOAs to enact their own constitutions including homeowners' covenants and HOA rules and procedures, and provide models to help homeowners in this task. As soon as HOAs are established and their constitutions are approved at the first general membership meeting the temporary homeowners' covenants prepared by the developer expire and the new rules apply. In general almost all HOA constitutions are similar within a city because most HOA preparatory groups draft these constitutions from the standard model prepared by the local housing administrative department. The enactment and modification of these constitutions require approval from at least half of the owners and from homeowners whose exclusive dwelling areas account for more than half of the total area of neighbourhood buildings.

The 2003 Regulations also specify 'preliminary property management' in new neighbourhoods, meaning the property management activities undertaken by a management firm after the first homeowner moves in and before a HOA is established. Developers are required to select these firms. Before the establishment of a HOA, the monthly service fee is decided by the developer in the temporary homeowners' covenants. Property management firms collect monthly management service fees from homeowners, with the developer paying the service fees for unsold housing units. After a HOA is established, the HOA and the management firm negotiate and agree the service fee.

The 2003 Regulations describe some functions all property management firms should carry out in new neighbourhoods. For example, they should prevent any violation of the laws and regulations related to public security, environmental protection, housing decoration and the use of real property; report illegal acts to government agencies; and assist local governments in maintaining public security. The management firm may contract out some of these services to other firms.

The 2003 Regulations further require that HOAs should actively cooperate with residents' committees in self-governing neighbourhood processes, support residents' committees' work, and subject themselves to direction and supervision by residents' committees. Moreover, HOA committees should inform residents' committees of all their decisions and receive 'suggestions' from residents' committees. In this way HOAs are designed into the framework of local governance.

Most importantly, the 2003 Regulations identify the responsibilities of a HOA, its committee, and its members. In the West, HOA boards of directors or managers are the primary decision makers (Davis 1991, Dilger 1991); whereas in China, ordinary HOA members are empowered to make many decisions on matters of common interest in new neighbourhoods. The 2003 Regulations specify that the only governing body of Chinese HOAs is the HOA committee, elected directly by homeowners with a simple majority vote. The HOA committee is defined as the executive body of the HOA, which implements decisions made by HOA members at general membership meetings, and whose director and vice director should be elected from the committee members. The 2003 Regulations provide that the committee should perform the following duties: convene HOA general membership meetings and report to members on the status of neighbourhood property management; sign the property management service contract with the property management firm which has been selected by the HOA; listen to the opinions and suggestions of homeowners and tenants, and monitor and assist property management firms in fulfilling service contracts; monitor the implementation of homeowners' covenants; and any other duties assigned to it by the HOA.

Given that the decisions of the general members of the HOA carry such weight in China, the rules on voting are extremely important. The amended 2003 Regulations prescribe that decisions regarding the collection and utilization of special maintenance funds, as well as regarding the repair, reconstruction and rebuilding of buildings and accessory facilities, must get approval from 'two "two-thirds"': that is, at least two-thirds of the total homeowners; and approval of homeowners whose exclusive dwelling areas account for more than two-thirds of the total area of neighbourhood buildings.

The 2003 Regulations also require that final decisions with regard to the following matters must receive approval from at least half of the homeowners and from homeowners whose exclusive dwelling areas account for more than half of the total area of neighbourhood buildings: the enactment and modification of HOA constitutions including HOA rules and procedures and homeowners' covenants; the election and impeachment of HOA committee members; the employment and dismissal of property management firms; and other major and important matters with regard to the co-ownership and rights of common property.

Newly Developed Residential Neighbourhoods: The Research

A recent study carried out by the author examined how the current HOA regulations impact on the power relationship between HOAs and other organizations. The study used archival research and interviews to gather quantitative and qualitative data about HOA relationships with other neighbourhood institutions and governments. Various documents relating to HOAs were reviewed and analysed. These documents included central government regulations, a series of rules published by the Beijing municipal construction department and district governments, newspaper articles, homeowner activists' blogs and HOA online forums. Face-to-face interviews with Beijing HOA leaders were also conducted from March 2006 to February 2007. The interviewees were asked how they perceived the attitudes of other organizations, including local government agencies, residents' committees, developers and property management firms toward HOAs, the neighbourhood problems they had faced in the past two years and their problem-solving processes and results.

The sample consisted of 92 newly developed neighbourhoods that had registered HOAs in Beijing, selected randomly from a list of HOAs registered with district governments in Beijing by 2005. The neighbourhoods sampled were located in both urban and suburban areas. The largest neighbourhood had 3,728 households, the smallest 40 households. The average size was 985 households. A range of older and newer neighbourhoods with a range of socio-economic statuses were included.

Newly Developed Residential Neighbourhoods: The Findings

The research found that it was very common for new neighbourhoods in urban areas to face multiple, serious neighbourhood problems involving relationships among developers, local governments, property management firms and homeowners themselves. Table 8.1 provides further detail on the nature of these problems.

HOAs and Residents' Committees

The interviews showed that most surveyed HOAs did not have good relationships with residents' committees, despite the requirements of the 2003 Regulations which were discussed above. In many cases, HOAs and residents' committees did not communicate with each other at all. Many HOA leaders reported that they had no cooperation with residents' committees on neighbourhood affairs. Only 25 per cent of sampled HOAs (23 in total) received support and guidance from the residents' committees in their operation. The remaining HOAs stated that residents' committees' attitudes toward them were either indifferent or unsupportive.

HOAs and Developers

The interviews showed that developer-related issues were one of the most common and serious problems faced by the surveyed neighbourhoods in the past two years. The interviews indicated that 92 per cent of HOAs reported that they had issues with developers over common property. Of these, 83 per cent were said to have affected their neighbourhood life in a serious manner. For example, developers sold neighbourhood parking lots to others, leaving local residents no parking spaces. Problems relating to construction defects and deeds were noted by 55 per cent of respondents. Surprisingly, despite the seriousness

Table 8.1 Issues Raised by Self-governed Urban Neighbourhoods in China

Actors	Themes	Specific Issues
Government	Public service delivery	1. Increased use of schools and hospitals 2. Increased use of public transportation and shopping facilities 3. Lack of local police (e.g. neighbourhood public safety problems)
	Land development	4. Neighbourhood environment adversely affected by the new land development
Developer	Common property	5. Breaching agreement, such as decrease in green space 6. Changing approved development plan (e.g. the planned kindergarten replaced by shopping centre) 7. Lack of common facilities (e.g. no heating facilities installed, etc.) 8. Common property rights
	Construction quality and deeds	9. Construction defects (e.g. leaking roof) 10. Deed problems (e.g. delays; smaller units than agreed)
Property management firm	Property management services	11. Problems with the provision of water, heating and electricity services 12. Problems with neighbourhood environmental improvement 13. Problems with neighbourhood security services 14. Problems with neighbourhood transportation and parking management 15. Problems with other services (e.g. road maintenance)
	Fees and common income	16. Property management fee 17. Common income problems (e.g. management firms retain income by renting out neighborhood common areas)
Homeowner	Disputes between homeowners	18. Occupation by individual homeowner of common areas, such as stairways 19. Neighbours' conflicts 20. Use of residential apartments for small businesses

Source: Constructed by the author.

of developer-related problems, many HOAs chose not to take action to resolve the problems. Of those neighbourhoods facing serious problems over common property, one third of HOAs did not take any action. When facing construction quality and deeds problems, 48 per cent attempted to resolve the problems with developers. For those HOAs that took action, very few had success in resolving the problems.

HOAs and Property Management Firms

HOAs also faced serious problems caused by, or involved with, property management firms. The research showed that 97 per cent of the sampled neighbourhoods had faced property management service problems in the past two years. Seventy-six per cent indicated issues concerning management service fees (such as unreasonably high management fees set up by the management firms) and common revenue (such as income from renting out common areas is retained by the management firm).

Although most HOAs took action to resolve these problems (79 per cent took action to resolve property service delivery issues, and 69 per cent took action over management fees/common revenue issues), issues relating to property management firms have increased greatly over time. For example, the Chaoyang District Court of Beijing reported that the disputes regarding property management dramatically increased by 400 per cent every year from January 2003 to June 2006 (Qin 2007).

Local Governments' Attitude toward HOAs

When interviewees were asked to describe government attitudes to HOAs in addressing neighbourhood issues, 43 per cent indicated that attitudes were supportive. The remaining 57 per cent described government as either delaying or quibbling with respect to resolving neighbourhood issues caused by developers and management firms. Moreover, all HOA leaders mentioned that government officials were not willing to enforce regulations in a way favourable to HOAs. For example, based on the 2003 Regulations that HOAs have the right to choose property management firms, in September 2005 one HOA discontinued the service contracted with the preliminary management firm designated by the developer and hired a new management firm through an open bidding process. However, the preliminary property management firm refused to leave the neighbourhood and continued to occupy underground parking lots and community property designated for the property management firm's use. Meanwhile, the new property management firm moved into the neighbourhood. The HOA Committee requested that local government agencies force the preliminary management firm to leave the neighbourhood many times, but as its committee director commented: 'They [the government officials] did not have sympathy with us [homeowners]. They don't want to help us resolve the problems at all. They just shirk responsibility.' At the time of the interview, these two property management firms had co-existed in the neighbourhood for ten months. Finally, the new management firm hired by the HOA left because it could not use the community property and other facilities occupied by the preliminary management firm. This is not a special case. Many HOAs have similar difficulties.

Discussion

This section analyses how the current Regulations on Real Property Management, in terms of content, clarity and enforceability, have led to the existing imbalance of power relationships between HOAs and residents' committees, developers and property management firms.

HOAs and Residents' Committees

The HOA regulations are the very source of conflict between HOAs and residents' committees. The 2003 Regulations establish the guiding role of residents' committees over HOAs. Legally, residents' committees are autonomous neighbourhood organizations, rather than governmental or quasi-governmental organizations. Therefore, many HOAs do not feel that residents' committees, as neighbourhood organizations, have the legitimacy to provide guidance for them and to interfere in their daily operation. In some cases, residents' committees attempt to guide HOAs' daily administrative operations. HOAs reject these attempts which can eventually lead to uncooperative or oppositional relationship between these two organizations.

HOAs and Developers

The absence of laws that define private property, particularly common assets in new neighbourhoods, results in major problems. Unlike Western countries where property rights are well established, the principle that citizens' lawful private property is inviolable, although recognized by the Constitution in 2004, has not been operationalized in China. Under this legal environment, although HOAs' authority for managing their own property is recognized, most HOAs cannot exercise this power without adequate legal protection. In most cases, developers do not register common assets with local housing administrative agencies, or define the common property that belongs to homeowners. As the Regulations are silent on how to register or use public assets within neighbourhoods, developers can claim ownership of common assets (such as parking lots and building basements) without any evidence and also make large profits by occupying them. The absence of legal protection of property rights and the incomplete nature of HOA regulations regarding common property management, exacerbates the imbalance of power between HOAs and developers and is becoming an increasing concern with the rapid growth of new neighbourhoods.

Facing serious developer-related issues, many HOAs chose not to take action. One reason for this was that the Regulations do not provide HOAs with a clear legal status. Neither the 2003 Regulations, nor the newly passed Property Rights Law 2007, define the legal status of HOAs, without which they are not eligible to bring a lawsuit against developers. Legally, HOAs are neither social nor business organizations, because they cannot register with the local Bureau of Civil

Affairs, the only government agency managing social organizations, nor with the local Bureau of Industry and Business Administration that manages business organizations. Similarly, HOAs' elected committees have no clear legal status. According to the 2003 Regulations, a HOA committee can only take legal action related to property management. Therefore, neither HOAs nor their committees can bring a lawsuit against developers, although homeowners collectively are able to bring class action lawsuits against developers.

The absence of laws that guarantee HOAs' legal rights has greatly impeded the capability of HOAs to address developer-related issues. Rather than litigation, HOAs have to use strategies such as negotiation, contacting government officials and media, and group demonstrations and petitions, to deal with developer-related issues. Without strong economic, political and organizational power, HOAs have demonstrated very low levels of effectiveness in solving these types of problems (Wang 2007).

Furthermore, the current Regulations fail to provide clear and complete guidance for managing the new neighbourhoods, which places HOAs at a disadvantage when interacting with developers. First, the language of central government rules is vague when it comes to regulating developers' behaviour, which leaves room for developers not to follow the rules. For example, Article 24 of the 2003 Regulations stipulates that 'the state *advocates* that developers select a property management firm through a bid process according to the principle of separation of real estate development and property management' (emphasis added). The word 'advocates' gives developers the freedom of whether or not to follow the principle of separation. In practice, many developers appoint a subsidiary to provide neighbourhood services. In the research reported on in this chapter, 85 per cent of management firms were either a developer subsidiary or had very close relationships with developers. Second, HOA regulations do not specify detailed rules to guarantee that general principles are put into practice, which weakens HOAs' rights. For example, Article 6 of the 2003 Regulations prescribes that homeowners have the right to know of, and supervise the use of, common property and facilities; however, without detailed rules to ensure implementation, these rights hardly extend beyond the paper they are written on. As a result, developers can hide information from homeowners and easily infringe upon homeowners' common property rights.

Temporary homeowners' covenants were discussed earlier. To change these preset covenants, homeowners must reach a high voting threshold, which further tilts the balance of power towards developers. Although the Ministry of Construction provides a covenant model for developers, they can choose not to adopt the model. Most developers select articles that regulate homeowners' behaviour, while ignoring the articles that constrain their own behaviour. For example, most developers choose not to clarify what constitutes the common assets owned by homeowners. Moreover, if homeowners want to terminate or change the content of temporary covenants they require at least two-thirds of the total votes to do so. For a neighbourhood with hundreds or thousands of households, high participation costs (Cooper 1979) and collective action problems (Olson 1965) make it very difficult to garner this number of votes. Some interviewees testified that they had failed several times to reach these stringent voting requirements and were therefore unable to replace the temporary covenants with new homeowners' covenants.

HOAs and Property Management Firms

Problems with property management services are common in new neighbourhoods. One reasons for this is the difficulty homeowners have in replacing their current property management firm. Given that preliminary property management firms manage neighbourhoods before the establishment of HOAs, these firms are well established in service delivery, and the control and use of common property and accessory facilities at an early stage. As they can earn significant profits from these activities they tend not to disclose information about common property ownership to HOAs. Information asymmetry greatly disadvantages HOAs in their interactions with preliminary property management firms. When homeowners are not satisfied with services delivered by these firms, they have only one choice: to establish a HOA and empower the HOA committee to select another management firm. However, as discussed, the high voting requirement makes it difficult to change a property management firm. Among the HOAs surveyed in this study, only 22 HOAs (24 per cent) had successfully switched from the preliminary management firms to other management firms.

Another reason for severe service delivery problems is the lack of market mechanisms; free choice and the principle of competition. However, under the 2003 Regulations, HOAs do not have the right to choose how their services are delivered or to hire multiple professional service enterprises to deliver different types of services. In a word, homeowners must accept the mandatory and monopolistic services provided by professional property management firms. The problems were articulated by one research participant as follows:

> If allowed, we want to organize our own management body. We do not need professional services delivered by the current property management firm. In our neighbourhood, we have many retired and unemployed people. We can hire some of them to clean the public spaces or manage parking lots. They can do better jobs than the current property management firm … We [homeowners] do not need to pay that much service fees. Now, we have to pay for whatever services the property management firm delivers regardless of the quality or whether they are really needed.

While the Regulations stipulate that management firms can contract out some services to other professional service enterprises, HOAs are not granted the same right. As a result, regardless of the quality of service and level of satisfaction, HOAs can only select one property management firm. In interviews with HOA leaders, 15 interviewees expressed their wish to hire multiple service providers, but by 2006 only one HOA had successfully signed a three-party contract between itself, a property management firm and a cleaning service firm. So far, this is still the only case where a HOA has selected a specific service enterprise on its own in Beijing (Zhou 2007).

The current Regulations ensure that property management firms have more power than HOAs. In particular, preliminary property management firms have substantial power in managing the neighbourhood. These powers which include assisting local governments in maintaining public security, managing heating, electricity and water services and stopping homeowners from violating the use of real property, are both transferred from developers, and granted under the 2003 Regulations. When HOAs have disputes with property management firms over service delivery issues they are often in a difficult and disadvantaged position.

Having no clear legal status also impedes HOAs' ability to resolve property management service problems. As they are not an incorporated or social organization, a HOA and its committee cannot open a bank account to manage its own operating funds. In China, HOA committees have no rights to collect management fees from homeowners. In the absence of clear property rights, the majority of HOAs cannot share any profits from developing common property with developers or management firms. Therefore, HOA operating funds usually come from individual homeowner donations. Some HOAs receive a portion of common profits from management firms through tough bargaining. For most HOAs these funds are managed by their property management firms, making the operation of HOAs highly dependent on management firms. Among the surveyed HOAs, only one HOA committee had opened an independent bank account, and that was through a member's personal connection with a bank. Some HOA committees entrust one of their members to open a personal bank account for HOA funds to allow full discretion over the use of their money. In some cases however, the property management firm establishes a separate account for the HOA committee. In others, no separate account is established. When they need money, HOAs must obtain approval from their management firms. Such dependency for resources significantly disadvantages HOAs in their interactions with property management firms and impedes their ability to operate and resolve management firm-related issues. Interview data from a HOA leader highlights this lack of autonomy. She said:

> Our funds come from 2 per cent of the management service fees with a total of about RMB78,000. But we cannot manage our own money. If we want to buy some office supplies, we must submit an application to the manager of the property management firm. After his approval, the firm's staff will send the office supplies to us. You see, it is impossible at all to get money from the firm for the use of hiring lawyers to sue it. It is just like 'bargaining with the tiger for its skin' [asking somebody to act against his own interest].

Governmental Attitudes Toward HOAs

It is up to local government to deal with issues not addressed in the Regulations on Real Property Management. In practice, local governments are responsible for regulating HOAs and property management firms. Their attitudes toward HOAs and how they interpret and implement the Regulations have enormous impacts on neighbourhood governance. However, the research found that related local government departments are often not willing to give substantial support to HOAs.

The long-standing discriminatory culture against citizen-initiated, non-governmental organizations makes local governments hesitant about supporting HOAs. Moreover, any action taken by HOAs in resolving neighbourhood issues might be troublesome for local governments, which make officials unwilling to side with HOAs. To protect common interests infringed upon by developers and property management firms, HOAs take various actions to counter those outside forces, such as organizing demonstrations and petitions and suing government agencies for their administrative nonfeasance. These activities draw considerable attention from media and higher-level governments. Therefore, local governments usually consider HOAs an unstable social force that interrupts the establishment of a harmonious society. For example, in one interview, the head of a street office commented that HOAs are 'just causing more problems', and 'they are not able to resolve any problems but mess things up'.

Conclusion

The interests of developers, property management firms and local governments usually conflict with HOA interests. Therefore, these organizations have incentives to prevent HOAs from operating as the homeowners would desire. Without the advantage of economic and political power HOAs must seek legal and institutional power to legitimize and support their actions. However, the research carried out into new neighbourhoods found that currently, legal rules and regulations do not provide Chinese HOAs with the kind of favourable environment that allows them to grow and develop. Incomplete and ambiguous regulations do not grant equal powers to HOAs and other organizations and are enforced in a way unfavourable to the development and operation of HOAs.

This study suggests that a favourable legal and institutional environment needs to be created to facilitate the development of HOAs. Governments can amend the current Regulations to achieve this. Currently, no specific laws or regulations exist to discipline the conduct of developers and property management firms. The absence of such laws or regulations has left significant gray areas where developers and property management firms can take advantage of their political and economic advantages to impinge upon homeowner rights.

In sum, the absence, incompleteness and ambiguity of laws and regulations that govern HOAs, developers and property management firms have led to a case-by-case approach to resolving conflicts between homeowners and developers and property management firms. The outcome of this approach greatly depends on the discretion of government agencies and courts and varies greatly from case to case. Being in a politically and economically disadvantaged position, homeowners often feel that government agencies and courts treat them unfairly. This feeling leads directly to such mass action as protests and demonstrations through which homeowners utilize the media and public attention to gain leverage. Manifested at the societal level, the development of homeownership has increased social unrest in China's metropolitan areas. Therefore, to achieve a more harmonious society, which is the current leadership's political goal, laws and regulations that govern HOAs, developers and property management firms need to be improved or established. Such laws and regulations could help alleviate uncertainty, form mutual understanding and expectations and reduce public conflict.

References

Beijing Municipal Bureau of Statistics. 2002. *Beijing Statistical Yearbook 2002.* Beijing: China Statistics Press.

Beijing Municipal Bureau of Statistics. 2007. *Beijing Statistical Yearbook 2007.* Beijing: China Statistics Press.

Chen, A. 1996. China's urban housing reform: Price-rent ratio and market equilibrium. *Urban Studies*, 33(7), 1077–92.

Chen, Y. 2007. Property rights and self governance: A case study on homeowners' organizations in transition of Chinese society, in *Nonprofit Sector: Governance, Sector Interaction and Social Innovation*, edited by C. Qiu. Taipei: Taiwan Best-Wise Publishing Co. Ltd, 89–120.

Cooper, T. 1979. The hidden price tag: Participation costs and health planning. *American Journal of Public Health*, 69(4), 368–74.

Davis, J. 1991. *Contested Ground: Collective Action and the Urban Neighborhood.* Ithaca, NY: Cornell University Press.

Dilger, R. 1991. Residential community associations: Issues, impacts, and relevance for local government. *State and Local Government Review*, 23 (Winter), 17–23.

Ding, C. and Song, Y. (eds) 2005. *Emerging Land and Housing Markets in China.* Cambridge, MA: Lincoln Institute of Land Policy.

Guo, Z. and Pan, W. 2008. A study on urban old residence community management modes (chengshi jiu zhuzhai xiaoqu guanli moshi yanjiu). *Special Zone Economy (Tequ Jingji)*, 6, 121–22.

Lee, J. 2000. From welfare housing to homeownership: The dilemma of China's housing reform. *Housing Studies*, 15(1), 61–76.

Leung, J. and Wong, H. 1999. The emergence of a community-based social assistance programme in urban China. *Social Policy and Administration*, 33(1), 39–54.

Liu, X. 2007. A report on Nanjing homeowner association committees in the past ten years (Fengyu Shinian, Nanjing Yeweihui Diaocha). *Modern Report (Xiandai Kuaibao)*, Nanjing.

Olson, M. 1965. *The Logic of Collective Action: Public Goods and the Theory of Groups.* Cambridge, MA: Harvard University Press.

Qin, B. 2007. *Hallway Democracy (Zoulang Minzhu)*. Paper presented to the International Conference on Community Governance: Multi-Cultural Perspectives, Beijing, China, 24–25 June.

Quan, Z. 2006. Institutional transformation and marketisation: The changing patterns of housing investment in urban China. *Habitat International*, 30(2), 327–41.

Wang, F. 2007. *The Determinants of Effectiveness of Chinese Homeowner Associations in Solving Neighborhood Issues: An Empirical Exploration.* Paper presented to the Academy of Management Annual Meeting: Doing Well by Doing Good, Philadelphia, PA, 6–9 August 2007.

Wang, F. 2008. *Social Functions of Private Neighborhood Associations: The Case of Homeowner Associations in Urban China*. Unpublished Ph.D. Dissertation, University of Southern California, Los Angeles.

Wang, Y.P. and Murie, A. 1999a. *Housing Policy and Practice in China.* London: Macmillan.

Wang, Y.P. and Murie, A. 1999b. Commercial housing development in urban China. *Urban Studies*, 36(9), 1475–94.

Zhou, S., He, Z.H., Han, Y. and Li, S. 2005. A study on service quality improvement of property management in China. *China-USA Business Review*, 4(8), 8–12.

Zhou, X. 2007. *Duoyuanhua Wuguan Moshi Huhang Yezhu Zizhi.* The multiple property management types protect the homeowners' self-governance. [Online: Xinjing News, Beijing 20 November]. Available at: http://www.thebeijingnews.com/economy/hjls/2007/11-30/018@093534.htm [accessed: 10 January 2008].

Chapter 9
Governance and Residential Satisfaction in Multi-owned Developments in Sydney

Michael Bounds

Introduction

This chapter focuses on the legal arrangement associated with property ownership in multi-owned developments in the Australian state of New South Wales and the implications of these arrangements for residential satisfaction. In keeping with the theme of the text it deploys the analysis of power relations among residents, developers and strata managers in multi-owned developments and focuses on the question of control as a factor in residential satisfaction in multi-owned developments.

The New South Wales state government introduced the Strata Titles Act in 1961 as a means of giving security of title to residents in multi-owned developments. This legislation has since become the model for multi-owned management in many parts of the world. When the Strata Titles Act was introduced, multi-owned dwellings were a relatively small proportion of the tenure mix in New South Wales (and in Australia as a whole). Over the past two decades however, multi-ownership has greatly expanded and promises to become the dominant form of tenure in Sydney, Australia's largest city, thus bringing a majority of Sydney residents under the rights and obligations of the strata title legislation.

The chapter takes issue with critics of multi-ownership who claim that resident satisfaction with multi-owned developments cannot match that of detached dwellings, arguing instead that residents in multi-owned developments in inner city areas can display high levels of satisfaction. The argument draws on research into people's neighbourhood preferences, which suggests that home type and the characteristics of a neighbourhood's residents are much more important factors in residential preferences than housing density per se (PRP Architects 2002). People seek different forms of housing at different times of life and their preparedness to remain in medium density housing is increasing. While decisions to live in intensive residential developments are often based on amenity and cost, they also reflect the changing social character, education and life style preference of buyers, and the increasing desirability of inner city areas where most multi-owned developments are located. It is also argued in the chapter that the virulent opposition to medium density development still evident in Australia derives from a variety of continuing anti-urbanist sentiments (Bounds 2004: 93).

As Baldassare (1982) argues, the principal area of concern in relation to residential satisfaction in multi-owned developments relates to the residents' sense of control over the management of their dwellings. Where owners of detached dwellings have freehold ownership and are in control of their domain, owners in a strata scheme are subject to the control of the body corporate to which they belong. This has implications for owner control, ontological security and residential satisfaction. As Giddens (1985: 50) argues, ontological security and autonomy of bodily control with predictable routines is required in day-to-day life, to enable trust and to secure our place in the world. Dupuis and Thorns (1998: 43) contend the material environment of the home is a powerful influence in this construction of this sense of security.

In part these implications for owner control in multi-owned developments are an outcome of the structure and demands of the body corporate which impose unfamiliar and stringent obligations on the residents. In part they are a product of what Blandy, Dixon and Dupuis (2006: 2374) define as the 'embedded power of the developer'. In numerous instances management control has brought about power struggles and conflict between developers and residents of multi-owned developments. These conflicts have led to recent changes in the legislation to protect the rights of residents as cited below.

Drawing on cases of developer-resident conflict in Sydney strata developments, and based on interviews and research in Pyrmont-Ultimo in Sydney, the chapter discusses the implications of strata title regulations for residential satisfaction, effective property rights and control over their domain for residents of multi-owned developments in Sydney.

Governance and the Strata Titles Act of New South Wales

Before the Strata Titles Act was introduced in 1961, flats, units or apartments could be owned through three different forms of title. These were through *company title* which provided the owner with shares in a company with title to the full development, *leasehold title* allowing use of the dwelling and common property for a long period, or *tenancy in common* where joint owners of a development agreed to exclusive use of the residences and common use of the common property.

While there was large scale construction of multi-owned developments in the post-war period in response to housing shortages, these three legal schemes did not provide owners with a secure ownership of separate title to sell. Since the Act's introduction it has been amended four times, the most recent changes contained in the Strata Management Legislation Amendment Act 2008 coming into effect in August 2008. Multi-owned developments subject to strata title, under which the units are owned by the individual owner and the common property is owned by the owners collectively, are governed by a board of representatives of the residents called a body corporate (also see Sherry, Chapter 10).

Prior to the first amendment in 1973 there were 8,500 plans or developments registered under the Act. Between 1973 and 1997 there were 41,500 registered plans in New South Wales (Ilkin 2004). Over the past decade the volume of property under strata titles as a proportion of total housing stock has increased significantly, as has the proportion of residents settling in multi-owned developments. In the next decade, as people retire to smaller dwellings, many more will become subject to governance by bodies corporate. In terms of opportunities for participation in governance there is perhaps no similar area that offers an enabling opportunity to participate in shared management. Yet few people know what a body corporate is and few who are subject to the rule of a body corporate know of its functions.

The body corporate of the strata scheme imposes three kinds of levies to fund the operation of the scheme. These are an administrative levy for day-to-day costs of administration and maintenance, a sinking fund for anticipated costs of repairs and upkeep and special levies where immediate costs exceed the funds available from the other levies. While it is mandatory in New South Wales for the strata scheme to have a sinking fund plan and exact appropriate levies to maintain it, new entrants into the scheme may find that the sinking fund is under-funded for the maintenance requirements of the property, leading to unanticipated demands for special levy payments.

The role of bodies corporate in the decline or enhancement of the environment has attracted little interest (also see Alterman, Chapter 5). Bodies corporate impact on the wider issues of urban governance in respect of the maintenance and decline of the built fabric, but also with respect to the behaviours policed within the residences and the common property of multi-owned developments. In particular, with the popularity of 'lifestyle developments', bodies corporate in redeveloped areas in Sydney such as Pyrmont-Ultimo and Breakfast Point (which are discussed later in this article), have an enormous proportion of the open space and recreational facilities in these areas under their collective management.

The Residential Satisfaction Debate

The academic literature on residential satisfaction has a long history and is characterized by two opposing positions. On the one hand are those who connect residential satisfaction to strong community and social networks. On the other hand are those who link residential satisfaction more closely with notions of ownership and quality of housing. Put simply, the debate could be cast in terms of the importance of the social versus the physical infrastructure.

Few who are familiar with the history of social concerns in urban development would be unaware of the debates on urban renewal in the 1950s and 1960s. The principal concern at the time was the displacement of traditional communities in the process of slum renewal. Extensive studies of established, high density inner-city communities in the US and the UK demonstrated the close social networks and trust relations that existed among the residents of these areas and the manner in which density facilitated such interactions and interrelations. While the physical fabric was weak and deteriorating, the social fabric was strong. People valued social interaction, sitting on doorsteps, visiting each other, interacting on street corners and in pubs. Slum living, as it was called, was characterized by expressiveness and group integration among people who were person oriented (Michelson 1976: 67).

The virtues of such high density living were identified by Michelson (1976: 68) as: checking and reinforcing of behaviours; constant surveillance; binding social networks; physical proximity breeding interaction; and common retail paths facilitating interaction. The residents of these areas saw suburbs as undesirable and 'having no action'. For example, Gans's (1962) study of the *Urban Villagers* found that young inner-city boys visiting wealthy suburban developments had no idea why anyone would want to live in such dreary places. The inner city neighbourhood, and what it offered, was more important than the condition of their housing. Gans also found that when residents of the West End of Boston were displaced they sought out similar high-density and mixed-use areas in which to live. Young and Willmott's (1962) study of Bethnal Green in East London reached similar conclusions. The move to suburbia broke up social networks and close family support; interactions became more dominated by secondary social networks. The move to suburbia was a move away from the extended family to the nuclear family and the private future.

In Australia, Healey and Birrell (2004) are advocates for the position that privileges housing quality and the detached residence in low density suburbs. They argue that a central aspiration of the suburban history of Australia was the provision of a healthy residential environment, an aspiration that was associated with home ownership, open space and the garden city. In this context low density development, underpinned by an abundance of land, high incomes and state provision of transport and other infrastructure, became associated with social progress. Town planning became a central part of social reform associated with the garden city combining the virtues of town and country. These authors, together with many others (for example Davison 2000), argue that low density suburbia remains the preferred option for Australians. Michelson (1976: 84) summed up the debate neatly when he suggested that those who embraced the future of the nuclear family and managing the interactions with suburban neighbours found satisfaction in suburbia. Those who sought high culture and the city lights did not find satisfaction

The broad move to urban consolidation and the process of multi-ownership or apartment development represents both a move to urban efficiency and a swing away from the focus on suburban development that characterized much of the twentieth century. In Australia, urban intensification was spurred on by the 'Better Cities Program' of the Labor Federal government of the early 1990s, which aimed to encourage more just and economically efficient cities. The aspiration for a compact city is linked to the global interconnectedness of cities and the agenda to make them more internationally competitive, flexible and responsive. In the Australian context part of this global agenda is migration and the growth pressures this has placed on the largest cities, in particular Sydney which, constrained by the availability of land, has little choice but to consolidate to address environmental concerns and to enable continued growth.

Despite the fact that the majority of settlers in Australian capital cities now purchase medium density housing there are still commentators who criticize this form of urban development. For example, Healey and Birrell (2004) reflect the view that any claim for medium density is, by definition, questionable, whereas the virtues of urban sprawl are beyond doubt.

The Question of Control and its Relation to Satisfaction

Baldassare's influential study on resident satisfaction claimed that '[m]ost surveys of the general population have found only moderate effects of neighbourhood density on attitudes toward the residential area, health, mental health and personal relations' (Baldassare 1982: 96). However, a key finding from his work was that high density and low social control result in least residential satisfaction, noting that '[w]ith a lessened ability to control events in the dense area, the neighbourhood becomes unpredictable, more stressful, and ultimately more dissatisfying to residents' (Baldassare 1982: 96).

With respect to resident satisfaction with high density living, Baldassare found that residents' responses varied in relation to the social situation in which high density occurs. Some individuals are perceived as having definable social attributes which offer better opportunities for adjusting to high density neighbourhoods. In terms of retaining control, he argued that individuals are capable of adjusting to environments of excessive stimuli, making choices whether to withdraw or engage in encounters. They can selectively maintain relations and avoid overload and as individuals or a group define and manage the use of their environment. The capacity to exercise this control is the key to avoiding the adverse impacts of density.

Multi-unit Development and Strata Titling

Urban consolidation and compact city policies are not novel planning innovations in the Australian context. Debates over urban consolidation have been actively raging since the late 1970s (Bounds 2004). By the late 1980s however, urban consolidation was the centre piece of most metropolitan strategic plans and in spite of localized resistance, local governments were compelled by state authorities to plan for increasing densities. In the Sydney context this was backed by prescriptions for allocated areas of medium density development. Most importantly this legislation underpinned the right of developers to appeal local government refusal of their development plans.

From the early 1990s on, as Sydney and other Australian cities emerged from the property collapse of 1989–1990, the rate of inner urban medium density development escalated. For example, dwelling approvals as a proportion of capital city approvals rose from 2.4 per cent in 1987–1988, to 16.1 per cent in 2001–2002. Table 9.1 provides a breakdown of residential building approvals for Sydney for the years 2001–2005.

Table 9.1 Average Annual Residential Building Approvals in Sydney (2001–2005)

Type of Residential Building Approved	Outer Ring %	Middle Ring %	Inner Ring %	All Sydney %
Houses	56.9	20.9	6.6	37.7
Semi-detached, row or terrace houses, townhouses	19.7	22.8	7.3	18.6
Flats, units or apartments	23.3	56.3	86.1	43.7
Average annual approvals (%)	100.0	100.0	100.0	100.0
Average annual approvals (#s)	14,161	7,794	5,548	27,503

Source: Australian Bureau of Statistics: Building approvals, Australia, 2005 (ABS cat. no. 8731.0).

The table highlights the high proportion of multi-owned building approvals in the city's inner ring and an increasingly lower proportion of these approvals moving outwards to the middle and then outer ring of the city. State Government policy alone cannot account for the increase in, and pattern of, medium density development. Both supply and demand factors also were important. Contributors to supply included: the availability of brownfield sites, a classic characteristic of the post-Fordist city; major developers geared up to the production of apartments; an oversupply of office space leading to an imperative for conversion to residential units; and the reallocation of development capital from the commercial to the residential property sector. Demand factors included: vastly increased housing values and tax incentives on property investment enabling ageing home owners with high equity in their own homes to borrow against them and buy investment properties as a hedge against retirement; the reconcentration of high-value occupations in inner urban areas; the settlement of migrant groups accustomed to high density living; the ageing population looking to reduce costs of home maintenance and to access the entertainment benefits of the inner city; and the marketing of medium and high density developments as lifestyle dwellings.

In the future it is expected that higher density development will be the main driver of residential growth in Sydney, with 70 per cent of new housing being erected on brownfield sites. It is estimated that by 2030 multi-unit dwellings will account for 45 per cent of Sydney's housing stock, whereas now they account for about one third of the housing stock (Randolph 2005).

Currently there is an over-representation of renters in multi-unit developments; 55 per cent of flats are rented while the figure is 14 per cent for detached houses (Randolph 2005: 7). This skews the income distribution, as flat dwellers are disproportionately young and single. Approximately 43 per cent of flatters have incomes under $600 per week, compared to 29 per cent of residents who live in houses. At this point too, multi-unit developments are dominated by the investment property sector and renting. Many of those resident in apartments are transient, a low proportion of occupants having lived in their flats for five years or more. This reflects both the transitional character of the market and the age of most flats.

There is also a disproportionately high percentage of recent migrants living in multi-owned developments, reflecting a cultural propensity for living in flats, the availability of rental accommodation in this sector and the desire of migrants to live in close proximity to the employment hub of the CBD. New multi-unit developments are, in the main, located on brownfield sites in the inner city at present. This is a product of suburban resident and council resistance to multi-unit development and the availability of locationally desirable brownfield sites for development.

Strata Governance and Conflict

Baldassare's (1982) arguments regarding the control of events epitomize the relation of many strata scheme residents to their body corporate (also see Sherry, Chapter 10). While the strata title legislation establishes a process of governance and management to defend the equity and rights of residents, in practice it may not necessarily provide security or resolve the problems of power and conflict inherent in multi-owned developments. It could be argued that resident involvement in the body corporate is necessary to ensure they do not feel impotent, anomic and isolated. Yet many residents do not have the political or business experience which would equip them to deal with the meeting procedures, interpersonal politics and responsibilities of bodies corporate.

For many residents the experience of bodies corporate is one of failure on the first encounter which discourages further attempts to exercise their right to management through the body corporate. The following examples from Sydney's Pyrmont-Ultimo, Regis Towers and Breakfast Point developments, illustrate the frustrations of residents that undermine their sense of securing their world and erode their satisfaction with multi-owned developments.

Pyrmont-Ultimo

In the past the Pyrmont-Ultimo peninsula was a major industrial area, but with the decline in industry in more recent times, the area became run down. The process of rapid development that has since occurred in the Pyrmont-Ultimo area has been part of the City West Urban Strategy and is a product of an historic agreement between the New South Wales and Commonwealth governments signed in 1992, whereby $241 million under the Building Better Cities program was directed to the development of physical and human infrastructure on the peninsula. Currently there are about 18,000 residents in Pyrmont-Ultimo, although it is intended that the population will be slightly higher once development is completed. In many ways Pyrmont-Ultimo is an archetype of urban consolidation and can be taken to represent the Sydney of the future.

Research undertaken by the author and others on the social impact of development in Pyrmont-Ultimo consisted of a literature search, surveys and a number of interviews conducted between 1998 and 2005 (see Bounds and Morris 2005, Bounds et al. 2000, Bounds and Morris 2000, Bounds et al. 1999, Bounds, Searle and Stapleton 1998). The 1996 post occupancy survey of Pyrmont-Ultimo revealed a youthful, highly educated population from diverse origins. It found that the 'major reasons for living in the area are lifestyle advantages and proximity to work. Nearly 90 per cent of the survey sample reported that they like living in the area. By far the most common reason was the type of housing offered' (Cox and Miers 1996: 48). A conclusion of the research was that despite voicing concerns, respondents enjoyed living in Pyrmont-Ultimo. They enjoyed the easy access, the ability to walk to work and to many facilities and the increasing number of cafes (Bounds et al. 2000). In general the respondents had prior experience at some time in their lives of living in medium or high density accommodation, often while living abroad.

Three-quarters of respondents felt that their quality of life in Pyrmont-Ultimo was good or very good. Typical reasons for satisfaction offered included: the experience of apartment living abroad or elsewhere; the desire to move away from suburbia once children had left home; the appeal of pedestrian and low car use life style; the proximity to the entertainment district and the facilities of the Sydney Harbour; boredom with the country and seeking an urban lifestyle; being attracted by a sense of mystery of the inner city; and a desire to flee suburbia.

Yet one of the major concerns of residents was the shortcomings of bodies corporate. For a number of respondents levies had increased far beyond their expectation since they had taken up residence. This rendered properties difficult to sell, as it increased the costs for prospective buyers and created the perception for new purchasers that levies might spiral out of control in the future. These levy increases were particularly hard on older residents on fixed incomes who had bought in the expectation of limiting their outgoings by reducing the costs of upkeep and maintenance on a detached dwelling.

This problem was exacerbated for some who found that within a relatively short time structural problems emerged in the multi-unit developments, imposing major costs for repairs and for conducting litigation against the developers. Issues to do with litigation were often made more difficult because of the conflict of interest among the various parties involved. Typically the developers contracted the strata managers assisting the body corporate. The managers then enjoyed a closer relation with the developer than with the owners. In one instance the body corporate was impeded from repairing structural faults and taking action against the developer as the developer had still not fulfilled the legal requirement of lodging plans for the building after six years. These are instances of developers taking advantage of what Blandy, Dixon and Dupuis call 'instances of legal silence' which facilitate the exercise of power (2006: 2371). They are experienced by owners as an impotence which inheres in the management of multi-owned developments in contrast to the ownership of a detached dwelling. The emotional and economic cost to owners of pursuing legal action under these circumstances are enormous, as illustrated in the case of Regis Towers below.

Regis Towers

Typical of the type of difficulties facing bodies corporate in inner city development, and indeed more generally across the city, is the case of Regis Towers located in Castlereagh Street, about a kilometre South of the Sydney Central Business District. This 653 unit development was constructed by one of the major Sydney apartment developers, Meriton Apartments. Meriton is also responsible for a large part of the redevelopment of Pyrmont-Ultimo and for many other multi-owned developments up the East coast of Australia.

In the case of the Regis Towers, numerous defects in the construction of the building have led to the body corporate suing the developer for compensation. The costs of litigation have exhausted the funds of the body corporate, undermining its capacity to fulfil its functions. The ensuing publicity has damaged the developer and the potential to sell the remaining apartments in the development (Condon 2005: 23). The strata scheme has now been declared insolvent with debts of $500,000.

At the heart of the matter is the capacity of the system of governance constituted by bodies corporate to deal with developments such as Regis Towers, which is worth $400 million and has a strata levy budget of $3.2 million (Davies and Nichols 2003). In this case the owners of the building fell out with the managing agents over the pursuit of the developer, the managing agent refusing to increase the levy to cover the costs of litigation and thus defying the owners for whom the managing agent worked.

The issues faced by the owners of Regis Towers give some insight into the multiple responsibilities and the political and financial stakes involved in the politics of the bodies corporate. Such differences between the owners and managing agents are all too frequent and apparently inherent in the process of establishing bodies corporate and appointing managing agents. In the majority of instances it is the developer who establishes the body corporate and appoints the managing agent at the time of completion of the development. As at this point, the developer still owns much of the property in the development and the agent is beholden to the developer for the appointment and often for future appointments. In new developments the responsibility of the agent in advising the owners and in pursuing the developer for faults is sometimes mediated by a conflict of interest.

Breakfast Point

The majority of new residential building in Sydney is in multi-owned developments and the majority of these new developments are large scale lifestyle developments with large elements of infrastructure and open space. The Breakfast Point development is a $1.65 billion, 52 hectare, lifestyle development on the Parramatta River in the Local Government area of Canada Bay in Sydney's inner

West. It currently houses 2,000 people with an estimated final population of 5,000 by 2018. On completion of each stage of the development, bodies corporate of residents become responsible for the maintenance and upgrade of these facilities as part of their common property.

Developers under agreement with the local government council make developer contributions to the council prior to completion, to fund the extra demands placed on council resources by the new development. They will also at times enter into agreements with the council to provide facilities which will be available to both the residents of the development and the public at large. As individual purchasers are not aware of the agreement entered into by the developer and council they are unaware of the liabilities, which may be considerable, that await them in respect of the maintenance and care of public facilities, nor of the responsibilities undertaken by the council to provide facilities for the residents of the development in consequence of payments by the developer (Community Associations in City of Canada Bay 2007).

In Breakfast Point, and other developments, these matters have now become issues of dispute, pitting state, local government, developers and bodies corporate against one another. At stake are the liabilities, amenities and exclusive rights of residents in multi-owned developments and the responsibilities of state and local government for the provision of urban services. These politics are played out in the meetings of bodies corporate, in community politics and in Parliament. In the case of Breakfast Point the residents were fortunate to have a Member of Parliament, the Upper House Labor MP Ian West chairing the body corporate, and a strong advocate in the local state Member of Parliament Angela D'Amore. On 31 August 2006 the New South Wales State Minister for Planning, following lobbying by Angela D'Amore, declared the $1.5 billion residential development by Rosecorp at Breakfast Point to be a Major Project under the provisions of the Environmental Planning and Assessment Act 1979, resulting in the state government taking over development approval of the site from local government.

The master plan for Breakfast Point includes a village green, a playing field and community hall; guaranteed public access along the entire foreshore of the site; a waterfront park and sporting facilities; a retail precinct and community shopping centre; a sport and recreation club; gardens; and wildlife corridors and native species plantings. Angela D'Amore asserted that the declaration of Breakfast Point as a Major Project would ensure that development applications 'will be assessed within a reasonable time, and approved or rejected without the 450-day delays that had begun to occur under Canada Bay Council's jurisdiction. It will provide certainty for local residents, who will get the public benefits they paid for, in full and within a reasonable time frame' (Parliament of New South Wales 2005).

However, the continuing concerns of Breakfast Point residents over these matters and the relationship of multi-owned developments with the council in Canada Bay led to a joint meeting of community associations with Angela D'Amore in July of 2007. At this meeting a number of issues were raised, including the lack of transparency about where allocations from developers to the council had been spent; the fact that developers make deals with the council to get their development applications approved and future residents are then obliged to pay for things for which they had no part in negotiating; and the expectation that small communities should accept responsibility for the maintenance of roads, lighting, foreshore walkways and other facilities to which public access must be granted.

Many of the issues for residents derived from the Master Plan. This plan was specifically contrived to require public access to pathways and open space created for the development, but to 'to isolate itself from any potential liability related to the historic industrial use of the land' (Giles Tribe Architects and Urban Planners 2005) as much of the site for the development had been subject to industrial contamination which remains capped under the village green. Notwithstanding the intervention of the state member on behalf of the residents, when the residents attempted to sack the managing agent appointed by Rosecorp, the developer, Rosecorp was able to exercise enough proxy votes to stop the managing agent from being dismissed. Although the strata title legislation at the time of these events was intended to limit the voting power of the developer after 30 per cent of the entitlements had been sold, a requirement was included in sales contracts providing the developer with proxy voting rights of some of the residents.

Changes in the body corporate law stimulated by this and similar struggles to prevent developers obliging residents to give them their proxy votes on the body corporate, became effective in August 2008. Yet still the developer Rosecorp found a legal loophole to regain control of the body corporate by purchasing further lots in the strata to increase its voting power after the change in the law (Creagh 2008). The developer argued that the community included more than the current residents and extended to future residents and others who used the common property, a compelling argument. The residents saw the developer's control as a purely commercial interest to maximize Rosecorp's return on the development (Creagh 2008). Both parties have interests to defend but such struggles give little assurance to residents in multi-owned developments that they will find the kind of ontological security and control over their domain which they would enjoy in a detached dwelling.

Conclusion

There is nothing intrinsically more satisfying about a detached dwelling over an apartment in a multi-owned development. What principally differentiates the two forms of tenure is the level of sovereignty the resident has over their domain. In multi-owned developments sovereignty is mediated through the body corporate. It is here that many decisions are determined which will affect the quality of life and satisfaction of residents. The success of this process of governance is a key factor in residential satisfaction within multi-owned developments. Yet many residents purchase apartments with little understanding of the commitment they are undertaking to maintain the common property and to participate in the management of the development. Some are neither financially nor managerially equal to the task. Moreover, many master planned developments take a number of years to complete and throughout that time the developer retains an equitable interest in the image, care and maintenance of the development. The Strata Management Legislation Amendment Act 2008 is intended to limit the power of the developer and to deal with the instances of 'legal silence' (Blandy, Dixon and Dupuis 2006: 2371), but the total exclusion of the developer from the body corporate and governance of the development would not reflect the developer's continuing equitable interest or ensure the quality of the completed development.

The views offered and the examples discussed in this chapter illustrate the all too common failure of bodies corporate as a means to ensure good governance in the interests of residents. The 2008 change to the strata legislation has had some success yet many issues remain to be resolved if bodies corporate are not to become a conspiracy of some residents against others, or a forum of conflict between residents, developers, the public and local government.

Residential satisfaction is contingent on the social characteristics and needs of the inhabitants. All people go through housing careers where different forms of accommodation are appropriate at different points in time (Bounds 2004: 290). For the foreseeable future more Australians will be spending more of their lives in some form of attached medium to high density housing in multi-owned developments by virtue both of supply and demand for its proximity to work, service and leisure. The principal concern that we should have with the question of satisfaction with multi-owned developments relates to control. At least part of the answer lies in education to acquaint prospective purchasers with what lies ahead, and whether it will provide the sense of control they expect in a home to secure their world, so they can make informed decisions as to whether to enter into this type of property ownership.

Such education could provide information to all purchasers in multi-owned developments, prior to the purchase of their individual plot, on what Blandy et al. (2006) term the bundle of rights and obligations. This would enable the purchasers to access the history of the body corporate so they were informed of the personalities, politics, power and financial legacies that would soon be part of their lives.

References

Baldassare, M. 1982. The effects of neighborhood density and social control on residential satisfaction. *Sociological Quarterly*, 23(1), 95–105.

Blandy, S., Dixon, J. and Dupuis, A. 2006. Theorising power relationships in multi-owned residential developments: Unpacking the bundle of rights. *Urban Studies*, 43(13), 2365–83

Bounds, M. 2004. *Urban Social Theory: City Self and Society*. Melbourne: Oxford University Press.

Bounds, M., Miers, S., Pfister, N. and Searle, G. 1998. *The Impact of the Sydney Casino on the Social Composition and Residential Amenity of the Residents of*

Pyrmont Ultimo, Stage 1 Report 1, November. University of Western Sydney, Macarthur: The Urban Studies Research Centre.

Bounds, M. and Morris, A. 2000. *The Impact of the Sydney Casino on the Social Composition and Residential Amenity of the Residents of Pyrmont Ultimo, Stage 2 Report 1, March*. University of Western Sydney, Macarthur: The Urban Studies Research Centre.

Bounds, M. and Morris, A. 2005. High-rise gentrification: The redevelopment of Pyrmont Ultimo. *Urban Design International*, 10(3/4), 1–10.

Bounds, M., Morris, A., McCormack, T., Moore, C. and Searle, G. 2000. *The Impact of the Sydney Casino on the Social Composition and Residential Amenity of the Residents of Pyrmont-Ultimo: Final Report to the Casino Community Benefit Fund.* University of Western Sydney, Macarthur: The Urban Studies Research Centre.

Bounds, M., Searle, G. and Stapleton, C. 1999. *The Impact of the Sydney Casino on the Social Composition and Residential Amenity of the Residents of Pyrmont Ultimo, Stage 1 Report 2, November*. University of Western Sydney, Macarthur: The Urban Studies Research Centre.

Community Associations in City of Canada Bay. 2007. Minutes of meeting held on Saturday, 7 July, 2007, at 10.00 am in The Pelican Point Community Centre, 164 Burwood Road, Concord, New South Wales.

Condon, T. 2005. Triguboff hangs onto his units in downturn. *The Australian*, 27 September, 23.

Cox , G. and Miers, S. 1996. *Post Occupancy Survey of New Residents of Pyrmont Ultimo.* New South Wales: Department of Urban Affairs and Planning, New South Wales Government.

Creagh, S. 2008. Villagers fight for strata control. *Sydney Morning Herald*, 1 October, 10.

Davies, A. and Nicholls, S. 2003. Meriton fight leads to strata collapse. *Sydney Morning Herald.* [Online, January 29]. Available at: http://www.smh.com.au/articles/2003/01/28/1043534057498.html [accessed: 18 October 2009].

Davison, G. 2000. Suburban character. *People and Place*, 7(4), 26–31.

Dupuis, A. and Thorns, D. 1998. Home, home ownership and the search for ontological security. *The Sociological Review*, 46(1), 24–47.

Gans, H. 1962. *The Urban Villagers.* New York: Free Press of Glencoe.

Giddens, A. 1985. *The Nation State and Violence: Vol 2*. Cambridge: Polity Press.

Giles Tribe Architects and Urban Planners. 2005. *Breakfast Point Concept Plan.* [Online]. Available at: http://www.planning.NewSouthWales.gov.au/asp/pdf/bp_breakfast_point_concept_plan.pdf [accessed: 18 October 2009].

Healy, E. and Birrell, R. 2004. *Housing and Community in the Compact City.* Melbourne: Australian Housing and Urban Research Institute.

Ilkin, A. 2004. *Strata Schemes and Community Schemes Management and the Law.* 3rd Edition. Sydney: LBC Information Services.

Michelson, W. 1976. *Man and his Urban Environment.* Reading, MA: Addison Wesley Publishing Co.

Parliament of New South Wales. 2005. *Hansard Papers 10 November 2005* [Online]. Available at: http://www.parliament.NewSouthWales.gov.au/prod/parlment/hansard.nsf/V3Key/LA20051110035 [accessed: 18 October 2009].

PRP Architects. 2002. *High Density Housing in Europe: Lessons for London, Report for East Thames Housing Group East*. London: Thames Housing Group Ltd.

Randolph, W. 2005. *Higher Density Communities: Current Trends and Future Implications*. Paper to the Strata and Community Title in Australia for the 21st Century Conference, September 2005.

Young, M. and Willmott, P. 1962. *Family and Kinship in East London*. Baltimore: Penguin.

Chapter 10

Long-term Management Contracts and Developer Abuse in New South Wales

Cathy Sherry

Introduction

There is a story of power imbalance and developer abuse that has been played out repeatedly in multi-owned housing across the globe and across time. It relates to the developer's ability to cause the body corporate to enter into long-term contracts at the inception of the development, when the developer as owner of all of the units controls the body corporate. The developer does this in order to gain financial benefit for itself and its related companies. However, these contracts frequently do not benefit the body corporate or the ultimate owners of the units and as a result, have caused considerable disharmony in multi-owned housing. In countries such as Australia and the United States, which rely heavily on the profit-dependent private sector to build the bulk of new housing, it is a practice that the law has struggled to contain effectively.

This chapter will present two legal case studies. The first sheds light on the current landscape of multi-owned housing in New South Wales, the most populous state in Australia. Like most Western countries, Australia has experienced a building boom in the past decade, with much development being high or medium density multi-owned housing. Real estate booms typically go hand in hand with dubious building and sales practices (see Federal Department of Housing and Urban Development 1975, for US examples) and Australia's boom has proved no exception (Parliamentary Joint Committee on Corporations and Financial Services 2005). Problems have been exacerbated by Australians' general lack of experience of multi-owned housing and by legislatures' failure to keep pace with current practice when enacting appropriate protections. Where legislation has failed, attempts have been made to use more general principles of law to identify and eradicate abusive practices. A recent leading case on the sale of long-term management rights by a developer is used to illustrate the successes and failings of both kinds of law. The second case study compares developer abuses through long-term management contracts and leases, in the United States in the 1960s and 1970s and in contemporary New South Wales, to demonstrate that developer practices across time and jurisdictions are uncannily consistent. It is suggested that there is much to be learned about effective methods to combat unacceptable developer behaviour from the United States, where a combination over time of legislation, judicial decisions and market backlash has helped to address particular abuses such as developer-formed contracts. However, while unrestrained developer control of bodies corporate remains, the spectre of abuse will never completely disappear.

The Legal Structure of Multi-owned Housing in Australia

In Australia, almost all high-rise buildings and increasing numbers of master planned communities are created under special state legislation, variously referred to as the Strata Title and/or Community Title Acts. In New South Wales, the first state in Australia to introduce effective legislation nearly 50 years ago, 'strata title' generally refers to high-rise development and 'community title' to low-rise master planned estates, although the latter term is also used to refer to developments with both high-rise and low-rise buildings. Developments begin with surveyors drawing up vertical or horizontal plans of subdivision, which designate the area of individual 'lots'. Physically, these lots may be apartments, town houses, freestanding houses, vacant building lots, or they may be commercial office spaces or even hotel rooms. Generally, any land within the scheme which falls outside these individual lots becomes 'common property'. When plans of subdivision are registered with the state lands department, the legal title to the lots and common property comes into existence for the first time.

Registration of a strata or community title plan of subdivision also brings into existence a body corporate, a legal entity made up of all the lot owners at any given point in time. In New South Wales strata developments, bodies corporate were originally called just that, but a 1996 change in legislation introduced the new term 'owners' corporation'. In community title developments, the body corporate may be called a community, precinct or neighbourhood association. As long as they are created under the strata or community title legislation, all of these bodies are essentially the same and so this chapter will use the generic term 'body corporate' in reference to them all. Bodies corporate are set up by legislation to manage and maintain the common property for the benefit of all of the individual owners. They may make or amend by-laws that govern use and management of both the common property and individual lots. However, they can only act in both their management and rule-making capacity to the extent that the legislation authorizes them to do so. They have no source of power outside the Acts that create them.

In relation to strata and community developments, Australia's legislative structure stands in contrast to other countries'. For example, in the United States, while developments will be affected by condominium or common interest ownership legislation, governing bodies in communities are not *created* by legislation. Thus they owe their existence to documents drafted by developers' lawyers, and the powers of the governing body will vary according to the choices made by the developer. In the US, the body is typically an incorporated association, but it may be unincorporated or be a board of trustees (Hyatt and French 2008: 31–3). In the United Kingdom, despite the enactment of the Commonhold and Leasehold

Reform Act 2002, most high-rise (Davey 2006) and master planned developments (Atkinson et al 2003: 41–5) remain leasehold and the structure and powers of the governing body will vary according to the terms of the lease (see Blandy, Chapter 2). Consequently, the legal relationships within multi-owned housing in the United States and United Kingdom are more diverse than in Australia.

As McKenzie demonstrates in Chapter 4, there have been hard-fought battles to have governing bodies regulated by legislation in the US, whereas in Australia governing bodies that owe their very existence to legislation are more easily controlled. For example, bodies corporate cannot acquire liens over properties for unpaid levies and foreclose on residents' homes as a result. This is because Australian legislatures have never considered it desirable for governing bodies to have this power and, as in Israel (see Alterman, Chapter 5) the body corporate cannot give itself this power.

The fundamental role played by legislation in Australia has led to a desirable uniformity of legal structure and governance in multi-owned housing (in contrast with the position in New Zealand: see Dupuis and Dixon, Chapter 12; and in England and Wales: see Blandy, Chapter 2), as well as to significant restrictions on governing body power. Unlike the push to secure some government oversight that McKenzie (Chapter 4) describes in the United States, Australia already has detailed legislation with a strong vein of consumer protection. In New South Wales, the ongoing management of multi-owned housing falls within the auspices of the Department of Fair Trading which provides mediation and arbitration services for residents and bodies corporate. The Director-General of the Department has powers of investigation and intervention. However, the dominance of legislation has arguably led to an assumption in lawyers' minds that answers to all legal dilemmas can be found within the statutes. Unlike the United States, Australia has very little case law in which lawyers have sought to argue that relations between the participants in multi-owned housing – developers, builders, owners and occupiers – are regulated by general principles of law and equity. This is unfortunate, because in common law jurisdictions many of those general principles have been developed over centuries, specifically to combat abuse of power. While the legislation has been drafted with the prevention of abuse in mind, as any clever lawyer knows, it is possible to pick one's way around legislative provisions. If it can be argued that a fact scenario falls outside the section under consideration, rather than being protected by a legislative safety-net, a consumer will be in free-fall. In contrast, protective principles of common law and equity are potentially more elastic and more able to capture and remedy behaviour when its true quality is abusive.

Management Rights and Power: Two Contracts

One aspect of strata and community title developments in Australia which has been particularly prone to abuse concerns management rights (see also Cassidy et al., Chapter 11). Management rights, typically in large developments, encompass the business associated with physical maintenance and management. Landscaped gardens, pools and other facilities need to be maintained, and caretaking or building manager businesses have sprung up to meet this need. The 'management rights package' may also include use or ownership of a front desk, foyer and/or residential lot. Legally speaking, management rights are the subject of a contract between a management company and the body corporate of a community, known as a management agreement. By this contract, the management company promises to perform certain tasks for the body corporate and the body corporate promises to pay a stipulated annual fee.

However, the *sale* of management rights takes place in a separate contract made between a developer and a particular management company, prior to the sale of any apartments or lots. By this first contract the developer agrees to cause the body corporate to enter into a second contract, namely, the management agreement between the body corporate and that particular management company. The developer is able to commit the body corporate to this second contract because, as original owner of all the lots, the developer controls the body corporate during the 'initial period', which is defined in the Strata Schemes (Freehold Development) Act 1973 as the time before one third of the lots are sold. The developer causes the body corporate to enter into this agreement for two primary purposes. The first and perfectly legitimate reason is to ensure that at the inception of the development, there is a management service in place. The second, more questionable reason is that management companies are often prepared to pay developers a large fee for causing the body corporate to become contractually bound to their management company. Although no research has specifically surveyed this practice, it is made explicit through contested cases (see discussion of the Arrow case below). Further, the management rights to established developments are openly advertised for sale at high prices by one management company to another, making it obvious that the initial sale of management rights by the developer would also have a high value.

In New South Wales, in specific recognition of the vulnerability of communities to developer abuse in the early life of the project, there are statutory restrictions imposed on the body corporate while it is controlled by the developer. The legislation regulates a range of activities, including the incurring of debts and the making of agreements with third parties, during the 'initial period'. Using community title as the example here, the Community Land Management Act 1989 provides that any agreement with a third party made by the body corporate during this initial period must terminate at the first annual general meeting, being the first meeting at which the new owners, rather than the developer, have the opportunity to control the body corporate.

Unfortunately the statutory prohibition on forming agreements in the initial period is not absolute and termination is not guaranteed. Termination can be avoided if the agreement is either 'ratified' or 'disclosed'. Ratification can occur when the body corporate, no longer controlled by the developer, confirms that it agrees to be bound by the agreement. Disclosure, a typical consumer protection technique, particularly in the corporate sphere, is required in the 'community management statement' which sets out the by-laws for the community. These are attached to sales contracts and are also publicly available on the title register once the subdivision is ultimately registered. Disclosure is based on the philosophy that if the purchasers have full knowledge of the management agreement and proceed to purchase, they can have no grounds for complaint afterwards (Natelson 1990: 54–65).

Realistically, as a result of Australia's land registration system, the disclosure requirement is not particularly workable. Developers face a 'chicken and egg' dilemma. It is the body corporate (not the developer) which will be the party to the management agreement; however, the body corporate does not come into existence until the registration of the community scheme. Registration of the community scheme cannot occur unless the community management statement is lodged at the time of registration and it is this document that must disclose the effect of any management agreement. So, developers must disclose the effect of an agreement that by definition cannot exist because one of the parties to the agreement, the body corporate, has not yet been created. Developers' lawyers have tried to overcome this dilemma by stating in the community management statement that the body corporate 'intends' to enter into a management agreement and that it 'may' be for a certain period and for a particular fee. However, in the case of *Hudson Property Group Pty Ltd v Community Association DP 270238*[1] the New South Wales Court of Appeal confirmed that statements such as this disclosed no more than 'possibilities', and this was not sufficient for the purposes of the legislation.

Arrow's Case

Not surprisingly, this potential conflict of interest between the developer and body corporate in relation to management rights, and the complexity of the attempted legislative protection, has produced a number of disputes in communities. The most significant dispute to run as far as the New South Wales Supreme Court is *Community Association DP No 270180 v Arrow Asset Management Pty Ltd and Ors*[2] (Arrow's case). The case illustrates the problems with the existing legislation in practice and the potential of general principles of common law and equity to provide a measure of protection to purchasers. This case involved a dispute over the sale of the management rights to Balmain Shores, a new community title established under the New South Wales Community Land Development Act 1989. The Balmain Shores development is made up of eleven strata schemes (apartment blocks), with a shared gym, landscaped gardens, indoor and outdoor pools. It was built (like many recent examples of city redevelopment around the world) on a large disused industrial site, fronting a once working river.

1 [2005] NSWCA 374.
2 [2007] NSWSC 527.

Australand, the developer, sold the management rights to Balmain Shores in 1998 to Arrow Asset Management Pty Ltd in return for a payment of AU$190,000. A separate management agreement bound the body corporate (in this legislative scheme called a 'community association') for ten years, with two options to renew of five years each, and obliged the body corporate to pay a fee of AU$168,200 in the first year, increasing each year with the Consumer Price Index, with a minimum annual increase of 5 per cent. At the court hearing, expert witnesses were called by both the developer and the body corporate to establish the true value of the services provided. Despite the questionable nature of the expert testimony, the court decided that the agreement was unusual for the industry at the time and that the remuneration payable exceeded, and was likely to continue to exceed, the true value of the services provided. The judge, Justice McDougall, concluded that the remuneration was 'excessive'.

By 2000 it had become clear that the body corporate, now constituted by apartment owners rather than by the developer, was unhappy with Arrow's work and the cost of the services. However, Arrow wanted to assign its management rights to Bondlake, an associated company. The body corporate reluctantly agreed to the assignment of the management agreement to Bondlake on certain conditions. Presumably continuing to be unhappy with the services provided, the body corporate subsequently litigated to challenge the validity of the management agreement on the following grounds.

Non-disclosure of the Management Agreement and Absent Ratification

The decision in *Hudson*, which as described above established that disclosure of 'possible' management contracts was no disclosure at all, came after the developer's lawyers had drafted the community management statement for Balmain Shores. However, following the decision in *Hudson*, Arrow was forced to concede that as the Balmain Shores community management statement did not differ in any material respect from that in *Hudson*, the management agreement had not been properly disclosed. Yet Arrow argued that this did not matter, as the management agreement had been ratified at the first annual general meeting of the body corporate. This suggestion was rejected by the court because there was no evidence that the management agreement had even been tabled for consideration at that meeting.

The position of the Balmain Shores body corporate was that the management agreement was unenforceable; it should have terminated at the first annual general meeting as it had been neither disclosed nor ratified as required by the legislation. In response, Arrow and Bondlake (which had now taken over the management rights from Arrow) put forward a technical argument based on estoppel. Estoppel is a doctrine of law and equity that prevents people from relying on their strict legal rights, if it would be unfair to do so. Arrow and Bondlake argued that the body corporate had acted at all times as though the management agreement were binding and enforceable, both in its dealings with Arrow and, in particular, when it agreed to allow Arrow to assign the management rights to Bondlake. They asserted that the body corporate could not now claim that the agreement had terminated under the legislation. The court agreed, saying that it was plain that both Arrow and Bondlake would suffer detriment if the body corporate were allowed to subsequently change its position in this way and assert that the agreement should have terminated for non-disclosure.

It is arguable that this conclusion was incorrect on a number of grounds. Firstly, as a matter of common sense consumers should not be denied the protection of a consumer protection provision enacted for their benefit just because they failed to take advantage of it at an earlier point in time. If it was enacted to protect them, their own ignorance or inadvertence should not prevent them from being protected. Secondly, this common sense approach is reflected in the law. There is a general rule that it is not permissible to argue estoppel in relation to a provision in a statute, if that statute represents social policy enacted in the interests of the public generally or some section of the public (see *Kok Hoong v Leong Cheong Kweng Mines Limited*).[3] This principle had already been applied to another New South Wales management agreement, in the case of *Owners – Strata Plan No 51487 v Broadsand Pty Ltd.*[4] In this case the management agreement had been illegal from the beginning because the manager was unlicensed, although for some time the body corporate had been unaware of this fact. The court refused to accept that the body corporate should be estopped from denying the validity of the management agreement, saying that the purpose of the legislation was to provide a protection for the public, in particular protection from the risks associated with being tied for a long period of time to a manager that the developer (rather than the owners) had selected at a time when the developer controlled the body corporate.

This decision should have been directly applicable in Arrow's case. An important issue of public policy underlies the legislative provision: bodies corporate (and the owners who ultimately make them up) should not be bound by management agreements made by developers, unless the agreement was disclosed at the time of purchase or subsequently agreed to by the body corporate after the initial period. Neither had occurred in Arrow's case and thus the agreement should not have been enforceable. Finally, the Balmain Shores body corporate realistically had little choice but to treat the management agreement as enforceable. The members of the body corporate were new purchasers in a new and relatively unknown form of title. It is unlikely they were familiar with management rights businesses and their prior sale by developers, let alone with the complexity of the community title legislation or its provisions designed to protect consumers. Even if they were aware of the protection in the legislation, they could reasonably have assumed that they had no rights under it. This is because the Court of Appeal decision in *Hudson*, which established that the disclosure of 'possible' provisions of a future management agreement did not prevent the termination of a management agreement, was not

3 [1964] AC 993.

4 [2002] NSWSC 770.

decided until five years after the Balmain Shores body corporate found itself in this dilemma. In these circumstances, there was nothing unreasonable or unfair about the body corporate, having tried to make the management agreement work, subsequently arguing that termination had occurred. There should have been no reason to estop the body corporate from relying on the legislative protection.

The court's concern was that both Arrow and Bondlake would suffer detriment if the management agreement were not enforceable. However, the legislature must have envisaged that possibility when it enacted the termination provision in the Community Land Management Act 1989. It made a decision that, as between a body corporate and a party such as Arrow, the body corporate was more in need of protection. Given the fact that body corporates may enter into management agreements when under the control of the developer this seems a reasonable legislative provision which should not be undermined by the courts.

The decision in Arrow's case seems to weaken the legislation's ability to protect residents. However, there is another aspect of the decision which is more helpful to owners, as body corporate members, which will now be discussed.

Fiduciary Obligation

The court in Arrow's case decided that a developer stands in a fiduciary relationship to a body corporate that it creates. This decision provided some satisfaction to the Balmain Shores body corporate, but more importantly has far-reaching implications for the whole strata and community titles industry.

Fiduciary duties exist in all common law systems and have been described as 'the obligations of trust and confidence that equity imposes on a person in circumstances where the person, the fiduciary, is bound to act for the benefit of another' (Evans 2003: 122). A 'fiduciary' (someone who owes a fiduciary duty) must not allow their personal interests to prevail over those of the person to whom they owe a duty. There are accepted categories of people who owe fiduciary duties in common law systems: for example, lawyer to client, trustee to beneficiary, employee to employer, director to company and in some jurisdictions (including Australia) promoter to the company being promoted. However, fiduciary duties are not limited to these categories and much judicial and academic time has been spent trying to define the characteristics of a relationship that will make it fiduciary.

In Arrow's case the body corporate successfully argued that, just as a promoter owes a fiduciary duty to the company promoted, so too a developer owes a fiduciary duty to a body corporate. Many cases that push the boundaries of what constitutes a fiduciary relationship have involved relationships between unrelated commercial entities, which have a certain ability to protect themselves. In contrast, at the inception of a development, the developer does not simply influence the body corporate; as the owner of all lots it *is* the body corporate. As such, it can cause the body corporate to act in the developer's interest rather than the interests of the body corporate as ultimately constituted by the owners. The facts of Arrow's case demonstrate the danger of this vulnerability perfectly. The body corporate had an interest in securing management services on the best commercial terms possible because it (or its members) would have to pay the annual fee. The developer had an interest in making that annual fee as high as possible, as the more a management company could charge for services, the more it would be prepared to pay the developer for those rights. There was a direct and obvious conflict between the interests of the developer and the Balmain Shores body corporate and, given the 'excessive' annual fee to be charged to the owners for management services, the developer obviously preferred its own interests to those of the future owners.

Significantly, once a court decides that a relationship between a developer and a body corporate is fiduciary, it will not matter if a management contract is sold to a third party on terms which are good for the body corporate. A fiduciary is never entitled to make a profit in circumstances where duty and interest conflict. In order to persuade fiduciaries not to fall foul of this rule, courts require them to pay back any profit they have made, even when they have acted honestly. The developer in Arrow's case was ordered to pay the Balmain Shores body corporate the AU$190,000 fee it earned from the sale of the management rights.

Clearly a developer is entitled to make a profit from the development as a whole, so it is necessary to define the scope of the fiduciary duty. In the context of multi-owned housing it would seem reasonable that the duty should apply to any activity that the developer performs when it acts as or controls the body corporate. When acting as the body corporate the developer should always act in the long-term interests of the ultimate members of the body corporate, the owners. In other respects, the developer should be entitled to act in its own interest.

It is possible to remedy a breach of fiduciary duty by obtaining the informed consent of the party to whom the duty is owed, by making full disclosure of all information relevant to the transaction. Arrow argued that the references to the management agreement in the community management statement that was attached to all contracts of sale, and the annexation of the management agreement itself to the minutes of the inaugural general meeting, constituted full disclosure. However, the court's decision was that breach of fiduciary duty could only be remedied by disclosure of the terms of the *initial* contract between the developer and Arrow, whereby the developer sold the management rights to Arrow before the residents had come into the picture.

The implications of this aspect of the Arrow decision are significant. Many developers have altered their practices fearing that the fiduciary relationship will make them liable for a range of obligations they could potentially impose on bodies corporate. To the extent that this discourages them from concluding management agreements that are not in the body corporate's interest or that it forces developers, when acting as the body corporate, to only do as the body corporate would do for itself if it could, this is a positive change. Unfortunately, there are also some contracts that could be concluded by the developer that might be in the community's interest which developers are now avoiding; for example, contracts for the bulk purchase of electricity or telecommunications products. The developer could form these contracts so long as they are properly disclosed;

however, the prevalence of off-the-plan sales in Australia makes this extremely difficult. Developers' financing is often dependent on sales contracts being in place very early in the development process, well before the housing is built or even the strata or community plan is registered. It is at the point of contract for purchase, not completion of the sale, that disclosure would be required and this is too early for service contracts to have been negotiated. Of course even if developers are not creating contracts beneficial to the body corporate, the community of owners can always negotiate them at a later date, so long as the necessary consensus can be achieved. It is arguable that the body corporate as constituted by owners is *always* the appropriate body to negotiate these agreements, as it is the owners who will bear the responsibility of paying for the services and dealing with any problems with service delivery.

Despite the decision in Arrow, there are some contracts that developers cannot avoid committing bodies corporate to, as they are required by state governments as a condition of development consent. For example, a developer might be required to provide a private bus service to a new community where there is little or no existing transport infrastructure – greenfield development in Australia often suffer from the same kinds of infrastructure deficits as suburban sprawl in the United States (Duany, Plater-Zyberk and Speck 2000). These contracts are a good illustration of the complex nature of housing development. While developers, particularly large ones, wield significant power, they operate within a larger political and social framework over which they have limited control. So, while some developer-created services provided to communities by the body corporate such as 24 hour security are luxuries which form part of the developer's marketing package, others are basic necessities like roads, sewerage and transport. Governments are eager to outsource the latter services, and individual developers cannot realistically be held responsible for decades of political pressure in favour of privatization. So long as these contracts are negotiated in the body corporate's long-term interests and the developer does not profit from them directly (other than in increased housing sale prices), a developer should not be liable under the fiduciary principle.

In terms of further litigation, the Arrow case has not resulted in a spate of cases with communities challenging their management agreements on the grounds that their formation was a breach of fiduciary duty. There could be a number of explanations for this. First, some communities are no doubt satisfied with management services in place. Others, while dissatisfied, may not be prepared to litigate, the cost to the community being excessive. Finally, some dissatisfied communities, for example in *Yedway Pty Ltd v Owners Corporation of Strata Plan 62871*,[5] are managing to terminate agreements on the terms of the contracts themselves, the managers indeed being incompetent. This potentially gives communities greater satisfaction than the decision in Arrow, where the body corporate recovered the profit made by the developer from the sale of management

5 [2009] NSWSC 8.

rights, but was still stuck with the existing management company. That said, the estoppel finding in Arrow, which bound the body corporate to the management agreement, is arguably open to challenge, and this may well be taken up by other communities in the future.

Before moving to the next section reference must be made to the legislation in Queensland, the state in Australia that has the second most high-rise developments after New South Wales. Here the sale of management rights is more common and lucrative than in New South Wales, and is specifically permissible by statute (see Cassidy et al., Chapter 11). The sale of management rights cannot *per se* amount to a breach of fiduciary duty in Queensland, but the developer is nonetheless obliged to act in the best interests of the body corporate as constituted after the period of developer control. In Queensland, therefore, the scope of any fiduciary duty is confined by the legislative context which provides a standard of behaviour for developers. However, there is no reason that breach of fiduciary duty could not be argued if, for example, a Queensland developer caused the body corporate while under developer control to enter into long-term leases for the benefit of the developer or an affiliate, which were ultimately detrimental to the body corporate.

United States Experience

One of the great ironies of management rights sales and litigation in Australia is that it is a case of history repeating itself. And repeating itself. In the United States, landlords converted large numbers of tenanted apartment buildings into cooperatives during the building boom after the Second World War (Urban Land Institute 1977). In this booming market, developer abuses included retaining a majority of shareholder votes in their own hands, using money collected from shareholders for their own purposes, understating ultimate maintenance costs and arranging lucrative long-term management agreements with developer-owned or affiliated companies (Notes and Comments 1971).

In 1962 the Federal Housing Administration authorized insurance on family units in multi-family structures. This, combined with pressures from developers seeking to make profits from increasingly expensive and smaller plots of land, led to an exponential growth of condominium and common interest housing in the 1960s and early 1970s (McKenzie 1994) which, in turn, 'resulted in a concomitant growth of "flagrant and subtle" abuses by developers' (Batsel 1973: 351). Two specific abuses were prevalent: the signing of long-term management agreements with associated companies for inflated fees (known as 'sweetheart contracts'), and the creation of long-term leases of common facilities. Both types of abuse were made possible by the control which developers had over governing bodies prior to the sale of units.

Concern about developer abuses was so great that by 1974 the Federal government directed the Secretary of Housing and Urban Development (HUD) to conduct a study of 'the problems, difficulties, and abuses or potential abuses applicable to condominium and cooperative housing'.[6] The resulting *HUD Condominium and Cooperative Study* (Federal Department of Housing and Urban Development 1975) uncovered significant problems with construction defects, misrepresentation by developers and sales staff, misuse of deposits, complexity of documents, lack of warranties and understatement of maintenance expenses. Some or all of these may sound familiar to those with experience of contemporary development in Australia. While sweetheart management contracts were a problem in some US markets, most dissatisfaction centred on long-term leases. Typically, the developer would maintain ownership of common facilities and during the period of developer control, cause the unit owners association to enter into a long-term lease of the facilities. Objections arose when unit owners realized that the lease payments were high in comparison to the value of the facility and as a result of 'escalator' clauses in the lease, were getting higher. Developers were permitted to, and often did, have a lien on the condominium as security for non-payment and thus could foreclose on individual units.

The subjects of long-term leases were geographically specific. In the warm southern states, in particular Florida, common facilities leases were over pools and club houses, presumably an integral part of the marketing package for holiday or resort-style living. In contrast, in high density New York, long-term leases in either condominium or cooperative conversions were granted over facilities such as garages, health clubs and retail stores. In these circumstances, the coop or condominium might own the facility, but during the initial period of developer control, the developer would cause the governing body to grant the developer a long-term lease at well below market rent. The developer, as lessee, would then sublet the facility to other parties at much higher market rates, generating substantial ongoing income (Poretz and Weiss 2000).

Potential solutions to these problems were sought and sometimes found in a number of places. First, by the time the HUD study was released, adverse market reaction had stymied the practice of long-term leases and management contracts in many markets. In Florida, in particular, widespread adverse publicity about long-term leases of collectively owned recreational facilities and a correspondingly more informed consumer body forced developers to change practices. Adverse market reaction was coupled with a concerted effort on the part of the HUD, the Urban Land Institute and the newly formed Community Association Institute to improve developer practice for the sake of the fledgling condominium and common interest community industry (McKenzie 1994). These organizations, in conjunction with the Urban Land Institute, published *Creating a Community Association: The Developer's Role in Condominium and Home Owner Associations*, a handbook which strongly exhorted developers to take a balanced approach to the transition from developer to community control and to resist the urge to dominate the association. The handbook advised that 'the disadvantages of developer-related

6 s 821, 88 Stat. 740, 42 U.S.C. s 3532 (1970 ed., Supp. IV).

management outweigh the advantages for both the developer and owners' and that 'the outside management company or the association-paid staff is usually the best choice for the developer' (Urban Land Institute 1977: 49). It also noted that abuses in relation to sweetheart management contracts had led to lenders requiring independent management, especially for large projects. Adverse market reaction could benefit only future purchasers of units, so existing owners were left to other remedies, specifically litigation.

Fiduciary Principle Litigation in the US

A number of legal actions that communities in the US pursued, including actions based on fiduciary duties, predated the Arrow case in New South Wales by almost 40 years. After some initial failures, the US courts ultimately agreed with a number of commentators who had argued that developers did or should owe fiduciary to associations (Batsel 1972–1973, Young 1976). In *Raven's Cove Townhomes Inc. v Knuppe Dev. Co, Inc.*[7] the Court of Appeals of California held that the initial directors and officers of the association had a fiduciary relationship to the homeowner members, analogous to that of a corporate promoter to the shareholders. In the Arrow case, by contrast, the court found that the developer owed a fiduciary duty to the association, not individual members. The Raven's Cove case involved developer liability for construction defects, but in other cases, such as *Avila South Condominium Association Inc. v Kappa Corp.*,[8] the Florida Supreme Court held that officers and directors of a condominium associations who contracted on behalf of the association with themselves or with companies in which they had a substantial interest, might be liable for the profit they made as a result.

Legislation in the US: First Attempts to Address Developer Abuses

By the 1980s, the importance of fiduciary principles to strike down abusive management contracts had been overtaken by legislation in the US. The first and arguably least effective were state condominium legislation or federal securities legislation requiring disclosure. The philosophy of disclosure is that if a person is apprised of all the relevant information and proceeds to purchase regardless, they cannot then complain about the obligations and conditions by which they are bound. They have given their informed consent and must accept the consequences. Unfortunately, disclosure legislation had limited success, for the following reasons.

Firstly, the US federal securities legislation only captured a proportion of the condominium market, namely that section that looked like securities: an investment opportunity with a promise of earned income as a result of third party endeavour. Typically, only resort or holiday condominiums with a rental pool answered this description so that condominiums that were primary residences escaped

---

7 (1981) 114 Cal App.3d 783.

8 (1976) 347 So.2d 599.

the security disclosure provisions. Parallels can be drawn with contemporary Australian regulation, where some strata developments fall within the purview of the Australian Securities and Investment Commission (ASIC) which considers 'management rights schemes', that is, holiday letting arrangements for strata units, to be 'managed investments schemes' under the Corporations Act 2001 (ASIC 2007). Like US regulation, this only covers part of the tourist strata market and even experienced lawyers struggle with the question of whether particular developments fall within the disclosure provisions. ASIC certainly does not regulate the sale of residential developments such as the one in the Arrow case above.

Secondly, even when disclosure was extended to all developments, as it was in Florida in the early 1970s (and currently is in New South Wales), there remains a question of whether disclosure works. Presenting purchasers with a battery of information in highly technical sales contracts and brochures will not necessarily protect them:

> For a regulatory system to work, a potential purchaser must be equipped with the basic tools with which to analyse and evaluate the underlying investment. Even the most efficient scheme of full disclosure cannot be of any substantial value to an investor incapable of reacting to information in an appropriate and rational manner (Note 1975: 667).

Most people purchase real estate a few times in their lives and thus, by definition are unlikely to be experienced. This is all the more so for new forms of title such as strata title, condominiums and common interest developments (see McKenzie, Chapter 4) where purchasers themselves are unlikely to be familiar with the title, are unlikely to have friends or family members who are, or even have a lawyer who understands the complexities. This is illustrated by the fact that the potential terms of the management agreement in Arrow's case were disclosed but, from the course of the litigation, it does not seem that purchasers fully appreciated what this meant, including some who were reputedly lawyers.

There has been much debate amongst North American legal scholars about the efficacy of disclosure and consent in condominium and common interest communities, in particular whether there can ever be valid consent in relation to complex covenants and restrictions. Part of the debate centres on the potential power imbalance between experienced, repeat player developers and inexperienced purchasers and whether the latter's consent will ever be anything other than partially coerced (Alexander 1988). However, even if one accepts that there can be genuine consent with adequate disclosure as Ellickson (1982) and Natelson (1990) appear to do, there are some obligations which are intrinsically abusive or contrary to public policy, to which purchasers should never be asked to consent. The sale of management rights arguably falls within this category. It could be said that the entity that has the most legitimate right to exploit the business associated with maintaining the collectively owned property of the community is the community itself. That is, management rights are never the developer's to sell. By a circuitous route, this is the policy that a successful breach of fiduciary duty case implements. In Arrow's case, by forcing the developer to disgorge the profit it made in the sale of management rights, the court was reallocating money to the entity which should have made the profit in the first place – the collective body of owners.

Alternatively, even if one argues that having built and funded the structure that needs to be maintained, the developer is entitled to make money out of the sale of management rights, it is still possible that, at least in residential developments, this causes more problems than it is worth. Buying an apartment and finding that you are collectively bound to employ the same management company for ten years, not chosen by you or your neighbours, is analogous to buying a freestanding house and finding that you are compelled to keep employing your vendor's cleaner. Most people would find this objectionable. People expect to be able to control their home environment and while this ability will inevitably be partly circumscribed by the dual ownership (individual and collective) inherent in multi-owned developments, it is not inevitable that it needs to be circumscribed by a developer choosing a long-term management service for the community. Ultimately, this is the conclusion that legislatures came to in the United States.

Legislation in the US: Second Attempts to Address Developer Abuses

Second attempts to remedy developer abuse through legislation utilized the more direct route of allowing communities to terminate developer-made contracts. The first legislation was the Condominium and Cooperative Conversion Protection and Abuse Relief Act in 1980 which, amongst other things, allowed for the termination of some management contracts which had been entered into by the unit owners or association and by the developer or a developer affiliate, during the time that the developer controlled the association.

While the benefits of the Abuse Act are still being felt 20 years later, particularly in New York City (Poretz and Weiss 2000), the most significant change came with the Uniform Condominium Act in 1980, subsumed by the Uniform Common Interest Ownership Act in 1982. While there are a myriad of limitations with the Acts in others respects, in the states that have adopted one or other of them, they seem to have had some positive effect in relation to developer-formed management agreements and leases. Problems with these agreements loomed large in the US litigation and literature of the 1960s and 1970s and now seem largely absent. The Acts provide that any management contract, employment contract or lease of a parking or recreational facility which was entered into by the developer, can be terminated by the homeowners' association at any time on 90 days notice. Further, while there is by no means uniform acceptance of this, the Acts set a fiduciary standard for any member of the executive board appointed by the developer (the 1982 Act makes developer appointees 'trustees', which are a recognised category of fiduciaries). In practical terms, this means that if the fiduciary standard applies, developer appointees are bound to act in the interests of the unit owners, not in the interests of the developer.

While state enactments consistent with the Uniform Acts demonstrate that appropriately stringent legislation can provide some protection to consumers, developer abuses continue. This is because developer misuse of power comes in a variety of forms, not just the imposition of management contracts or leases. Developers failing to hand over control of associations to avoid liability, failing to maintain adequate reserve funds and failing to hand over records all remain a problem in the United States (Hyatt and French 2008: 607–39). The temptation to use their ability to act for the community for their own advantage, seems to be one that many developers cannot resist.

Conclusion

The landscape of housing development is complex. Australia, like many Western nations, relies heavily on the private sector to build the bulk of new housing, a sector which is legitimately and necessarily self-interested and profit-driven. However, as private developers are making a profit from land, the patrimony of the nation, it is equally legitimate for governments to regulate the way in which that profit is made, particularly in order to protect citizens from abusive or socially disruptive practices.

Viewed in this framework, it can be argued that the trajectory of developer-formed contracts in United States' cooperatives in the 1950s and condominiums in the 1960s and 1970s, as well as in strata and community title developments in Australia at the turn of the twenty-first century, were inevitable. Developers were always going to use every means at their disposal to make a profit and in multi-owned housing, the existence of a separate legal entity under the developer's control, presented an additional opportunity to do so.

However, once it became clear that there were problems with developer control of bodies corporate, legislatures should have acted more decisively, particularly in relation to developer-made contracts. Qualified forms of regulation such as disclosure frequently do not work. As the Arrow case demonstrates, the practical aspects of disclosure are difficult when development happens over an extended time period, particularly if purchasers commit at an early point in the process. Further, purchasers frequently do not appreciate what is being disclosed when presented with a bundle of complicated documents in a relatively new form of title. Finally, it is impossible to disclose the true nature of the services that have been committed to until they are actually performed. The problems with developer-formed contracts rarely relate to services that are well-priced and well-performed, but rather poor services relative to fees that are only revealed when the contract of service is carried out.

Rather than relying on qualified forms of regulation, Australian legislatures should take the same step as the United States and allow for termination of all developer-made service or employment contracts by residential communities. This would not mean that developers could not market housing with any services in place, it would simply mean that whatever contracts were in place would have to have been negotiated on the understanding that if the community is not satisfied with the service, it will be entitled to terminate it. Developers may not profit from the sale of management rights but given the problems associated with their sale, this is an acceptable outcome.

Further, courts should continue to apply the principle that developers owe bodies corporate a fiduciary duty. It is entirely appropriate that when acting as the body corporate a developer must act in the body corporate's long-term interest, not its own. To do otherwise is an abuse of a legal structure that exists for the benefit of the ultimate owners of multi-owned housing, not the developer. Also, the fiduciary principle, unlike specifically worded legislation, is elastic enough to capture a range of harmful, self-serving behaviour on the part of developers, which we know from the US experience continues to exist even once multi-owned housing is no longer a novel form of title.

Finally, it is important to remember that poor development and sales practices can only exist with willing purchasers. In property booms, those purchasers are often as profit-driven as developers, in addition to being naïve and careless. The experience in Florida in the 1970s suggests that the process of consumer education and resulting market backlash can be a significant force in eradicating specific developer abuse. In Australia, multi-owned housing is still a minority of the housing sector and most purchasers, at least those who are sufficiently affluent to be buying homes or investments in developments with services, can exercise choice to purchase elsewhere. Countries like Australia, with a relatively new multi-owned housing sector, should actively engage in consumer education so that informed consumers can vote with their feet.

References

Alexander, G. 1988. Freedom, Coercion and the Law of Servitudes. *Cornell Law Review*, 73 (July), 883–905.

Atkinson, R., Flint, J., Blandy, S. and Lister, D. 2003. *Gated Communities in England: Final Report of the Gated Communities in England New Horizons Project*. London: Office of the Deputy Prime Minister.

Australian Securities and Investments Commission (ASIC) 2007. *Management Rights Schemes*. Consultation Paper 81. Sydney: ASIC.

Batsel, G. 1972–1973. Florida Condominiums – Developer Abuses and Securities Law Implications Create a Need for a State Regulatory Agency. *University of Florida Law Review*, 25(2), Winter, 350–67.

Davey, M. 2006. Long Residential Leases: Past and Present, in *Landlord and Tenant Law: Past, Present and Future*, edited by S. Bright. Oxford: Hart, 147–70.

Duany, A, Plater-Zyberk, E. and Speck, J. 2000. *Suburban Nation: The Rise of Sprawl and the Decline of the American Dream*. New York: North Point Press.

Ellickson, R. 1982. Cities and Homeowners Associations. *University of Pennsylvania Law Review*, 130(6), 1519–80.

Evans, M. 2003. *Equity and Trusts*. Sydney: Lexisnexis.

Federal Department of Housing and Urban Development. 1975. *Condominium/Cooperative Study*. Washington: Federal Department of Housing and Urban Development.

Hyatt, W. and French, S. 2008. *Community Association Law: Cases and Materials on Common Interest Communities*. 2nd edition. Durham: Carolina Academic Press.

McKenzie, E. 1994. *Privatopia: Homeowner Associations and the Rise of Residential Private Government*. New Haven and London: Yale University Press.

Natelson, R. 1990. Consent, Coercion and Reasonableness in Private Law: The Special Case of the Property Owners Association. *Ohio State Law Journal*, 51(1), 1–88.

Note. 1975. Condominium Disclosure: Beyond Disclosure. *University of Pennsylvania Law Review*, 123(3), 639–75.

Notes and Comments. 1971. Cooperative Housing Corporations and the Federal Securities Laws. *Columbia Law Review*, 71(1), 118–39.

Parliamentary Joint Committee on Corporations and Financial Services. 2005. *Property Investment Advice – Safe as Houses*? Canberra: Senate Printing Unit, Parliament House, Commonwealth of Australia.

Poretz, T. and Weiss, A. 2000. Terminating Sponsor Leases: Regaining Control of Your Garage. *The Cooperator: The Co-op and Condo Monthly*, 20(8). [Online]. Available at: http://cooperator.com/articles/557/1/Terminating-Sponsor-Leases/Page1.html [accessed: 9 July 2009].

Urban Land Institute and Community Association Institute. 1977. *Creating a Community Association: The Developer's Role in Condominium and Home Owner Associations*. Washington: Urban Land Institute and Community Association Institute.

Young, J. 1976. Areas of Dispute in Condominium Law. *Wake Forest Law Review*, 12(4), 979–1006.

Chapter 11
Multi-titled Tourism Accommodation Operations in Australia: The Queensland Context

Kelly Cassidy, Chris Guilding and Jan Warnken

Introduction

The objective of this chapter is to examine the phenomenon of multi-titled tourism accommodation in Australia, with a particular focus on the legal framework and the experience of owners in Queensland. The examination will review the reasons behind the substantial growth of this sector in the last 25 years, outline the legislative context, and overview different types of multi-titled tourism accommodation complex. In addition, the chapter explores an idiosyncratic facet especially associated with this particular type of accommodation, that is, management rights. Management rights in multi-titled tourism accommodation are an entitlement that can be sold and purchased, as specifically permitted under the Body Corporate and Community Management Act 1997 (see Sherry, Chapter 10, for consideration of sale of management rights more generally). The holder of the management rights of a building is typically entitled to draw a salary for maintaining the building, earn a commission on managing the building's letting pool and own a unit that is typically located on the ground floor of the complex. The chapter also outlines challenges arising in the sector with particular importance attached to power issues between the stakeholders in multi-titled tourism accommodation.

The term 'multi-titled tourist accommodation' is used to denote any tourist accommodation premises that has a multi-titled, multi-ownership structure tied to a common property. This definition distinguishes such complexes from the many other forms that can be assumed by traditional holiday homes (Coppock 1977), and also from hotels or motels which are generally built on a single land title that is either leased or owned by a single party. The definition also distinguishes multi-titled tourism accommodation from timeshare, because timeshare investors rarely acquire a property title (Woods 2001). In Australia, most multi-titled tourism accommodation complexes comprise self service high-rise apartment complexes, although the recent past has also seen a growth in tourism-oriented hotels, golf resort communities and villa complexes owned by way of a multi-titled arrangement.

Growth of Multi-titled Tourism Accommodation

The growth of these complexes represents a significant extension to our conventional conception of forms of short-term accommodation. They may take a variety of forms and appear to be proliferating in many parts of the world.

Some of the likely factors accounting for the growth in multi-titled tourism accommodation complexes appear to be closely aligned with those recognized to be fuelling growth in second home ownership and self-catering stays including greater levels of individual disposable wealth, increased mobile pursuit of leisure activities, more and shorter holidays (Johns and Lynch 2007) and an increasingly aged population seeking seasonal migration to escape extreme summer or winter climates (Williams et al. 2000, Irvine and Cunningham 1990). Other factors relate to property development and marketing issues, for example, developers accessing broader markets of potential investors by unitizing tourism accommodation ownership (Nicod, Mungall and Henwood 2007: 248) and improvements in short-term accommodation marketing available to small operators as a result of new internet-based technology (Thomas and Hind 2007: 331).

Unfortunately, the growth of multi-titled tourism accommodation has not been captured well in the statistics compiled by tourism analysts or government bodies. A systematic search for information concerning the growth of multi-titled tourism accommodation has revealed that although the Australian Bureau of Statistics provides an accommodation database, the information collected is far from ideal. Figure 11.1 plots the number of new strata title schemes in Queensland over the period 1965–2006. Also graphed is the cumulative number of units in Queensland strata title schemes. While these data suggest growth in multi-titled tourism accommodation in Queensland, the evidence is not conclusive as the data presented pertains to all strata title schemes, that is, those that can be viewed as tourism focused as well as those that have a large proportion of long-term residents.

Internationally, most national tourist accommodation accounts or surveys focus on traditional service-related categories such as hotels, motels and caravan parks (usually by star-rating), or they combine holiday homes and holiday apartments into one segment. To obfuscate record-keeping matters further, mixed-used complexes with serviced rooms and condominium style apartments have emerged and these can be variously classified. Agencies managing the compilation of such data sets exhibit little interest in different ownership configurations and frequently fail to capture the subtle difference between a conventionally owned hotel or large motel and a professionally managed multi-titled tourism accommodation complex. This has likely been a significant factor contributing to the lack of recognition afforded to the increasing significance of this type of accommodation. Despite the problems obtaining accurate data concerning detailed trends, Warnken, Guilding and Cassidy (2008) provide grounds to suggest there has been significant multi-titled tourism accommodation growth in Australia and also internationally.

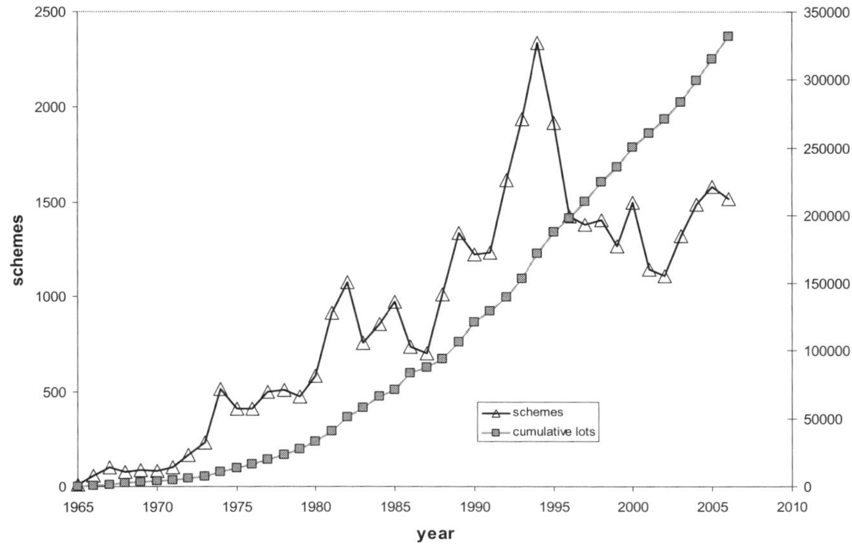

Figure 11.1 New Strata Title Schemes and Cumulative Number of Lots (Units) in Queensland (1965–2006)

Source: Information compiled by authors from an extract of the Queensland Titles Database, Queensland Department of Natural Resources and Water, provided by special permission in August 2006.

The Legislative Context for Multi-titled Tourism Accommodation

In Australia, it is estimated that three and a half million people either live or work in strata titled properties (National Community Titles Institute 2009). The collective ownership of buildings or complexes is legally possible using a wide variety of legal arrangements such as covenants, home unit corporations and tenancies in common (also see Blandy, Chapter 2). However, in Australia many of these alternative legal arrangements have been unable to survive the test of time and the preferred framework is now by way of a community titles scheme (also known as 'strata title'). The legislation in each Australian state's jurisdiction has been responsive to industry and stakeholder concerns and, as a result, always to the detriment of uniformity (Everton-Moore et al. 2006). In a cross-state examination of strata title law in Australia, Everton-Moore et al. make the claim that Queensland is the most advanced state in terms of developing legislation that lays the basis for effective, yet flexible, strata industry regulations. Despite this, Everton-Moore et al. (2006) also perceive shortcomings in the Queensland legislation.

The extent of inter-state inconsistency becomes still more evident when the failure to standardize terminology across the states is considered. As an example of this problem, 'body corporate' is the recognized terminology in Queensland,

Victoria and Tasmania; however, in New South Wales and the ACT, the term 'owners' corporation' is used; in South Australia it is the 'strata corporation'; in Western Australia it is the 'strata company', and in the Northern Territory it is referred to as the 'management corporation'.

Multi-titled Tourism Accommodation in Queensland

For illustrative purposes in this chapter, the legislation for Queensland is detailed. In Queensland, the Body Corporate and Community Management Act 1997 provides for the ownership of a 'lot' (as the Act terms the single parcel or unit) in a building or complex, together with a legal arrangement providing for the governance of relations between lot owners which also grants them a corporate interest in the management of common property.

Operationally, the legislative framework comprises one 'umbrella Act, supported by separate regulatory modules that are tailor-made for specific types of development' (Queensland Hansard 1997: 1136). The Body Corporate and Community Management Act 1997 is supplemented by four Regulations, referred to as Modules:

- the Body Corporate and Community Management (Standard Module) Regulation 1997 (Qld) (the Standard Module)
- the Body Corporate and Community Management (Accommodation Module) Regulation 1997 (Qld) (the Accommodation Module)
- the Body Corporate and Community Management (Commercial Module) Regulation 1997 (Qld) (the Commercial Module) and
- the Body Corporate and Community Management (Small Schemes Module) Regulation 1997 (Qld) (the Small Schemes Module).

The Body Corporate and Community Management Act 1997 provides a general legal framework for community title empowering the four Regulation Modules which contain the specific policies, procedures and rules for a community title scheme (when first introduced, the Act and its accompanying Regulation Modules were administered by the Department of Tourism, Fair Trading and Wine Industry Development).

This regulatory structure is based on the fundamental recognition that different community title schemes have different requirements, problems and demands and that no single piece of legislation is likely to be able to adequately address the diversity of multi-titled accommodation encountered in a state such as Queensland. Consequently, each Regulation Module contains detailed and individualized provisions on the rules, policies and procedures for corporate governance, which include amongst other things: the constitution of the Body Corporate Committee; the scheduling, conduct and reporting of committee meetings; and the regulatory requirements for financial and property management. The specific content of each Regulation Module is guided by the type of Community Titles Scheme it is intended to govern. For instance, the Standard Module is a generic module designed for residential schemes consisting mostly of owner-occupiers. By contrast, the Accommodation Module is appropriate for schemes comprising residential complexes, serviced apartments, hotels or resorts. The Commercial Module is used when the lots are mainly intended for business purposes. The Small Schemes Module is the least prescriptive and applies only to buildings where there are no more than six lots included in the scheme and there is no letting agent.

The final noteworthy aspect of community title governance surrounds the engagement or authorization of a body corporate manager, service contractor and/or letting agent. Although the body corporate is expressly prohibited from delegating its powers, it is authorized to appoint a body corporate manager to deliver administrative services or exercise the authority of an executive member of the committee.

Community Titles Scheme

A community titles scheme is defined under The Body Corporate and Community Management Act 1997. Ardill et al. (2004) characterize community title as constituting freehold land subject to a single community management statement recorded by the Registrar of Titles, where the land comprises two or more lots and contains common property that is not a part of these lots. The Community Management Statement is the constitution for the body corporate and must comply with the requirements of the Body Corporate and Community Management Act 1997 and the pertinent Regulation Module for that scheme.

The Body Corporate and Community Management Act 1997 provides that the Community Management Statement must:

- contain the identifying name for the scheme
- identify the name of the body corporate
- state the unique identifying number for the scheme
- identify the regulation module applying to the scheme
- include a contribution schedule and an interest schedule
- identify the lots included in the scheme
- specify the common property for the scheme
- identify the lots affected, or proposed to be affected, by a statutory easement and state the type of statutory easement
- specify bylaws unless the default bylaws in the Act are nominated
- specify any future stages to be developed whereby a lot is made into a subsidiary scheme and
- include anything that the regulation module applying to the scheme says it must include, and may include anything that the regulation module applying to the scheme says it may include.

Power and Practice

The developer (or original owner) of the property is responsible for devising and registering the Community Management Statement. This document is critically important because it distributes the power and requires responsibility on the part of individual lot owners to contribute toward the costs associated with the complex. It also presumes lot owners will participate in the governance of the scheme through the body corporate. Experience suggests, however, that few lot owners actually undertake their responsibilities and the motivation and views of some frequently depart radically from the majority of lot owners.

Types of Multi-titled Tourism Accommodation

Warnken et al. (2008) describe the range of complexes and advance a typology that can assist in providing a sense of the range of manifestations that multi-titled tourism accommodation can assume. The typology includes five types that are based on key factors such as building style, location, maintenance arrangements and so on.

Type 1

These complexes represent a higher density extension of the traditional 'holiday home' sector: they provide accommodation units in low-rise buildings, generally without lifts or recreational facilities such as pools, gymnasiums. A-frames, duplexes, townhouses, villas in up-market holiday (resort) villages and small apartment complexes (for example ski chalets) can be all categorized within the Type 1 classification.

Type 2

In Australia, most of these type of complexes tend to be referred to as 'three storey walk-ups'. They usually comprise more than 24 units arranged in an 'L' or 'U' configuration. These complexes typically have several staircases, underground car parking, basic recreation facilities, no conference or meeting facilities, but may have a snack food or small retail outlet located on the ground floor. Many type 2 complexes can be found in regional tourism seaside destinations (for example the Whitsundays or Cairns in Australia), or in the immediate periphery of tourist centres.

Type 3

Type 3 complexes are larger, tending to have more than 50 units (mostly high-rise). Some units in these complexes can be occupied by long-term residents (renters and owners) and they are usually sufficiently large to warrant the engagement of a full-time resident manager. These complexes are prolific along the eastern seaboard of Australia and in particular, Queensland. This type, together with Type 4, are the most common type of complexes where management rights businesses (discussed in detail below) are established and sold. Due to these complexes' mix of uses, the potential for conflict between unit owners is quite high.

Type 4

These complexes can be found in buildings that are physically similar to the Type 3 complexes. The key distinguishing facet of the Type 4 complex is that it is managed by a specialist multi-titled tourism accommodation operating company with an established brand name. The vast majority of units in the Type 4 complexes are in the short-term letting pool, that is, they will have a low ratio of resident unit owners to investor unit owners. The mix of uses in a Type 4 complex is not as great as in a Type 3; therefore conflict is usually lower due to greater alignment of unit owner interests. The balance of power in this type of complex is usually weighted towards the majority of investor owners; however, in some instances resident owners can disrupt this power balance as a result of their regular on-site presence in the complex and at body corporate meetings.

Type 5

In this type, complexes provide a hotel front-end reception staffed with a concierge, full service in-house bar, restaurant and retail facilities, daily room cleaning and service and tend to be located in the centre of a tourism hub or central business district. Some recently constructed Type 5 complexes also provide dual key apartments with small kitchen and laundry facilities that can be separated into two units, each the size of a standard hotel room. It is evident that many traditional hotels are being reconfigured and ownership titles subdivided in order to facilitate conversion into 'condotels' (Smoke and Burk 2005). This new ownership/management model – with the hotel's ownership not being represented by way of a single property title, but by as many property titles (and owners) as there are accommodation units in the complex – has become extremely popular. However, the new model is likely to place new administrative demands on hotel operators due to the additional burden of attempting to maintain harmonious working relations with the many independent parties that represent the hotel's ownership.

Resident Management Rights

This section serves to introduce and explain the specifically Australian phenomenon of resident management rights. Management rights evolved initially in the Sunshine State of Queensland approximately 30 years ago, but have recently expanded rapidly and can now be found in all Australian states and territories. Management

Rights' operators represent only one element in the tourism accommodation supply chain; however, their role, which is integral to the workings of any multi-titled tourism accommodation complex, can affect and be affected by the various other stakeholders involved in the provision of such accommodation.

What are Resident Management Rights?

The day-to-day maintenance of larger buildings requires the appointment of a caretaker. This person is primarily responsible for maintaining a complex in good technical working order and the upkeep of common property, which usually includes gardens, pools, hallways, undercover car parks, walkways, stairways and so on. Tourism complexes with a number of units in the short-term letting pool also require an onsite resident manager with a limited letting agent's license to manage and promote the short-term letting pool. In Queensland, in many cases, these two functions are covered under a single management rights contract that can be purchased, with the purchaser of the contract receiving a rental commission for the sub-letting of units. The purchaser of a management rights contract also becomes the owner of a unit located close to the main entry of the complex. Management rights can assume considerable value; some recent sales of resident manager rights in large Australian complexes have commanded prices in excess of a million dollars (Guilding et al. 2005).

The management rights model has been justified by using the rationale that purchase of rights increases the incumbent's motivation to maintain a building in good working order and also augments the building's short-term letting pool income. A shortcoming of the system concerns the limited capacity of unit owners to force a poor performing resident manager out of a building.

Management Rights Contracts

The management rights contract is generally drawn up by the building's developer on behalf of the body corporate. It can be purchased by individuals or companies that have the requisite qualifications. When operating their businesses, resident managers will be keen to derive a maximum return by appropriately trading off the different sources of return that they can earn from their management rights investment. These three sources of return are:

- the opportunity to secure a capital gain earned upon sale of the management rights
- the opportunity to earn commissions from letting (holiday or long-term stays) investor owner units that are placed in the complex letting pool and
- the opportunity to receive salaried income in connection with the provision of general building service and maintenance functions.

It is particularly apparent with respect to his or her function as a letting agent that the resident manager's interests are closely aligned with the tourism role of a multi-titled tourism accommodation complex (Guilding et al. 2005). This is because higher occupancy rates result in higher commissions earned by the manager. This signifies that it is in a manager's interest to convert resident owners into investor owners who place their unit in the letting pool.

It follows that management rights' contracts in buildings with a high proportion of units in the letting pool tend to sell for more than management rights in buildings with a low proportion of units in the letting pool. It is also noteworthy that the way that a resident manager structures day-to-day operations and the use of sub-contractors represents a further opportunity to increase their return on investment.

Challenges Identified in Research Literature

There are significant challenges arising in management rights businesses and the affiliated network of stakeholders involved in multi-titled tourism accommodation complexes. This section reviews the published literature that outlines these challenges. Ardill et al. (2004) documented some of the issues arising in connection with the promotion of equitable power distribution between multi-titled tourism accommodation stakeholder groups. Guilding et al. (2005) utilized an agency perspective to examine owner/manager relationships in multi-titled tourism accommodation complexes. Cassidy and Guilding (2007) noted tension arising due to the autocracy of managers in regard to control over setting unit prices. Most recently, Warnken et al. (2008) addressed the challenge for destinations with a dominance of strata titled accommodation and the extent to which such dominance can carry an adverse implication for a destination's profile. The contributions of each of these studies are now outlined in turn.

Ardill, Everton-Moore, Guilding and Warnken (2004)

Ardill et al. (2004) examined the community title reforms in Queensland for commercial, residential and tourism stakeholders. The paper outlined the imbalance of power between various multi-titled tourism accommodation stakeholders with particular examples cited to illustrate the imbalance between a) the developer and lot owners, b) service providers and lot owners and c) differing types of lot owners.

The authors noted a perception that the original owners of a multi-titled property (the developers), have the balance of interests tilted in their favour. In particular, they could typically sell service rights, thereby encumbering future unit owners with long-term management rights or other service agreements, which carries a particular resonance with the 'embedded power of the developer' discussed by Blandy, Dixon and Dupuis (2006). Ardill et al. (2004) also noted that regardless of whether a body corporate inherits a contract governing services from a developer, it can become encumbered by the long-term arrangement associated with the delivery of sub-letting and maintenance services under a management rights contract (see also Sherry, Chapter 10). They also highlighted the distinct interests of investor owners and resident owners and the likely tensions that can be expected to arise between these two parties. The investor owners can feel disillusioned if their returns do not meet expectations, especially when increasing amounts are being paid for residential management services. The resident owners similarly, can feel disillusioned if the resident manager is concentrating on the needs of the investor owners. As already noted, the commissions earned from sub-letting signify that the resident manager's interests are likely to be more aligned to the interests of investor owners than resident owners.

Guilding, Warnken, Ardill and Fredline (2005)

Guilding et al. (2005) adopted an agency theory model and Lambert's (2001) four dimensions of principal-agent conflict to explore the relationship between resident managers and multi-titled tourism accommodation unit owners. In addition to extending some of Ardill et al.'s (2004) commentary concerning the inconsistent motivations between resident owners and investor owners, Guilding et al. also revealed a potential for tension between investor owners. In effect, investor owners are competing for the same sub-letting rental income and in many buildings there is no obligation for the resident manager to assign holiday tenants across the available letting pool. This has to be the case as some owners refurbish their units to higher standards than others and a regime requiring equitable allocation of sub-lettings across the available letting pool stock of units would negate much of the motivation for owners to appropriately maintain their units. This means that investor owners may be tempted to induce the resident manager to prioritise the sub-letting of their unit over other units in a building.

Guilding et al. (2005) also noted the potential for a resident manager to place building maintenance contracts with particular sub-contractors in return for a 'back-hander' received from the sub-contractor. The scope for this type of activity was seen to be constrained by the possibility of a resident manager needing to terminate a sub-contracting arrangement due to poor service; the sub-contractor might then elect to inform the body corporate of the resident manager's unscrupulous behaviour in placing the sub-contract. A further moral hazard potential in this agency context concerns the possibility of a resident manager not recording a short-term rental of a unit and failing to make the appropriate reimbursement to the unit owner. Guilding et al. (2005) also expressed a concern over the possibility of resident managers overstating the cost of maintenance or housekeeping, and keeping the difference between the costs reported to the unit owner and the payment made to the tradesperson.

The same authors also considered the relative risk profiles of resident managers and unit owners. It is generally held that principals bear the greater risk in agency relationships. The worst case scenario for agents is that they may lose their jobs; however a principal can have considerable capital at stake. The dynamics of the owner/manager relationship in the provision of multi-titled tourism accommodation do not appear to conform to this conventional risk differential, however. A resident manager can be seen to bear more risk than a typical unit owner, as the initial outlay to purchase management rights is substantially greater than the outlay of a unit owner to purchase a unit. Further, the resident manager's livelihood is dependent on the successful operation of a building. It is unlikely that a unit owner would have their main livelihood implicated by the degree of success achieved by a building's letting pool.

Cassidy and Guilding (2007)

A key finding of the study by Cassidy and Guilding (2007) concerned the lack of power experienced by a unit owner with respect to setting short-term letting rates. It was found that the resident manager in multi-titled tourism accommodation complexes exercises complete autocratic power with respect to the setting of unit letting rates. This example of compromised power of a unit owner can be added to those examples cited by Blandy et al. (2006). Cassidy and Guilding expressed a cautionary note in connection with an apparent imbalance in the degree of power assumed by resident managers and the extent to which they possess requisite accommodation management skills. In other short-term accommodation management contexts, such as the large hotel sector, the prerequisite for securing a managerial position is the possession of experience combined with a minimum level of pertinent education or training. At present, the prerequisite for employment in the multi-titled accommodation management field is no more than the capacity to fund the purchase of the management rights business and the possession of a letting license.

Warnken, Guilding and Cassidy (2008)

A challenge noted by Warnken et al. (2008) relates to the mix of tourists and resident owners in a multi-titled tourism accommodation complex. Warnken et al. note that a protracted downturn in tourism demand for a particular destination is likely to result in investor owners letting out to long-term tenants or selling to resident owners. Such a development would change the resident profile of a building away from tourism. If a tourism destination is heavily populated by multi-titled tourism accommodation complexes, it would appear that it is vulnerable to a reduction in its stock of tourism accommodation should a tourism downturn occur.

The Role of Government

Governments have to wrestle with the competing interests of multi-titled tourism accommodation sector stakeholders. The conflicts of interest and issues about the balance of power can become highly emotive and they are frequently afforded extensive media coverage. This interest from the government and media alike can be expected to continue as a significant number of voters live or work in multi-titled tourism accommodation properties. Further, in areas such as South East Queensland, the powerful developing lobbying group has a major interest in the commercial sustainability of this accommodation sector. Tourism is one of Australia's biggest export earners and a major provider of employment. These factors underscore the likely continued public debate and interest in the efficient and effective workings of multi-titled tourism accommodation properties.

The Body Corporate and Community Management Act 1997 was 'meant to strike a balance between the developer and future owners of individual lots' in Queensland (Ardill et al. 2004: 18). The Act was also designed to provide flexibility that would enable subsequent revisions and amendments. The Queensland government has a strong record of consultation in advance of passing legislation relating to multi-titled properties. In 2003, Robertson, the minister (then) responsible for the Body Corporate and Community Management Act 1997, stated that:

> The issues that have generated most discussion relate to management rights – where a resident manager provides caretaking services for a scheme and acts as a letting agent for owners who wish to use that service. A scheme's success, and the success of related investments, relies on a strong working relationship between the resident manager, the body corporate and individual owners. Unfortunately this does not always happen. With two distinct owner types – those who live in their properties, and those who use them as investments – tensions can arise because of their different priorities, especially if one group feels the resident manager is concentrating on the needs of the other. Investor owners can feel disillusioned if their returns do not meet their expectations, especially if they are paying an increasing amount for resident management services. Bodies corporate can feel trapped in long-term agreements that fail to meet their needs. This bill seeks to bring balance to the management rights issue, proposing new codes of conduct to govern the activities of letting agents and service contractors like resident managers (Queensland Hansard 2002: 5225).

The legislative amendments that took effect in 2003 were designed to balance the owners' responsibility for self-management with a degree of access to a manager's support and expertise. Further amendments, like those of 2007, have been implemented as part of an on-going attempt to improve the existing legislative framework pertaining to multi-titled tourism accommodation. It is notable that the government maintains an open dialogue with industry bodies (representing most stakeholder groups) to foster and encourage discussions and solutions to the complex challenges presented by such properties. Consistent with the recent past, one can anticipate that frequent legislative review of multi-titled accommodation complex arrangements will be a continuing feature of all Australian state governments for some years to come.

Conclusion

In this chapter, the concepts of law, power and practice within the multi-titled tourist accommodation sector have been discussed and critically appraised in the context of the Australian state of Queensland. The chapter represents an attempt to further our understanding of the dynamics of multi-titled tourism accommodation operations in Australia and also some of the particular issues that arise from a business contract widely referred to as a 'management rights business'. This uniquely Australian construct presents a very particular set of challenges with respect to power and practice. This set of challenges is compounded by the diversity of state based jurisdictions that populate the Australian accommodation development and management landscape. These challenges have spawned the beginnings of academic enquiry that has been reviewed in this chapter. It should be evident from this review that much further legislative reform is to be expected before the multi-titled tourism accommodation can be perceived to have achieved a level of 'steady state' existence that characterizes most other spheres of commercial enterprise. In light of many Australian state governments' unveiling regional development plans that flag rapid inner city development, signifying the construction of more multi-titled properties, the onus on academic researchers to document multi-title challenges and on legislators to engineer multi-title solutions would appear to be considerable.

In the context of this book concerned with multi-owned properties and the distribution of power between parties involved, it should be noted that in their examination of property rights in multi-owned residential developments that drew on field study data collected in England and New Zealand, Blandy et al. (2006) comment on the restricted power of unit owners relative to managing agents. Part of this limited power stems from the fact that unit owners who purchase from a developer 'inherit' a managing agent who has been engaged by the developer to provide management services to the multi-owned property for a period typically up to three years. This temporally-related source of power for the managing agent pales when compared to the 25 year management rights contract widely used in Queensland. The length of these contracts signifies that this aspect of the owners' 'bundle of rights' is more severely compromised than in the English and New Zealand jurisdictions commented on by Blandy et al. (2006).

A further factor highlighting the restricted power of unit owners in a multi-titled tourism accommodation Queensland property context where the management rights have been sold off, concerns the very muted ability of unit owners to influence who becomes a new manager should the holders of the management rights choose to sell their investments to another party. Unit owners have to mount a very strong case if seeking to veto the sale of the management rights to a particular individual or company. The onus for unit owners to demonstrate due cause warranting the prevention of a management rights sale to a particular party is not minor. The owners' case would have to be based on serious grounds such as the purchaser having a legal record signifying a compromised capacity to manage a building.

The issue of equitable allocation of power between the potentially competing investor owner and resident owner interest groups discussed in this chapter adds a further key demarcation in the distribution of property related power, to those noted by Blandy et al. (2006) whose focus was restricted to relationships between developer, owners and managing agents as unitary groupings.

References

Ardill, A., Everton-Moore, K., Fredline, E., Guilding, C. and Warnken, J. 2004. Community titles reforms in Queensland: A regulatory panacea for commercial, residential, and tourism stakeholders. *The Queensland Lawyer*, 25(1), 13–27.

Blandy, S., Dixon, J. and Dupuis, A. 2006. Theorising power relationships in multi-owned residential developments: Unpacking the bundle of rights. *Urban Studies*, 43(13), 2365–83.

Cassidy, K. and Guilding, C. 2007. An exploratory investigation of tourist accommodation price setting in Australian strata titled properties. *International Journal of Hospitality Management*, 26(2), 277–92.

Coppock, J. 1977. *Second Homes: Curse or Blessing?* Oxford: Pergamon.

Everton-Moore, K., Ardill, A., Guilding, C. and Warnken, J. 2006. The law of strata title in Australia: A jurisdictional stocktake. *Australian Property Law Journal*, 13(1), 1–35.

Guilding, C., Ardill, A., Fredline, E. and Warnken, J. 2005. An agency theory perspective on the owner/manager relationship in tourism-based condominiums. *Tourism Management*, 26(3), 409–20.

Irvine, C. and Cunningham, B. 1990. *Second Homes*. New York: Bantam Books.

Johns, N. and Lynch, P. 2007. The self-catering accommodation market: A review of electronic and other resources. *International Journal of Hospitality Management*, 26(2), 293–309.

National Community Titles Institute. 2009. *Fast Facts* [Online]. Available at: http://www.ncti.org.au/institute.html#fastfacts [accessed: 6 May 2009].

Nicod, P., Mungall. A. and Henwood, J. 2007. Self-catering accommodation in Switzerland. *International Journal of Hospitality Management*, 26(2), 244–62.

Queensland Hansard. *Introduction to Second Reading of the Body Corporate and Community Management Bill by the Minister for Natural Resources*, 30 April 1997, 1136. [Online]. Available at: http://www.parliament.qld.gov.au/view/legislativeAssembly/hansard/documents/1997/970430ha.pdf [accessed: 6 May 2009].

Queensland Hansard. *Body Corporate and Community Management and Other Legislation Amendment Bill*, 3 December 2002, 2552. [Online]. Available at: http://www.legislation.qld.gov.au/Bills/50PDF/2002/BodCorpLAB02.pdf [accessed: 6 May 2009].

Smoke, A. and Burk, R. 2005. Assessing the impact of condotels in Waikiki, in *Wings of Change in Tourism Research: Voyages of Inquiry and Discovery*, edited by D.L. Spears, *Proceedings of the 4th Annual Asia Pacific Forum for Graduate Studies in Tourism Research*. Manoa, University of Hawai'i, 287–303.

Thomas, R. and Hind, D. 2007. The self-catering accommodation sector in Yorkshire, England. *International Journal of Hospitality Management*, 26(3), 328–35.

Warnken J., Guilding, C. and Cassidy, K. 2008. A review of the nature and growth of multi-titled tourism accommodation complexes. *International Journal of Hospitality Management*, 27(4), 574–83.

Williams, A., King, R., Warnes, A. and Paterson, G. 2000. Tourism and international retirement migration: New forms of an old relationship in southern Europe. *Tourism Geographies*, 2(1), 28–49.

Woods, R. 2001. Important issues for a growing timeshare industry. *Cornell Hotel and Restaurant Administration Quarterly*, 42(1), 71–81.

Chapter 12

Governing Multi-owned Residential Developments in New Zealand: New Forms of Private Governance

Ann Dupuis and Jennifer Dixon

Introduction

The experience of governing multi-owned residential developments in New Zealand is relatively new. It is only in the last 15 years that residential intensification has become prevalent as a new form of housing in a context where detached dwellings on individual sections or lots has long been the norm. This trend is particularly evident in New Zealand's most populous urban area, the Auckland region. The most common form of legal entity created to manage multi-owned residential developments is that of the body corporate, where owners share responsibilities for the management of commonly owned property. This arrangement is established under what is known as strata title, under the Unit Titles Act 1972 (hereafter referred to as UTA). There is evidence however, that new forms of entities are being created by developers in circumstances where strata title may not be appropriate or desired, or where developers wish to avert the regulations of the UTA, or have quite specific problems which they deem the UTA cannot cover adequately. We have termed these entities 'proto-institutions', which we define as entities brought about through the adaptation of already existing legal statutes, other than the UTA, to deal with the management and administration issues in the context of governing common property in private, multi-owned residential developments.

While research has established that the UTA in its current form 'is not sophisticated enough to successfully regulate the relationships, rights and responsibilities necessitated by common property ownership and management in multi unit developments' (Glaister Ennor and the ARC 2003: 1), it can be argued that the best way forward is reforming the UTA to ensure an already identified range of problems with the Act are rectified (Dupuis et al. 2002). Currently the UTA is under review so the process of reform is in train. Despite the acknowledged problems with the UTA, the fact that proto-institutions are being introduced on an ad hoc basis provokes some disquiet. A particular worry is the creation of proto-institutions occurring in the absence of a robust regulatory framework. It appears that in respect of the governance of multi-owned residential developments practice has run on ahead of law which could well result in the escalation and proliferation of problems rather than their amelioration.

This chapter draws on recent New Zealand research that investigated the emergence of proto-institutions and identified critical issues in respect of owners' rights and likely long-term prospects for good governance (Dixon, van Roon and Dupuis 2005, Lysnar et al. 2007, Dixon et al. 2008). Participants in this research included 14 lawyers, developers, residents and local authority staff, although in this chapter reference is made only to the views of developers and lawyers. Participants were selected because of their specialized knowledge. The remainder of the discussion is organized into four sections. The first section acts as a backdrop to the chapter and provides contextual material that discusses the circumstances that have led to concerns about the various ways intensive housing in New Zealand is governed. The second section sets out the key features of bodies corporate as they currently exist under the UTA and points to a range of problems and issues associated with bodies corporate. The third section discusses four proto-institutions: incorporated societies; residents' associations; limited companies; and trusts. Drawing on interview data with property lawyers the following section presents a range of views and perspectives on the use and value of proto-institutions. The final section concludes that while private urban governance has the potential to transform ways of living in intensive environments, it is important that neither the owners nor the residents who live in intensive housing are disadvantaged. While the chapter raises a number of questions around private urban governance it concludes that, as yet, the value of using proto-institutions for this purpose is still unclear and adds a caution as to the extent to which the use of proto-institutions, rather than improve the current situation, might simply add more complexity and confusion to what is already a sufficiently complex and confusing situation.

The New Zealand Context

Although it has been some decades now since New Zealand dwellings have been built on the legendary 'quarter acre paradise' (Mitchell 1972), New Zealanders have long been used to living in detached houses on individual sites with separate, invariably fee simple titles. Historically, unfettered individual ownership has therefore been the norm. The recent urban transformation brought about by the construction of intensive, multi-owned housing represents a significant shift in the traditional practices and values associated with housing in New Zealand. It is only recently therefore that the collective rights and duties involved in multi-ownership have come to the fore and strong concerns have been voiced by residents about their lack of control over the governance of their residential site, despite their rights of legal ownership.

Multi-owned housing is now evident in many areas across New Zealand, but the issues that have arisen to do with its management and operation are particularly pertinent in the Auckland Region which has the greatest concentration of both population and intensive housing in New Zealand. Over 1.3 million people, nearly one third of New Zealand's population, currently reside in the Auckland Region which is made up of seven discrete territorial authorities (Auckland, North Shore, Waitakere and Manukau Cities and Rodney, Papakura and Franklin Districts). Population projections indicate that over the next 20 years Auckland's population will increase by some 560,000, at which time the Region will be home to approximately 37 per cent of New Zealand's population (Statistics New Zealand 2007).

In 1999, the Auckland Regional Growth Strategy was implemented to manage Auckland's growth. The Strategy's aims are to restrict growth into rural areas, address urban sprawl and the associated problem of traffic congestion through urban containment and offer a wider mix of housing options than are currently available in a relatively expensive real estate market (Auckland Regional Growth Forum 1999). The Growth Strategy proposed that 70 per cent of new housing be constructed in existing metropolitan areas, especially around designated town centres and existing transport nodes, with medium and higher density housing as a fundamental platform of the Strategy. The future of Auckland was thus envisioned as one in which between 25–30 per cent of the Region's population would be living in multi-unit, medium and higher density housing (Auckland Regional Growth Forum 1999).

Since the adoption of the Strategy the proliferation of intensive housing has also presented stakeholders (developers, local authorities and housing consumers) with numerous legal and other issues that require consideration. Initially, most intensive housing developments constructed used the UTA as a means through which common property in developments was managed and administered. It was not long however, before a range of issues and problems with the UTA became apparent (Dupuis et al. 2002). While the UTA is still the most commonly used legal entity for governing common property in intensive developments there is evidence that, for a variety of reasons, developers and development companies are resorting to the use of other proto-institutions for this purpose.

The Unit Titles Act and Bodies Corporate

The UTA, the Act under which bodies corporate are established, was introduced in 1972 as a means of overcoming shortfalls in both the company share and cross lease forms of title. At its introduction the UTA was depicted as a measure intended to lessen urban sprawl and encourage the principled development of high-rise residential and commercial developments within city environments (Alston et al. 2000). The Act was amended in 1979, again in 1993 and is currently under review. The intention of the Act was to 'facilitate the subdivision of land into units that are to be owned by individual proprietors, and common property that is to be owned by all the unit proprietors as tenants in common, and to provide for the use and management of the units and common property' (Unit Titles Act 1972: 2).

The Act requires that land and buildings be subdivided into units and common property by means of the deposit of a unit plan under the Land Transfer Act

1952. The deposit of the plan creates in each unit a 'stratum estate', which allows for each unit to be transferred, leased or mortgaged in the same manner as the conventional fee simple estate. The Act also requires the District Land Registrar to issue a certificate of title under the Land Transfer Act for the respective stratum estate for each unit (McClelland 1978). Before the deposit of the unit plan every principal unit (unit designed as a place of residence or business) and accessory unit (e.g. shed, garage, pool, laundry, etc. that is designed for use with a principal unit) is assigned a unit entitlement, normally fixed by a registered valuer. The unit entitlement is based on the relative value of the unit in relation to each of the other units on the plan. Once assigned the unit entitlement is very difficult to change. Each owner's share in the common property, responsibility to pay for outgoings and obligation, liabilities and certain voting rights is determined by the unit entitlement (Glaister Ennor and the ARC 2003).

A body corporate comes into being upon creation of the stratum estate at the time the unit plan is deposited (Norton 1975). The legal responsibilities of a body corporate include the maintenance of common property, setting of owners' levies for their financial contribution, arrangement of insurance and valuation, preparation of annual accounts and the conduct of annual general meetings. In effect, and in law, owners of the units of the unit plan comprise the body corporate. In the first instance therefore, the developer, or the development company, is the body corporate. As units are sold, the individuals who make up the body corporate change and keep changing as subsequent unit sales occur.

Body corporate rules are set out in the Second and Third Schedules of the UTA. At the time the body corporate is established the rules can be amended. There is however, little flexibility for changing rules thereafter. Second schedule rules, which are largely to do with constitutional issues, can be changed in only two ways. The first is by a unanimous vote of all owners to agree to a rule change. The second way pertains to the situation where unanimity has not been achieved, but 80 per cent or more of owners support a rule change. In these instances application may be made-to-the Court to approve the change. Third schedule rules, involving more of the day to day running of the development, can be changed by a majority vote of owners.

An obvious implication of such inflexibility is that the rules set in place by developers are inherited by the first generation of owners and, assuming further sales, for subsequent owners. Commonly too, contracts and other arrangements are also set in place before any units are sold. For example, numerous instances have occurred whereby body corporate management companies have been contracted to manage a development for a decade, with the right of renewal for another decade – long after developers have severed any ties to the development. It is clear, therefore, that the developer is invested with power which has the possibility of shaping the lives of others long after completion of the development project and, in most cases, long after the developer has sold off all units and no longer has any legal responsibilities for the development itself.

Body corporate management companies manage bodies corporate on behalf of owners, usually through an agent who acts as the body corporate secretary, a term prescribed in the Act. Property management companies are also involved in maintaining properties and can be involved in tenancy management. The body corporate typically has an owners' committee, elected at the annual general meeting, whose major function is to employ others in connection with the control, management and administration of the common property on behalf of the body corporate. On-site managers may be employed by the owners' committee, although they can also be appointed by the developer, body corporate management or property management company.

Past research indicated a range of problem associated with bodies corporate in New Zealand. These include: a lack of clarity with respect to relationships between developers and body corporate management companies, developers and property management companies and developers and on- or off-site managers with the strong possibility of conflicts of interest arising in these sets of relationships; problems and deficiencies with the Unit Titles Act itself in matters such as the establishment of unit entitlements, body corporate rules and the regulation of, and practice by, body corporate management companies; and communication issues to do with various parties being poorly informed regarding roles, responsibilities and legislation, interpersonal difficulties, sometimes created by heavy handed practice and inadequate attention to administrative responsibilities by stakeholder groups (Dixon and Dupuis 2009, Glaister Ennor and the ARC 2003, Dupuis et al. 2002).

Within housing developments it is expected that developers have the ultimate power regarding the design and construction of the development and while most use the services of such professionals as architects, designers and project managers, the nature and quality of the completed development largely rests on the decisions made by developers or the company they represent. We have established however, that developers can also exercise continuing control over the development with respect to both the rules they lay down in the first instance and through the contractual obligations they enter into with management agents.

Proto-institutions

In this section we set out the key features of four different types of proto-institutions which have been identified as being used as an alternative to strata titles and the mechanism of bodies corporate for the management of multi-owned housing developments. We also refer to data from interviews with lawyers and developers with knowledge of both the UTA and proto-institutions.

Incorporated Societies

The first proto-institution examined is the incorporated society, defined as a group or organization registered under the Incorporated Societies Act 1908 (hereafter referred to as the ISA). Upon registration the group is authorised by law to run its affairs as though it were an individual person. A wide range of groups and organizations become incorporated societies including sports, social, music, cultural, special interest and activist groups. Any group of 15 or more persons may apply to become incorporated under the ISA, including natural (i.e. individual) persons and corporate bodies. Each corporate body counts as three persons for the purpose of making the minimum number of 15 members. An incorporated society can carry out any activity provided it is lawful and authorized by the 'objects' in the society's rules and provided the activities are not for the financial gain of the society's members. The ISA permits a society to raise money and employ people (including its own members) to carry out various duties, provided any profit from these activities is not distributed to the society's members. A set of regulations apply to the registration of incorporated societies. Rules of an incorporated society are set out in Section 6 of the ISA.

Incorporated societies can be used in a number of situations and can offer some advantages over bodies corporate. For example if more than one unit title/body corporate exists in a development, or there is a combination of titles such as unit title and fee simple titles, then a common set of rules may be required to include all the titles and residents (including residential and/or commercial residents) who own, lease, rent, work, or live at the development. In any of the above instances, the body corporate rules that exist and operate in relation to one unit title within the development have no authority over residents or workers who occupy any other title within the development. Under the ISA a common set of rules can be set in place. A second advantage is that an incorporated society is a legal entity separate from its members, and can therefore lease, rent, buy or sell property, borrow money and enter into contracts in the society's name. A third advantage is that with the exception of instances where debt or obligation is incurred from operations involving financial gain or as a result of unlawful actions, members have no personal liability for the debts, contracts or other obligations of their society. Fourth, the rules of an incorporated society must meet minimum requirements and therefore provide a degree of certainty in the way societies are run. Fifth, incorporated societies offer the advantage of perpetual succession, meaning they can continue despite membership changes. A sixth advantage has to do with the ISA being relatively straightforward and information about it easy to access. Compared with the information regarding bodies corporate and the UTA, information regarding incorporated societies is easier to obtain, the ISA itself is both shorter and more straightforward for the layperson to follow and a free government telephone number is available during business hours to provide information on the ISA. Finally, an incorporated society may be entitled to tax exemptions.

Incorporated societies can also exhibit features that are less advantageous when compared with bodies corporate under the UTA. First, whereas the UTA is property-specific in nature and concerned with such issues as subdivision and stratum estates, provisions relating to leasehold lands, and proprietors' duties and obligations with regard to commonly owned property, the ISA is more general in its approach and focuses on members' interests – rules and regulations pertaining to the running of the group. As a consequence it has been argued that the ISA does not deal with or provide any specific guidance in relation to how common property issues should be managed operated or maintained (Dixon, van Roon and Dupuis 2005). Second, certain aspects of an incorporated society can be considered ultra vires – in particular the requirement for residents to join an incorporated society if they share in the ownership of common property.

A third disadvantage with the ISA has to do with the issue of regular and transparent financial reporting. While the ISA states that every incorporated society must deliver a set of financial statements to the Registrar annually (section 23 Incorporated Societies Act 1908), there is no provision for the accounts to be audited. By comparison, the UTA contains a provision for the accounts of the body corporate to be audited annually by an independent auditor (rule 12[d]). It is however, possible to write a rule for such a provision for an incorporated society, as any rules for incorporated societies are very easy to change. This latter point leads to the fourth limitation of incorporated societies; the ease with which rules can be changed has the potential of creating a sense of uncertainty or instability with the society. The positive aspect of the ease with which rules can be changed is that if a developer were to establish a set of rules in the society that gave the developer or other another party undue advantage over future owners, then it would not be difficult to have those rules amended (Dixon et al. 2005). A fifth disadvantage of the ISA compare with the UTA is the ease with which the 'objects' of an incorporated society can be changed. The procedure is the same as that which is required for any rule change but also includes the provision that 'No alteration in the objects of a society shall be registered unless the Registrar is satisfied either that the alteration is not of such a nature as to prejudicially affect any existing creditor of the society, or that all creditors who may be so affected consent to the alteration' (section 21[4] of the Act). As with the argument made earlier in relation to the ease of rule changes under the ISA, it can similarly be argued that the ease with which the objects of an incorporated society can be altered could also lead to the possibility of unpredictability within an incorporated society. A sixth limitation relates to the weakness of the dispute resolution mechanisms within the ISA. If an incorporated society experiences problems or disputes about the way in which rules are being interpreted or applied, the Registrar is not empowered to intervene. While the ISA gives the Registrar the power to investigate breaches of the ISA by an incorporated society, the Registrar has no power over members who breach the rules of their incorporated society (section 34A and 34B). In instances where there is a dispute within an incorporated society, the authority lies with the High Court.

It is difficult to do much more than offer suppositions on the critical issues of owners' rights and the long-term prospects for good governance under ISAs. Nevertheless it is important to comment that, unlike the UTA, the ISA does not deal with, or provide any guidance in relation to the way common property should be managed, operated or maintained. Such issues still remain then as to who would run incorporated societies, the extent to which owners' rights are taken as a primary concern and the legal complexities in situations where more than one legal entity operate together – for example an ISA along with a body corporate.

Residents' Associations

Residents' associations take many forms in New Zealand and exist for multiple reasons. A common type of residents' association is that which is set up in relation to residential 'areas' such as streets, or small suburbs or perhaps (un)protected wetlands or areas requiring protection by interested parties who may live in the vicinity. While many residents' associations exist as 'incorporated societies' this is not mandatory by law. However incorporation does provide a group or association with a legal entity through which it can operate, and its members with protection from personal liability for legal costs should they be taken to court. A residents' association (which can also be referred to as a 'precinct society') can exist along with one or more bodies corporate set up under the UTA. A residents' association also allows for the participation of members other than unit owners. So, for example, the developer of the site could be a member of a residents' association, as could the on-site manager, and perhaps those who may lease private or commercial premises owned by the body corporate or developer.

A major disadvantage of residents' associations is that if not registered as an incorporated society, or under the umbrella of a body corporate, such an association would only be protected by the Privacy Act 1993 (in the case of a not-for-profit organization) or the Fair Trading Act 1986 (if the association has a fee-paid manager). While the Privacy Act comes under the jurisdiction of the Privacy Commissioner (who may only give a 'ruling'), the Fair Trading Act comes under the jurisdiction of the District Court. For comparison, both the UTA and the ISA come under the jurisdiction of the High Court.

As with ISAs, the few examples we have of residents' associations make it difficult to comment on the critical issues of owners' rights and the long-term prospects for good governance. However it appears that residents' associations provide only limited safeguards for owners. The extent to which this will result in problems in the future remains to be seen.

Limited Companies and the Companies Act 1993

Although the research project we draw on did not specifically investigate the set up of companies, trusts or joint ventures, our research participants referred to instances where developers chose to establish a limited company rather than an incorporated society; in such cases the Residential Exemption may not necessarily apply. However, during our research into proto-institutions an example arose of a developer who successfully applied for a Residential Exemption notice, and formed both an incorporated society and limited company within a development. Because the local territorial authority was not interested in taking on ownership or responsibility for the infrastructure within the development the developer formed a water company that owned and maintained the water ways and water facilities within the development. This was done on the rationale that the company had limited liability which enabled it to borrow. In this regard the company structure may be more beneficial as lending institutions are unwilling to lend to incorporated societies. While an incorporated society is viewed more as a community of interest amongst owners, a liability company is perceived as much more of a professional business which has a board of directors and a shareholding structure under the Companies Act.

It is not always straightforward for a company to be an owner of common facilities, especially in instances where every owner is a director and a shareholder. In such cases every time an owner sells not only does the property concerned have to be transferred, so too do the shares, resulting in rather a convoluted compliance procedure in terms of Companies Office records. By contrast, change of ownership within an incorporated society merely requires the register of the society to be updated internally, rather than the Companies Office being officially notified. A lawyer interviewed for the research noted that it depended on how a company was set up, as to whether an incorporated society or limited company would have priority if any problems arose between the two.

Trusts

Trusts are another form of legal mechanism that can be used to govern commonly owned property. The various acts which pertain to trusts are the Charitable Trusts Act 1957, the Public Trust Act 2001 and the Trustee Companies Management Act 1967. By setting up a Trust a legal deed is formed which sets out an agreement between a Settlor (developer), Protector (independent auditor) and group of Trustees (owners/residents). The Settlor creates a Trust Fund whereby the Trustees agree to hold, upon trust, the money and assets in the Trust, for the purposes and terms set out in the Deed. The Deed lays out the purposes of the Trust, the appointment, duties, powers, liabilities and other roles of the Trustees, and the procedures for meetings, voting, quorum, delegation, and annual reports and accounts. The role of the Protector is to monitor the activities of the Trustees and ensure the purposes of the Trust are being carried out. Like trusts devised for other purposes, these trusts too have beneficiaries: all the owners in the development, on whose behalf certain funds are protected by the Trust.

During the research on proto-institutions an example of a Trust being used to govern multi-owned property was identified, where the underlying land was fee simple and the owners had only a leasehold interest (in the form of a unit title). The Protector's role was to ensure that the lease did not expire or collapse. Although the UTA also protects the unit title owners, the Protector arrangement acts as a further safeguard with the appointment of a community recognized trustee (e.g. the New Zealand Guardian Trust). The use of such a trustee provides longevity of the arrangement and ensures that the rental for the lease does not get funnelled elsewhere.

It was also mentioned that with Trusts becoming more common, they had become more acceptable to lending institutions. Another advantage related to the use of charitable trusts as non-profit making organizations, thereby lessening the tax burden for the trust involved. The converse of this is when developers choose to form limited liability companies to govern commonly owned property within multi-owned developments, so that a profit can be made and returned to the shareholders, not as dividends but to benefit a collective pool. The shareholders could be unit title owners and/or the incorporated society, depending on how the management structure of the multi-owned development had been set up.

Views on Proto-institutions

This section presents a brief summary of the views of the developers and lawyers who were interviewed for the proto-institutions research, focusing on why they selected the particular legal and management structure for a particular development. For developers the decision to establish a particular type of proto-institution often appeared to be based on their past experiences, especially the issues they had with unit titles and bodies corporate. For example, one developer who had chosen an incorporated society as the legal entity to govern specific onsite features of a multi-owned development did so in order to establish freehold titles and commented on the importance of such titles which sit outside the UTA's legislative framework. His view was that with an incorporated society it is the people living in the development who run it. The implications for grass roots participatory democracy are clear from this comment. In other instances developers chose a legal entity they were already familiar with (such as a limited company), or because there was a belief that purchasers would be more familiar or comfortable with one type of entity.

Developers are often guided by the views of their lawyers. The interviews conducted with lawyers demonstrated three major points. First, that there is little agreement as to which type of legal entity is best suited for the governance of multi-owned developments. A view put forward by some lawyers was that the use of unit titles and bodies corporate is still the best means of governing multi-owned developments. In terms of commonly owned property the UTA legislation provides far greater protection than does the legislation of proto-institutions and will only improve once its review has been completed. Therefore, it would be better to continue with such legislation rather than set up alternatives which may result in even more problems than those associated with the UTA. It was also noted that overseas jurisdictions, especially Australian states, have successfully used unit titles and bodies corporate legislation. Conversely, the rules of other legal entities, like incorporated societies, could well be both inoperable and unenforceable. In addition, it was recognized that voluntary organizations, like incorporated societies, do not have the statutory backing that property legislation has, with incorporated society legislation emphasising the running of meetings rather than the protection of property. A property lawyer provided insights into problems that could arise with using incorporated society legislation when he commented:

> I really couldn't see the point of an incorporated society as an equivalent to the body corporate under the Unit Titles Act – because incorporated societies are general sorts of things. You have sports clubs, charitable associations, business associations, purely social clubs like the Naval Officers Association – that sort of thing – or Ex Naval Men's Association. There's a whole range of things. What we need here is a framework that's a lot more geared to living in a physically defined small community. It's not like the Ratepayers Association at all – an incorporated society is the ideal thing for a Ratepayers Association. But I think it's not specific enough … so you then … for each one, if you incorporate under the Incorporated Societies Act, for each one, you're going to have to make very, very specific rules, and lawyers being lawyers there'll be a totally different set of rules that each law firm will want to have for each one that it does. So you'd end up with maybe 300 different likely sets of rules – which is just hopeless, just hopeless.

Other lawyers favoured the use of proto-institutions. As one lawyer stated:

> I've never been a fan of bodies corporate as they operate on, in my opinion, now outdated concepts of participatory democracy. Many people don't have time to attend AGMs or stand for election to executive positions. That's why there's been the development of body corporate companies who carry out the dog work … For governance models, I'm leaning towards combining the principles of incorporated societies with those of trusts. The benefit of this model is that you can get the best of both worlds.

The second main theme that emerged from the interviews with lawyers was that legal entities themselves are complex, as are the issues that their use and implementation bring to the fore. The third theme was the extent to which positive long-term outcomes for multi-owned developments rests on the success of the legal entities used in the governance of these developments.

A number of other points were made during the interviews with lawyers. First, was that the model of combining proto-institutions, as some lawyers and developers had done, resulted in the 'best of both worlds'. Second, current statutory and legal frameworks lack subtlety and the question of how to limit liability in multi-owned developments has not been addressed within the legislation and, as one lawyer commented, is a 'time bomb' waiting to happen. Third, good governance mechanisms are inhibited by the present legislative environment. Especially in multi-layered developments tensions could easily arise because of a lack of understanding regarding how, for example, commercial and residential units could exist satisfactorily alongside one another. Given that such legal complexities could well be beyond the grasp of residents, the issue of sound and comprehensible information is crucial. Fourth, current legal entities do not adequately address or suitably resolve the legal relationships, rights or duties between the developer, owners and territorial authorities. The use and management of commonly owned assets are not established with rules that are secured by effective legal instruments and procedures in perpetuity. Such legal inadequacies have the potential to create risks to the physical and natural environment, the community within the multi-site development and the territorial authority against whom claims can be made if major problems arise. Finally, it was also pointed out that all legal entities exhibited advantages and disadvantages and that successful governance rested not on these entities but on having in place all of the following three feature: well organized and strong-minded owners; good design, layout and quality construction; and sound maintenance.

Conclusion

The research on which this chapter is based identified the many and complex ways that multi-unit residential property is being administered and managed in New Zealand. Nevertheless, it is still the case that most developments come under the Unit Title legislation and thus bodies corporate are the predominant mechanism through which multi-owned property is governed. Despite the problems associated with the UTA it must be acknowledged that it is a legal entity which, however inadequately, fulfils the necessary functions in terms of managing and governing multi-unit developments. Although there is evidence that developers are using various proto-institutions, the long-term prospects of the success of intensive housing, especially in the Auckland region, still rests on the adequacy of the UTA to meet the needs of all stakeholders involved in multi-unit developments.

While developers are resorting to a range of proto-institutions in their new developments, the lack of available information on these entities makes it difficult to assess the extent to which they are being used in place of the UTA. A similar lack of information inhibits an assessment of their success. It appears from interviews with lawyers that there is considerable disagreement in the profession as to the extent to which the UTA works well, or has the potential to work well and the perceived advantages and disadvantages of the proto-institutions.

In earlier work we highlighted the complex connections between property and law in multi-owned residential sites in New Zealand and England and found that despite differences in legal structures in the two countries similar kinds of issues arose in both jurisdictions with respect to power (Blandy, Dixon and Dupuis 2006). The discussion in this chapter on bodies corporate has demonstrated that owners' rights in terms of shaping the governing structures in which they operate can be limited. The extent to which this situation is ameliorated by the use of proto-institutions is a moot point. On the one hand these legal entities may provide greater flexibility with respect to changing rules and greater transparency in terms of financial reporting, but on the other hand they are not set up to deal specifically with property, require only voluntary membership and have relatively limited means through which rules can be enforced.

Given the instances of using combinations of both the UTA and various proto-institutions it is vital that suitable linkages are made between the various legal entities so that the rules of each entity work together rather than work in opposition, or so that one legal entity does not create problems for the smooth operation of another or other entities. The use of multiple entities also draws attention to the complexity that owners could face with respect to sets of relationships and responsibilities and the requirements for meetings. The need for well developed dispute mechanisms in these situations is evident. The recent experience in New Zealand of the leaky building syndrome in newer multi-owned (and individually owned) dwellings across the country, but especially in Auckland, highlights the importance of such mechanisms, particularly with regard to owner protection. Private urban governance of the sort discussed in this chapter has the potential to transform ways of living in intensive urban environments and could provide a new way forward as people take more control of their own affairs. It also raises a number of issues in the New Zealand context where it is still very much a novelty and where stakeholders are relatively inexperienced.

References

Alston, A., Bennion, T., Slatter, M., Thomas, R. and Toomey, E. 2000. *Guide to New Zealand Land Law*. 2nd Edition. Wellington: Brookers.

Auckland Regional Growth Forum. 1999. *A Vision for Managing Growth in the Auckland Region: Auckland Regional Growth Strategy, 2050*. Auckland: Auckland Regional Growth Forum, Auckland Regional Council.

Blandy, S., Dixon, J. and Dupuis, A. 2006. Theorising Power Relationships in Multi-owned Residential Developments: Unpacking the Bundle of Rights. *Urban Studies*, 43(13), 2365–83.

Dixon, J. and Dupuis, A. 2009. *Strata Title and Mixed Tenure: Tensions for Owner-occupiers*. Paper to the 4th Australasian Housing Researchers' Conference Sydney, 5–7 August, 2009.

Dixon, J., Lysnar, P., van Roon, M. and Dempsey, C. 2008. *The Privatisation of Sustainable Infrastructure: Implications for the Governance and Management of Multi-Owned Residential Developments*. Paper to the International Conference on Urban Drainage, Edinburgh, 1–5 September 2008.

Dixon, J., van Roon, M. and Dupuis, A. 2005. *Facilitating Maintenance of Stormwater Devices on Communally Owned Land*. Paper to the Fourth South Pacific Stormwater Aquatic Resource Protection Conference, Auckland, May 4–6.

Dupuis, A., Dixon, J., Lysnar, P. and Mouat, C. 2002. *Bodies Corporate and Housing Intensification in Auckland: A Preliminary Assessment*. Report for the Auckland Regional Council, Auckland City Council, North Shore City Council, Rodney District Council and the Waitakere City Council, Auckland.

Glaister Ennor and the Auckland Regional Council. 2003. *Unit Titles Act 1972: The Case for Review Discussion Report*. Auckland: Regional Growth Forum, and the Auckland Regional Council.

Lysnar, P., Dixon, J., Dempsey, C. and van Roon, M. 2007. *Managing 'Low Impact' Features on Multi-Owned Residential Sites*. Paper to the South Pacific Stormwater Conference, New Zealand Water and Wastewater Association, Auckland, New Zealand, 15–17 May 2007.

McClelland, L.H. 1978. *New Zealand Special Committee to Review the Unit Titles Act, 1972*. Wellington: Department of Justice.

Mitchell, A. 1972. *The Half-gallon Quarter Acre Pavlova Paradise*. Christchurch: Whitcombe and Tombs.

Norton, M.A. 1975. *Valuation of Unit Titles.* Wellington: Statistical Bureau Production, New Zealand Institute of Valuers.

Statistics New Zealand. 2007. *Demographic Trends 2006*. Wellington: Statistics New Zealand.

Chapter 13
Private Governance and Sustainability: Balancing Public and Private Rights and Responsibilities in New Zealand

Jennifer Dixon and Marjorie van Roon

Introduction

The private governance of sustainable design features, such as areas of retained indigenous forests or wetlands, rain gardens and swales, is becoming increasingly common as a practice in multi-owned residential developments in a number of countries. This practice is seen as a means of enhancing local sustainability while reducing environmental and infrastructure costs for local governments and communities. However, some critical issues are emerging in respect of their day-to-day management in relation to maintenance, liability and performance, and longer-term prospects as a means of improving sustainability of the local environment. In particular, thorny questions arise when legal entities put in place by developers do not work such as: when problems occur in respect of the ability of the entity to resolve conflict between its members; where liability lies if stormwater and ecosystem features are not properly managed and maintained; who picks up the costs if liability is not properly identified; and how ownership structures can be reorganized to accommodate a new generation of owners whose support is needed for an ageing community.

The chapter draws on research undertaken between 2005 and 2008 at multi-owned residential developments in Canada, Australia and Scotland, plus many sites in Auckland and Coromandel in New Zealand (Dixon et al. 2005, 2008, van Roon and Dixon 2006). Research methods used during this period included an examination of the commonalities and differences with respect to the various types of legal entities put in place to manage communally-owned property such as sustainability features; and for the New Zealand examples, in particular, a review of relevant statutes, entity rules and resource consent applications to councils. Lawyers, developers, professional advisors and council staff were interviewed and issues identified that need to be considered by policy makers and other stakeholders as these private arrangements become more commonplace.

The creation of private governance arrangements in most jurisdictions typically involves several steps. Developers seek approval for their projects from local authorities in order to construct their residential developments. This may result in conditions being imposed as part of the planning consent process for the on-site management of stormwater, water recycling and sewage disposal. In some peri-urban or rural cases where reticulated urban services are not yet available, consent will only be granted if the developer provides the infrastructure on-site. Once approval has been secured, the developers usually then set in place arrangements for the long-term management of the site, following the sale of the lots or units and conclusion of their involvement. This step can also occur sometime later as building gets underway. A critical element of this process is the setting up of the arrangements for new owners to take over and manage the site. The developers at this point wield considerable power in shaping the long-term management of the site, as the new owners are often yet to purchase, take up residence and become active in management decisions (Blandy et al. 2006).

While the type of property title may determine the type of arrangement that is established, developers are often free to determine what entity to put in place in relation to freehold title. Usually these arrangements involve the creation of a set of governing documents with by-laws or rules that will be guided by a statute that may be prescriptive or relatively flexible. The owners thus purchase their lots or units, subject to these developer-drafted restrictions. At this point, owners are often unaware of the conditions placed on development of their property or their obligations as owners who share an interest in the development (Dupuis et al. 2002, Blandy, Dixon and Dupuis 2006). Once ownership has passed on formally to the new owners from the developers, the owners then find themselves involved in management of their association or committee. The extent to which they can make modifications to the rules by which they are governed will be dependent on the arrangements put in place by the developer. Frequently the new owners will find contractual arrangements have already been arranged for the services of the professional managing company and property maintenance company and that they are not easy to modify without nearly unanimous support of the owners (Dupuis et al. 2002, Blandy et al. 2006). However, as many incoming residents have little experience in managing stormwater or ecosystem features, it is critical that adequate provisions for maintenance are set in place.

Blandy, Dixon and Dupuis (2006: 2372–3) suggest that there are three critical events, following the purchase of the site by the developer, in the establishment of a multi-owned site. These are: the establishment of the contract between the developer and agent; acquisition of property rights by the first and then subsequent owners and the simultaneous creation of the body corporate; and the transfer of the freehold in the whole property to the new legal entity by the developer. Our research suggests the inclusion of another step which is the granting of consent from local government councils setting out conditions governing the operation of the site. This event adds another layer of complexity to the long-term management of multi-owned sites.

Drawing on the New Zealand case study material, local government requirements, legal entity rules and subsequent contractual arrangements established to maintain and manage sustainability features are examined in turn to reveal the rights and powers of local government, developers and owners. The chapter concludes by exploring issues of public and private rights and responsibilities and considers whether contractual arrangements that are created both to implement local government requirements and enable owners to manage these features on-site require more active oversight by regulators and policy-makers.

Developments in Sustainability Practices

Internationally, attention to the sustainability dimensions of water management has been intensifying over the last decade. There is increasing emphasis by national and local governments on improving urban and rural-residential sustainability and encouraging sustainable design initiatives in neighbourhoods in the United Kingdom and New Zealand (see DETR and CABE 2000, DPMC 2003). These initiatives can also include the creation of open space for forest or wetland retention. As a consequence local authorities seek innovative ways of increasing the efficiency of water use and managing both quality and quantity of stormwater more effectively at source, rather than pursuing traditional 'end of pipe' solutions. The provision of features for stormwater management and water recycling is becoming the norm in many new residential developments.

The growing awareness of the need for multi-unit residential developments to become more locally sustainable, particularly in relation to the need to manage water resources and biodiversity more carefully, is leading to the construction of 'low impact' stormwater devices and vegetated corridors in these developments (Dixon et al. 2005). Often such features are required as a condition by consenting local authorities. Increasingly, however, long-term management and maintenance of these features then rests with the owners and managers of these developments. As a consequence, issues occur in relation to the efficacy of the legal entities for private governance and how well they might work in practice in addressing issues that arise with the management of these devices and ecosystems.

Low impact design features may incorporate a variety of approaches and devices such as swales, rain gardens, rain tanks, rainwater harvesting features, bioretention trenches, detention ponds, treatment trains, constructed and natural wetlands and forest patches. Ideally, the adoption of an holistic approach using a combination of these approaches should be used to achieve the benefits of combined water quality and quantity control as well as enhancing amenity (National SUDS Working Group 2004) and biodiversity. However this may not always be possible on specific sites. Of particular interest in this chapter is whether the governance arrangements created when privately owned developments are established are making sufficient provision for the management and maintenance of low impact design features.

What is known as Low Impact Design had its origins in North America (Shaver 2000) and has much in common with what is termed Water Sensitive Urban Design in Australia (Lloyd et al. 2001) and Sustainable Urban Drainage Systems in the United Kingdom (Martin et al. 2001). The Scottish Environment Protection Agency introduced a policy to require Sustainable Urban Drainage Systems for all new developments after its formation in 1996 (The Scottish Government 2001) although policy implementation has been slow. In New Zealand, the term Low Impact Urban Design and Development has been coined to embrace what is encompassed by Low Impact Design but also to deliberately strengthen connections with the fields of urban design and sustainable design. A strong driver has been the need to enhance sustainability of the built environment through an integrated approach to urban design and development (van Roon 2005). Low Impact Urban Design and Development aims to avoid a wide range of adverse physiochemical, biodiversity, social, economic and amenity effects, resulting from conventional urban and rural-residential development and, at the same time, protect aquatic and terrestrial ecological integrity (van Roon and Knight 2004).

Examples of New Zealand Sites with Sustainability Features

In this section of the chapter, we provide a selection of New Zealand cases that contain multi-unit and stand-alone housing where stormwater devices and protected areas of indigenous ecosystems are being managed by the owners and residents. Five sites have been chosen to represent a range of governance arrangements in place, as described in Chapter 12. These include examples of a body corporate, a trust, an incorporated society and two companies. All but one of these sites has been established recently. Examples of sites with long-established governance arrangements in place with sustainability features are relatively difficult to find (Dixon et al. 2008). The remainder of this section outlines current or proposed arrangements on these sites for managing common property that includes stormwater, water recycling and revegetation features. The following topics are canvassed for each site in turn: site description; planning considerations; legal structure for land ownership and governance; and potential issues arising.

Regis Park, Flat Bush, Manukau City

Regis Park is a low-density residential housing estate in headwater sub-catchments of Otara Stream in Flat Bush, Manukau City. The designers and developers of this estate have been intent on demonstrating a unique development style that includes many low impact design features and follows sound 'integrated catchment management' principles (van Roon 2007). The site is steep and before construction was vegetated in pastoral grasses with exotic trees in stream gullies. Of a total land area of 34 hectares, 19.5 hectares have been re-vegetated, mainly within ecological corridors, to aid evapotranspiration of stormwater, plus indigenous biodiversity and landscape enhancement (van Roon 2007).

Resource consents under the Resource Management Act 1991 were granted for this development within the Countryside Living Transition Zone of the Manukau

District Plan (MCC 2002) which allows for a mean lot size of 5,000 square metres and the restoration of re-vegetated stream riparian corridors. The consents provided for the clustering of 66 houses in order to free open space for indigenous re-vegetation, source control of stormwater within rain gardens (on every lot) and wetlands, and community sewage treatment. Sewage effluent is to be discharged to vegetated areas on-site until such time as the regional sewerage system is extended to this neighbourhood. Another design objective aimed at improving both ecological and economic sustainability was earthworks minimization and the exclusion of steep lands from the area developed. The Manukau City Council gave exemptions to road-gradient restrictions so that earthworks could be minimized (van Roon and Dixon 2006). As is usual, the developer delegated control for the earthworks to a project manager who, in turn, employed an earthworks sub-contractor. This sub-contractor used conventional earthworks techniques thereby negating the developer's wishes for minimal disturbance on unprotected areas and resulting in a sediment discharge downstream that breached standards set by the responsible regional council. The developer plans to maintain tighter control over contractual arrangements in future developments.

Open space areas and communal facilities are owned and managed jointly by residents. The structure for the management of the commonly-owned land is an Incorporated Society, known as the Regis Park Residents' Society, that is responsible for the costs and operation of the stormwater management system and the temporary wastewater treatment plant (Regis Park Residents' Society Incorporated 2006). Clause 18 of the rules sets out in considerable detail the powers of the committee in relation to management and maintenance of the site. A contract has been let with a maintenance company to manage the common property including replanted forests and wetlands. Potential problems with this development that will need to be addressed include long-term issues of tree maintenance, forest plant succession, and pest and weed management in the forest.

Point Ridge, Albany, North Shore City

This development is of interest in that it is one of New Zealand's largest, purpose-built gated residential communities. Owners and residents have taken up occupation over a period of several years from June 2005, with the first two stages of the development having now been largely sold and stage three currently being marketed.

The development company, Urban Developments Limited, had resource consent approved by North Shore City Council to construct 186 units on a six-hectare site. The consented development plan included provision for several swales, rain gardens, underground stormwater tanks and a stormwater pond. The development has been created under the Unit Titles Act 1972 in stages, with a body corporate created for each new set of unit titles. The development company is involved in management, although an external professional body corporate management company has been appointed. A residential manager also lives on-site and deals with day-to-day issues. Residents are encouraged to participate in a steering committee.

The development plans have been modified as construction of the site has proceeded and the original plans for low impact features have diminished somewhat as time has gone on. With lodgement of an application to vary a number of the original consent conditions, including the building of an additional 53 units and increasing the size of some existing units, less land has been available to incorporate planned-for rain gardens and swales. By way of amelioration underground rain water storage tanks have been installed (Dixon et al. 2005) and are reticulated to toilets in the additional units. Specific rules of the body corporate require compliance with the drainage requirements of North Shore City Council (Body Corporate No. 346275 2005: 3) and also require that the city water supply is not used for landscaping purposes. However the progression of time, variations to the original consent, and the establishment of more recent residential developments in the area, has meant that the local authority struggles to keep abreast of the various compliance and monitoring operations required. What was originally touted as a sensitive addition to the environment is now more accurately characterized as a 'low impact sustainability' approach as the various applications to vary the original resource consent have whittled away the original intentions for both low impact design *and* development.

This example shows how intentions to incorporate low impact features can be readily undermined in the development process to the detriment of strategic goals for long-term sustainability. It also demonstrates the critical role of local authorities in encouraging innovative practices and the protection of open space required to accommodate them. Complexity in terms of governance at Point Ridge arises not from the diversity of legal entities but rather from the large number of separate bodies corporate created over time.

Earthsong Cohousing Trust, Waitakere City

Earthsong is a cohousing village in the neighbourhood of Ranui in Waitakere City. (See Blandy, Chapter 2, for another example of a cohousing development). The village was constructed between 1998 and 2009 on a 1.67 hectare site that previously contained an organic orchard. The village includes 32 stand-alone and duplex two storey owner-occupied houses constructed of rammed earth and locally grown untreated timber, a communal meeting-house, orchard and native bush area. The clustering of buildings frees space for communal facilities and sustainability features and devices that include greywater treatment, swales and a pond for stormwater treatment, water tanks, solar water heating and a trial compost toilet.

Waitakere City Council (WCC) granted land use consent to Earthsong in 2000. This followed the establishment of the Auckland Regional Growth Forum in 1999 which promoted the urban containment strategy of revitalising transit-enabled town centres such as Ranui, and WCC's policy of increasing the density of housing around public transport nodes.

Existing systems such as planning rules or legal systems can and do hinder cooperative developments. Although WCC had committed itself to being an Eco-City and was largely supportive of the project, Earthsong nevertheless bore the financial burden of developing more sustainable systems and proving to the Council that they were viable. WCC has since recognized this as a major unnecessary impediment and Earthsong is now used as an example by the Council to educate their own staff and to encourage other developments to incorporate more sustainable systems. However, political and financial constraints did prevent a number of desired items from being included in the construction phase, including on-site wastewater treatment (opposed by the public water management body) and photovoltaic panels for the generation of electricity. Finally while designing neighbourhoods to be as sustainable as possible is important, the behaviour of the occupants is significant when it comes to the overall environmental impact (Building and Social Housing Foundation n.d.).

Earthsong was first established under a Trust Deed drawn up in 1997 (Earthsong Eco-Neighbourhood nd) but this was superseded by an 'Initial Organising Agreement' in 1998. In 1999 'Cohousing NZ Limited', a non-profit company, was established to create the development of the actual community. A Cohousing Agreement was then made between Cohousing NZ Limited as vendor and developer and Earthsong Eco-Neighbourhood. Membership of Earthsong Eco-Neighbourhood resulted in a shareholding of Cohousing NZ Limited with various rights attached concerning the development of the Earthsong Eco-Neighbourhood. Though the development of Earthsong Eco-Neighbourhood is now almost complete, the Cohousing agreement still exists for future buyers. It is expected that once the final aspects of the development have been finalised Cohousing NZ Limited will be wound up or shelved.[1] There is also a charitable educational trust, the Earthsong Centre Trust 2006, which jointly owns the common house with the Body Corporate, and runs all the outreach and educational aspects.

Body corporate rules prescribed by the Unit Titles Act exist alongside the Cohousing Agreement. Body corporate rules apply to owners (as the legal title of the Earthsong Eco-Neighbourhood land and property exists as a Unit Title) while the Cohousing Agreement covers shareholders of the company, that is, all those who have put money into the project. While the body corporate rules exist as the main legal entity and framework in terms of governance issues, including the ongoing operations and maintenance of commonly owned sustainability features, at Earthsong a considerable number of decisions are made at full group meetings where members are bound by the Initial Organising Agreement. In this respect Earthsong Eco-Neighbourhood is regarded as the main decision-making body with decisions being adopted as either body corporate or Cohousing NZ Limited or Earthsong Centre Trust decisions. Decision-making is by consensus and every household is represented (Sargisson and Sargent 2004). Under the

1 Personal communication to author from R. Allison, Earthsong Eco-Neighbourhood, Ranui, Auckland, July 2009.

unit titles legislation each co-owner holds a title to their house and a share of the communal property and associated sustainability features (Earthsong Eco-Neighbourhood n.d.).

This case demonstrates significant complexity of both governance structures and the number of entities that have evolved over time. There is a time-burden for members and hands-on participation by everyone is mandatory in contrast to the other cases. Residents are better skilled than those in other cases in maintaining low impact features as they have been integrally involved in the construction and operation of those features. However, the critical test of changing ownership and loss of knowledge in the long term has yet to be faced.

Paparoa Farmlands Ltd, Rodney District

The Paparoa Farmlands large-lot residential subdivision is 59 hectares in area and is located close to Warkworth, a small township in Rodney District. Houses have been built on mostly rolling pastoral sites. The subdivision has some sustainable design features. While there is no clustering of houses as seen in Regis Park, there is an extensive connected riparian corridor throughout all the gullies that have some native tree stands. The margins of the gullies up to the corridor fence line and the gaps in the riparian forest have been replanted. The landscape company, contracted by Paparoa Farms Limited early in the development, was required to maintain the plantings for several years ensuring no greater tree loss than 10 per cent.

Consent was granted under the Proposed Rodney District Plan (Rodney District Council 2000) for a 53 lot subdivision with an average lot size of one hectare. Under requirements of the resource consents, sewage is treated separately for each household using mostly up-market, modern on-site systems with irrigation fields. Stormwater detention is a requirement on every lot with gradual release to gulley vegetation. Road stormwater collection is conventional with curbs and gulley traps. Piping takes water from roads to a stormwater pond at the subdivision boundary. In 1999 a case was taken to the Environment Court, the judicial body that hears appeals in respect of planning decisions made by local authorities, by the development company to challenge some of the conditions imposed by the Council as part of the resource consent process (Paparoa Farmlands Limited and Rodney District Council).[2]

As a result of the above appeal, the Falls Road Body Corporate Limited company was set up in November 2004 following a Consent Order made by the Environment Court (25 February 2002). It ruled that a company had to be constituted under the Companies Act 1993 to manage specifically the removal and disposal of sewage. The Company also supplies water to shareholders for the purposes of stock troughs, gardening water, and optionally for toilet flushing. The shareholding of the company is limited to 54 shares. These belong to each

2 RMA 623/99.

person who bought a section from the development. Of the five directors only one actually lives in the development (Dixon and van Roon 2006).

Although called the Falls Road Body Corporate Limited, the company is not a body corporate created under the Unit Titles Act 1972, potentially confusing for people not familiar with the relevant statutes. The critical issue with this case is the disjunction between ownership of individual properties, the legal structure that governs the property as a whole and the on-going maintenance of the ecological corridors.

Wairahi Bay Station Limited, Great Barrier Island

The Wairahi Bay Station is 150 hectares in area and is located on Great Barrier Island 100 kilometres North-East of Auckland. Great Barrier is 285 square kilometres in area and has a population of approximately 850 people. The Wairahi Bay Station property is surrounded and isolated by state forest and tidal access, with no road entry. An oxbow river runs through a narrow valley defined by parallel steep ridges and emptying into a mangrove tidal estuary. There are 14 acres of property owned in common in cleared pasture dotted with ancient puriri trees on the valley floor which is just above sea level, and subject to annual flash floods. The valley is a habitat for the endangered brown teal duck, and large areas are in regenerating forest.

The only outside intervention in management and development is through the restrictions imposed by the Auckland City Council District Plan (that is, the statutory land use plan), which identifies sensitive natural areas and those suitable or approved for horticulture. Cooperative management of the catchment, storm water and sewage has not been necessary, as individual homes are sited far enough apart and residents put in place their own systems. This would, however, become a major planning driver if the housing density were to increase, and could put pressure on the community to evolve other management structures.

In 1971 the property was bought by a group of 20 loosely associated individuals who became company shareholders at a time when idealists were buying rural land cooperatively.[3] Governance arrangements with respect to this and a number of other properties on Great Barrier Island involved an arrangement under the Companies Act 1969 where all the land is held in common and there is a right to a dwelling site and a right to an arable site attaching to each share. Occupancy is thus under the tenants in common arrangement. In practice, however, each shareholder can develop dwelling and arable sites as they please once allotted. In 1996 the Company was restructured and reregistered under the 1993 Companies Act. A management plan was drawn up and the previous unanimous voting and consensus decision-making model moved to a majority democratic voting system.

The extreme isolation and low density of settlement (after 40 years there are 13 developed dwelling sites) has shaped the community. However, there have

3 Personal communication to author from D. Nash, landowner, Auckland, July 2009.

been similar problems to those of higher density housing in that the long-term management of common areas, and the rules by which daily life and interaction are governed, were not defined initially and remain a source of problems.

Furthermore inheritance of shares by families, the lack of enough suitable land to maintain the current low density housing plan in the future, and the requirement for new shareholders to agree and sign up to rules that some of the old shareholders will not observe, remain issues. Enforcement of rules is problematic, with few willing to act as enforcers. Governance issues in the community arise around the lack of any effective sanctions or consequences for breaking community agreed rules or guidelines. In addition, there is a tendency to deal with problems on an ad hoc basis as they arise, with minimal legal advice, which remains unsatisfactory. Nonetheless, the longevity of the community, the stable membership (more than half are original shareholders) and the history together where survival depends on each other, are testament to the ability of such communities to cope when there is no settled set of rules.

Governance, Management and Maintenance

The focus of this chapter is on legal entities and governance arrangements for the maintenance of sustainability features in multi-owner residential developments, but this is just part of a larger issue. Policy-makers in many countries are endeavouring to keep pace with changes in the form and management of privately governed residential developments. For example, in the UK, there has been considerable work undertaken on maintenance of Sustainable Urban Drainage Systems. An interim code of practice produced in 2004 is accompanied by model agreements for maintenance framework and model discharge agreements that can be adapted to suit (Ciria 2006). These can either be achieved as a planning obligation under town and country planning legislation or as a condition attached to planning permission (National SUDS Working Group 2004). For large developments, the code recommends use of the Act that requires negotiations and legal preparatory work to be carried out prior to development taking place and can only be varied by agreement. In England, while councils have been active in promoting Sustainable Urban Drainage Systems, they are not in the position of maintaining them and only a small number have been implemented, although this is beginning to change (Dixon and van Roon 2006). The existing Sustainable Urban Drainage Systems are maintained and operated mainly by caretakers and free lance contractors. There are three ways existing Sustainable Urban Drainage Systems maintenance is funded: by means of a local trust where the inhabitants pay an annual sum to the trust; where the developer keeps a commuted sum from the sale of the project and assures the operation and maintenance of the Sustainable Urban Drainage Systems; and third, where the developer gives a commuted sum to the local authority who adopts the Sustainable Urban Drainage Systems in order to assure future operation and maintenance costs. There are, however, uncertainties about the cost of maintenance of Sustainable Urban Drainage Systems. The calculation of the commuted sum is not easy and it is more a question of negotiations than accurate prediction (Dixon and van Roon 2006).

The following section discusses issues that arise from an examination of the New Zealand cases summarized above. Aside from the Great Barrier Island case, the sites reviewed above are all in the early stages of development so that it is too soon to determine how well the various maintenance approaches will work in practice. However, a number of observations can be made in respect of governance, management and maintenance issues relating to sustainable (or low impact) design features.

Variation in Legal Frameworks and Governance

Firstly, there is wide variation in approaches to the governance arrangements both across and within New Zealand examples (not all of which are described here), although common elements can be identified. Often little information is readily available on what are established 'good practice models' for developers proposing to construct agreements, as well as for consumers looking at buying into developments. In relation to low impact design practices, what is consistent is that maintenance agreements are designed according to specific sites and their crafting is highly dependent on expertise available in drafting rules.

In New Zealand, requirements for on-going maintenance can be set as a condition on the resource consent. However, it is very unlikely that this would require scrutiny by council staff of the governance or maintenance arrangements put in place by developers. Developers and their lawyers draft rules creating the body corporate, incorporated society or company that encapsulate any planning conditions which the new owners are obliged to follow, once the developers have concluded their involvement. Contracts for maintenance may then be constructed accordingly. For example, Regis Holdings Ltd wrote comprehensive rules specifically to address the issue of long-term maintenance for the Incorporated Society to manage which require the setting up of a maintenance contract with a company (Regis Park Residents' Society Incorporated 2006).

In addition, as noted in Chapter 12, it is clear that the development industry in New Zealand is creating models in response to the particular management needs of their developments and using the mechanisms available under several statutes which may not always be appropriate. Practice is ahead of law. One lawyer interviewed noted that all the potential options for use (such as bodies corporate and incorporated societies) were fairly blunt instruments. Whatever model is used, however, considerable scrutiny has to be given to the rights of owners which can be easily undermined by contracts and agreements put in place by developers who have a relatively short-term involvement (Blandy, Dixon and Dupuis 2006). The governance design of the Regis Park development reflected the experience and desire by the developers to create workable structures for the long-term but not all developers have the necessary expertise or interest in creating robust governance processes.

An Auckland legal firm, whose client base includes many local councils, has expressed concerns that the common ownership of infrastructure has increased the legal complexities and magnified the possibility of risk (Brookfields n.d.). They observed that there can be no settled set of rules, documents or structure for multi-owned developments as each development reflected the goals of the developer and was greatly determined by the geography and topography of each unique development site. Nonetheless, failure to properly address legal issues of ownership relations and the performance and operation of works (including maintenance and upgrade) leads to the risk of default in the provision, operation and maintenance over time (Brookfields n.d.).

Variable Management Expertise

Secondly, there are issues concerning whether property management companies have the requisite skills to properly maintain stormwater devices and ecosystems, and understand sufficiently the principles of integrated catchment management. There is concern on the part of one New Zealand developer that the current body corporate management industry does not have the necessary expertise to manage the low impact design systems in place.[4] This lack of expertise may be overcome by the involvement of third parties with the necessary skills, as demonstrated by the following example (who determines whether these skills are adequate is another issue). The company responsible for the development of Regis Park was so concerned about future maintenance of low impact features that it instigated the establishment of a company called Landpark Services to maintain indigenous tree plantations, stormwater devices and the wastewater treatment plant. The contract is in its fifth year and is reviewed annually.

Need for Education of Owners

Thirdly, a key dimension in the increasing privatization of stormwater and ecosystem features is the need to educate owners and ensure that they are aware of their responsibilities regarding management. While some owners may be well informed, others frequently blame councils for failing to inform them of the need to maintain these features. However, the council will not have any obligation to do so if they are privately owned, unless planning conditions are being breached. In fact, often owners are unaware of their obligations. Contractors too may be unaware of the impacts of their work activities, as demonstrated by filling up rain gardens with rubbish, parking on swales and damaging concrete paving and drains.

---

4 Personal communication to author from R. Bruce, Company Director, Regis Holdings Ltd, Auckland, April 2005.

While some new owners may be of the view that infrastructure management should be taken care of without their involvement, it can also be a selling point, as shown by Regis Park. The problem of poorly informed owners and residents has been noted generally as a major issue in respect of private governance in England and New Zealand (Blandy et al. 2006) and Australia (Consumer Affairs Victoria 2004). Legal advisors may not have advised prospective purchasers of all their obligations and often real estate agents are reluctant to inform interested buyers of what it means to buy property with a common interest. Once a development is established, there is the issue of educating successive generations of owners who may not be as supportive of the environmentally sustainable features of their developments as the initial owners. The Paparoa Farmlands case showed that only one company director remained living on-site so over time successive owners will need to be educated about the environmental features of the property. The issue is whether and how that communication might occur.

Lack of Oversight

Fourthly, there is no systematic government oversight of the creation of these agreements so that there is no independent assessment of how well they are likely to address both the needs of owners and management of the property. This in part reflects reluctance of governments to interfere with private property arrangements (Dupuis and Dixon 2006) and in part that property maintenance is not something planning processes have traditionally scrutinized. Rather the focus of the planning system is usually on the management of environmental effects of a development, achieved by monitoring of the receiving environment through conditions imposed on the council consent. In respect of the Great Barrier site, an added dimension would be the identification and protection of significant natural areas under the District Plan.

Councils have substantial experience in addressing the increasing range of technologies and strategies that avoid adverse effects on water bodies from stormwater runoff (such as sedimentation). However councils have much less experience with the operation and maintenance of 'low impact' technologies and strategies, particularly in relation to the private governance issues concerning the on-going management of 'low impact' features including forests and wetlands. A senior planner in a provincial jurisdiction was interviewed in 2006 for a research project on legal entities and mechanisms established to manage 'low impact' features (Lysnar et al. 2007). When he was asked who usually proposes the legal and management structure of 'low impact' features in residential multi-owned sites, he explained that they (the council staff) initially encourage the developers to come up with their own solutions and, if these do not solve the practical problems, then the council will intervene further. He was not concerned what legal structure was used, provided that the water and waste systems were fully functional and maintenance was adequate.

The shift towards 'soft' engineering and the use of devices and features on-site challenges traditional approaches to infrastructure management and places more responsibilities on owners and the entities created to manage 'low impact' features. It raises a new set of issues such as the need to ensure that: consent conditions are sufficiently comprehensive; the entity created is well suited for the development and the site; owners and other stakeholders are educated about long-term management and maintenance; the rights of individual owners are protected in relation to those of the entity with respect to changing rules; consent conditions are adequately monitored; liability for costs is clear if systems fail; and that there is sufficient provision for resolution of disputes where there is more than one entity on site (Dixon et al. 2005). The Point Ridge case highlighted the issues councils face in keeping pace with monitoring and compliance responsibilities which underscores the importance of setting up reliable systems at the outset that can be readily managed by owners or contractors.

Our research suggests that as long as the management of adverse effects on the environment is addressed, councils have little concern as to *what* type of legal entity or mechanism exercises that control. One council stormwater engineer we interviewed made reference to the complex and convoluted nature of consent issues and suggested it was not surprising that councils sometimes too easily accepted conditions for consent or did not adequately monitor compliance with conditions. It is critical, therefore, in discussions between developers and council staff prior to consents being considered, that development proposals do not largely drive and define issues addressed at the expense of broader council objectives and requirements.

Signals for the Future

An analysis of the private governance of common-property features reveals a series of complex layers of accountabilities and relationships in respect of law, private property rights and regulation. The quality of decision-making by various parties as the entity is created and rules developed, the physical design of low impact features and the consent conditions imposed by councils are all critical elements in shaping the long-term future of these sites. In addition, the ability of owners to manage and maintain their commonly-owned features is crucial, whether this is achieved by engaging experienced contractors or by the owners themselves. As noted earlier, many of these properties are at an early stage in their development. It is thus premature to assess how well the private governance arrangements, created in an ad hoc fashion, are going to work and which model best suits particular designs and sites. Nonetheless, the experience of the Great Barrier case reveals some major challenges for the owners as their community ages and signals more broadly the types of issues likely to arise in these situations. The other cases explored here are likely to experience similar issues in the long-term as ownership, technological practices and values change over time.

The forms of private governance being created are mostly new and taking place in largely uncharted territory while practices are moving rapidly ahead in the absence of any systematic oversight. Developers and their advisors are able to create legal entities within a minimalist statutory framework and set in place long-standing property rights and responsibilities for owners. They exercise considerable power that cannot easily be contested yet effectively predetermines how well sites may be managed. Councils are limited in their role in that they can only set conditions for long-term environmental management and monitoring. They need, however, to be more finely tuned to the nuances of the types of entities being created by developers. Planners have an opportunity to take a much more active role in mediating developments that are taking on responsibilities previously exercised by the public sector, particularly given longer-term uncertainties about as yet largely untried governance structures.

A major test for any of these types of entities is the extent to which they can accommodate changes in the long-term given rapidly changing environmental conditions, needs of owners and technologies, along with statutory planning policies governing site development. In the context of shifts towards the privatization of sustainable infrastructure, it is critical to have appropriate governance and management mechanisms in place to provide decision-making structures that will stand the tests of time and produce desirable environmental outcomes.

References

Blandy, S., Dixon, J. and Dupuis, A. 2006. Theorising Power Relationships in Multi-owned Residential Developments: Unpacking the Bundle of Rights. *Urban Studies*, 43(13), 2365–83.

Blandy, S., Dixon, J., Dupuis, A and Parsons, D. 2006. The Rise of Private Neighbourhoods in England and New Zealand, in *Private Cities: Global and Local Perspectives*, edited by G. Glasze, C. Webster and K. Frantz. London: Routledge, 190–205.

Body Corporate No 346275. 2005. *Body Corporate Draft Rules*, Auckland.

Brookfields. n.d. *Local Government – Complex Subdivisions*. [Online]. Available at: www.brookfields.co.nz [accessed: May 2007].

Building and Social Housing Foundation. n.d. World Habitat Awards: Earthsong Eco-neighbourhood. [Online]. Available at: www.worldhabitatawards.org/winners-and-finalists/?lang=00 [accessed: 29 October 2009].

Ciria. 2006. *Interim Code of Practice for SUDS*. [Online]. Available at: www.ciria.org/suds [accessed: 3 March 2006].

Consumer Affairs Victoria. 2004. *Future Directions Paper: Bodies Corporate*. Melbourne: Consumer Affairs Victoria.

Department of Building and Housing. 2004. *A Review of the Unit Titles Act 1972: A Discussion Document, November 2004*. Wellington: Department of Building and Housing.

Department of the Environment, Transport and the Regions (DETR) and Commission for Architecture and the Built Environment (CABE). 2000. *By Design: Urban Design in the Planning System: Towards Better Practice.* DETR and CABE. London: Thomas Telford Ltd.

Department of the Prime Minister and Cabinet. 2003. *Sustainable Development for New Zealand Programme of Action*. Wellington: Department of the Prime Minister and Cabinet.

Dixon, J., Lysnar, P., van Roon, M. and Dempsey, C. 2008. *The Privatisation of Sustainable Infrastructure: Implications for the Governance and Management of Multi-Owned Residential Developments*. Paper to the International Conference in Urban Drainage, Edinburgh, 1–5 September 2008.

Dixon, J. and van Roon, M. 2006. *Private Governance of Low Impact Design Features: A Comparative Investigation of Issues*. Paper to the International Sustainable Development Research Conference, Hong Kong, 6–8 April 2006.

Dixon, J., van Roon, M. and Dupuis, A. 2005. *Facilitating Maintenance of Stormwater Devices on Communally-Owned Land*. Paper to the New Zealand Water and Wastes Association 4th South Pacific Conference on Stormwater and Aquatic Resource Protection, Auckland, 4–6 May 2005.

Dupuis, A. and Dixon, J. 2006. 'Getting On': An Agenda for Living Closer Together, in *Living Together: Towards Inclusive Settlements in New Zealand*, edited by M. Thompson-Fawcett and C. Freeman. Dunedin: Otago University Press.

Dupuis, A., Dixon, J., Lysnar, P. and Mouat, C. 2002. *Bodies Corporate and Housing Intensification in Auckland: A Preliminary Assessment*. Report for the Auckland Regional Council, Auckland City Council, North Shore City Council, Rodney District Council and the Waitakere City Council. Auckland: Massey University and the University of Auckland.

Earthsong Eco-Neighbourhood. n.d. *Earthsong Eco-Neighbourhood.* [Online]. Available at: http://www.earthsong.org.nz/index.html [accessed: 30 June 2009].

Lloyd, S., Wong, T.H.F. and Chesterfield, C.J. 2001. Opportunities and Impediments to Water Sensitive Urban Design in Australia. *Proceedings of the Second South Pacific Stormwater Conference: Rain the Forgotten Resource*, Auckland, New Zealand, 302–9.

Lysnar, P., Dixon, J., Dempsey, C. and van Roon, M. 2007. *Managing 'Low Impact' Features on Multi-Owned Residential Sites.* Paper to the South Pacific Stormwater Conference, New Zealand Water and Wastewater Association, Auckland, New Zealand, 15–17 May 2007.

MCC. 2002. Manukau City Operative District Plan. Manukau City Council. [Online]. Available at: www.manukau.govt.nz [accessed: 12 October 2009].

Martin, P., Turner, B., Dell, J., Campbell, N., Payne, J., Elliott, C. and Reed, B. 2001. *Sustainable Urban Drainage Systems: Best Practice Manual*. London: Ciria.

National Sustainable Urban Drainage Systems Working Group. 2004. *Interim Code of Practice for Sustainable Drainage Systems.* London: National SUDS Working Group.

Regis Park Residents Society Incorporated. 2006. *Rules of Regis Park Residents Society Inc.* Flat Bush, Auckland: Regis Holdings Ltd.

Rodney District Council. 2000. *Proposed Rodney District Plan.* [Online]. Available at: www.rodney.govt.nz [accessed: 15 October 2009].

Sargisson, L. and Sargent, L.T. 2004. *Living in Utopia: New Zealand's Intentional Communities*. Aldershot: Ashgate Publishing Ltd.

The Scottish Government. 2001. *Planning Advice Note PAN 61: Planning and Sustainable Urban Drainage Systems.* [Online]. Available from: www.scotland.gov.uk/Topics/Planning-Building/Planning/15243/1416 [accessed: 12 October 2009].

Shaver, E. 2000. *Low Impact Design Manual for the Auckland Region*. Technical Publication 124. Auckland, New Zealand: Auckland Regional Council.

van Roon, M. 2005. Emerging Approaches to Urban Ecosystem Management: The Potential of Low Impact Urban Design and Development Principles. *Journal of Environmental Assessment, Policy and Management*, 7(1), 1–24.

van Roon, M. 2007. Water Localisation and Reclamation: Steps Towards Low Impact Urban Design and Development. *Journal of Environmental Management*, 83, 437–47.

van Roon, M. and Dixon, J. 2006. *A Policy Framework for Sustainable Urban Design and Drainage*. Paper to the World Conference on Accelerating Excellence in the Built Environment. Birmingham, UK, 2–4 October 2006.

van Roon, M. and Knight, S.J. 2004 *The Ecological Context of Development: New Zealand Perspectives.* Melbourne: Oxford University Press.

Chapter 14
Conclusions

Sarah Blandy, Ann Dupuis and Jennifer Dixon

Each of the chapters contributes a particular dimension to one or more of the themes identified in the Introduction: the power of developers and managing agents; the problematic status of owners; the potential and actual role of municipal planners; and the difficult issue of ensuring sustainable maintenance of multi-owned property, whether this consists only of buildings or also incorporates sustainable design features. Against the background of critical legal events in the life-course of these developments the real-life relationships among the key actors emerge as subtly different in each of the countries in which the chapters are grounded. In this overview of the issues raised by the foregoing chapters, we start with a consideration of the roles of the key actors, then explore the attempts to redress the balance of power among them and consider the significance of differences in legal and other aspects of culture, before reaching some conclusions and suggestions for a future research agenda.

Key Actors

In this section we consider the key actors involved in multi-owned housing: developers and managing agents or property management companies; owners; and various municipal authority stakeholders. Regarding the framework of critical legal events, this section highlights common issues and themes that have emerged from the preceding chapters with respect to the power imbalances that operate among these actors. We particularly concentrate on unravelling the bundle of rights involved in the processes associated with multi-owned housing.

Developers and Managing Agents/Property Management Companies

The initial critical legal event is acquisition of the site to be developed for multi-owned housing. The developer is then in a position to determine how various rights in the site will be allocated in the future. The most fundamental decision made by the developer is whether to retain a long-term interest in the site or to sell it on quickly, as was observed of leasehold ownership in England and Wales (Clarke 1998). In the US, for example, as McKenzie demonstrates in Chapter 4, developers routinely have only a short-term interest in the site. In these circumstances, the developer's lawyer would draft the Declaration of Covenants, Conditions and Restrictions and articles of incorporation for the homeowners' association, but these are often later changed relatively easily by the association. In contrast, in Singapore and Hong Kong (see Chapters 6 and 7 by Christudason and Yip) the developer's initial allocation of shares in the common parts, very important for owners as it determines their maintenance contributions, voting rights and proportion of ownership of common property, cannot be later redistributed by owners, however problematic it proves.

Our earlier research in both New Zealand and England found that many developers were able to retain a long-term interest in their sites either through retaining freehold ownership, or by embedding their power and rights in a property management company to which the developer sold the right to manage at the second critical legal event (Blandy, Dixon and Dupuis 2006). This transaction is often the main source of difficulties for owners and many contributions to this book focus on that issue. Sherry (Chapter 10) shows how the sale of management rights by a developer ties the body corporate to an ongoing contract with a management company, even though that contract was entered into at a point when the body corporate was not yet controlled by the owners. In Queensland (Cassidy, Guilding and Warnken, Chapter 11), management rights contracts entered into by the developer frequently last for 25 years and owners have virtually no say in the appointment of a new manager should the holder of the management rights choose to sell them. The power of managing agents, also known as property management companies, is extremely wide-ranging in most jurisdictions, causing many owners to feel that they lack control over their own housing. In Scotland, Robertson (Chapter 3) concludes that it is the property managers not the owners who make decisions in respect of multi-owned buildings and Wang (Chapter 8) shows how property management companies in China are embedded not merely by the developer but also by the state, which causes serious difficulties for owners.

It is not surprising that many developers have close links with the property manager with whom they make contracts for management rights, as the business of multi-owned developments is to their mutual benefit. These two key actors are then able to close ranks against individual owners. Bounds (Chapter 9) outlines the problems caused for owners when the managing agent fails to litigate against the developer for structural faults; and Blandy (Chapter 2) gives an example of the whole site being pre-sold by the developer to the managing agent, without the knowledge of the owners. These legal relationships can be traced through company structures in both England and in Hong Kong (Yip, Chapter 7). Developers in Hong Kong draft the Deed of Mutual Covenant which binds the new owners and appoint the management company at the same time. Although now theoretically possible, owners have found it extremely difficult to terminate management contracts because of the majority vote required. Powerful lobbying by the Hong Kong property management industry, backed by their big developer parent companies, has been successful in postponing legislative changes designed to improve the position of owners. Similarly, in the US, the property managers' trade association, the Communities Association Institute, resists regulation despite many instances of embezzlement of homeowner associations' funds.

Owners

The contribution by Bounds (Chapter 9) which focuses on residential satisfaction in Sydney, brings out very clearly the crucial issue of control for individual owners in multi-occupied property. The same issue applies in every jurisdiction considered in this volume. In this type of development, the use made by owners of their individual properties must be tempered by the fact that it will affect other owners on the site; even in a low density development, property values are interdependent. In some situations, for example as where the leasehold/freehold structure is used in England and Wales (Blandy, Chapter 2), another actor even has ultimate property rights over the individual owner's home. In this legal framework, the owners' rights over the common property and facilities may be limited to access. Even where the individual owner has rights of ownership over the common property and facilities, any decisions in respect of these can only be made in conjunction with the other owners.

The arrangements for collective ownership of common property vary widely amongst the jurisdictions represented in this book. At one extreme there are highly regulated frameworks which specify that in a multi-owned development, there must be a body corporate of a particular kind, as in Queensland (Cassidy, Guilding and Warnken, Chapter 11). At the other extreme are the legal frameworks which Alterman (Chapter 5) terms the 'simple' minimalist type, where no separate legal entity is created to which the owners must belong. Both Israel and Hong Kong fit this categorization, in which owners share the common property as co-owners. In Hong Kong there is no condominium law but the government encourages the formation of voluntary owner corporations. These have no legal status, but enable the owners to exercise the right to manage (Yip, Chapter 7). Israel's condominium law merely grants the elected representatives of the condominium legal authority to act on behalf of the other owners. Chinese homeowner associations have no legal status and no property rights over common property (Wang, Chapter 8). These associations have developed as voluntary bodies, similar to the voluntary residents' associations formed by owners in estate rentcharge schemes described by Blandy in Chapter 2. In England and Wales, as well as in New Zealand (Dupuis and Dixon, Chapter 12) collective bodies for owners may take a variety of forms chosen by developers and their lawyers from pre-existing common law and legislative frameworks.

The potential for conflict between individual owners and the collective entity to which they belong, and for conflict between different groups of owners, emerges very strongly in some contributions to this book. McKenzie (Chapter 4) outlines the strength of homeowner associations in the US, backed by draconian powers of foreclosure against individual owners who have no option but to join the association. Other chapters focus on the clash of interests between owners themselves. Christudason's case study in Singapore (Chapter 6) explores the conflict between minority residential owners and majority commercial owners over collective sales. Similar conflicts take place in Hong Kong (Yip, Chapter 7), whereas in Queensland

(Cassidy et al., Chapter 11) the differences in interests are between resident owners and investor owners in the same multi-owned tourist development.

There is, however, some evidence that the capacity for conflict can be minimized when owners have prior information about the type of housing they are moving into and particularly where they are committed to contributing time and energy to living collectively. Dixon and van Roon's case studies in Chapter 13 include a cohousing site run on these lines; Blandy describes a successful cohousing development in Chapter 2; and McKenzie (Chapter 4) makes a distinction between conflict-ridden condominiums and the more harmonious cooperative structure 'animated by a spirit of voluntary collectivism'. These echo the findings of Barton and Silverman (1994) that co-operatives represent the ideal of true community and democratic decision-making, in which all residents participate and vote. Perhaps the critical issue is that in these developments property was seen to be owned collectively rather than privately.

Municipal Authorities

The importance of municipal authorities has been highlighted in many contributions to this book. High density housing certainly finds favour at present with the planners who scrutinize developers' applications before granting consent. In the US, as McKenzie (Chapter 4) points out, homeowner associations are doing the work of municipal authorities which in turn encourage the growth of common interest housing for fiscal and other reasons. Other states, including Singapore, Hong Kong and China, rely on developers to provide the infrastructure for new areas. As Bounds comments in Chapter 9 in relation to multi-owned developments in New South Wales, this may result in the developer agreeing to obligations with the planning authority at the second critical event, which must then be carried out by the owners into the future. He also describes some onerous agreements obliging owners to maintain facilities that are not private but publicly accessible.

If arrangements for the maintenance by owners of buildings and large sites should fail, the implications are serious for municipal authorities. McKenzie reports that in the US there have been lawsuits brought by municipalities against homeowner associations over the maintenance of common property where, for example, neglected standing water provided a breeding ground for mosquitoes. Authorities should be concerned not just with the physical design at the commencement of the development, but with the arrangements for its continuing upkeep. Although seemingly few municipalities take on this oversight approach, Alterman describes the informal efforts made by local planning authorities in Israel to require developers to contract with a management company (Chapter 5). In Chapter 8, Wang explains how property management companies are required by law for new neighbourhoods in China.

It is instructive to note here the experience in Ireland, where the Planning and Development Act 2000 contains specific provisions for local planning authorities to grant planning consent subject to conditions for the continuing maintenance and management of the development, including the appointment of a management company. This condition came to 'be incorporated routinely as a condition of planning permission by a significant number of planning authorities throughout the country'; however, following owners' unsatisfactory experiences with property management companies, in 2006 the government issued guidance to local authorities that they should only require a management company to be appointed in exceptional circumstances (Mahon and Ó Cinnéide 2009: 6). It seems that solving one issue by changing the relationships between key actors, in this instance placing property management companies in an authorized and powerful position, may lead to further problems and unintended consequences.

Regulation of Multi-owned Developments

State regulation of multi-owned developments can be seen to operate in two separate phases: controlling which legal frameworks may be used to set up a development, and regulating developments once established. These chapters show how country-specific variations in property law have shaped the ways in which this type of housing may be legally established. As already noted, some jurisdictions provide for a statutory framework to which there are no alternatives: Singapore, New South Wales, and Queensland, for example. In other jurisdictions, developers have the opportunity to draft a legal framework that suits them. They form a powerful lobby against proposals to adopt a watertight statutory regime for multi-owned housing. In England and Wales, leasehold remains the major type of legal framework although it means an inevitable power imbalance between leasehold owners and the freeholder. Blandy (Chapter 2) describes how attempts to redress this balance over a long period have not been wholly successful. The recent introduction of commonhold legislation has resulted in a very low take-up by developers, as they prefer the flexibility of the alternative frameworks which remain available to them. The same process can be seen in Scotland. Robertson outlines in Chapter 3 the 2004 legislative reforms which ended Scottish feudalism, but neglected the opportunity to bring in a model management scheme setting up a body corporate structure, so the choice of legal framework still lies with developers and their lawyers. In New Zealand, where multi-owned housing is a relatively recent phenomenon, most new developments come under strata title legislation but, as Dupuis and Dixon explain in Chapter 12, given this arrangement is not mandatory, increasingly developers are setting in place other legal entities for governing this type of housing.

Regulation of Managing Agents/Property Management Companies

The difficulties which owners experience with property management agents or companies provide a recurrent theme in this book, even when they are licensed. However, the approach taken to this aspect of their regulation varies. For example, in the Australian state of New South Wales licensing became compulsory in 1941 whereas in Queensland no licensing is required for management rights businesses, despite the crucial role they play in that state's tourist industry (Cassidy et al., Chapter 11). One of the recent reforms discussed by McKenzie (Chapter 4) is the introduction of licensing for property managers in Florida. In both England and Wales, and in Scotland (despite the criticisms made by the Office of Fair Trading to which Robertson refers in Chapter 3), the government has not moved beyond self-regulation for the property management industry.

Consumer Protection Measures

McKenzie (Chapter 4) traces the attempts in three US states to provide individual owners with some protection against the 'quasi-judicial functions' and foreclosure powers of homeowner associations, noting some improvement in the position of owners but also some setbacks. In New South Wales there has long been strong consumer protection legislation for owners of multi-owned housing, but the ingenuity of developers is equal to it. For example, once 30 per cent of the lots have been sold, the developer should no longer be able to control the body corporate. However, in one instance Bounds (Chapter 9) notes that the sales contracts drafted by the developer provided the developer with proxy voting rights beyond this point, and in another a developer managed to regain control of the body corporate by purchasing more lots. In England and Wales, developers and freeholders have resisted attempts to even the playing field for leaseholders, making them fight through the courts for the statutory rights they are entitled to. The Office of Fair Trading has, however, taken upon itself the obligation to investigate particularly unfair standard clauses in leases relating to retirement accommodation (Blandy, Chapter 2).

Provisions for Dispute Resolution

The chapters explore a range of ways in which the inevitable disputes between key actors may be resolved. Typically, regulators and mediators provide the first tier, with the roles sometimes blurred, as in the Israel State Inspector of Condominiums whose powers encompass the regular civil means of enforcement of civil contractual obligations. In Florida a Condominium Ombudsman has recently been established. In England and Wales, there is provision for an Ombudsman for commonhold disputes, but so far this has not been put in place. In New South Wales there is provision for alternative dispute resolution of problems arising from strata and community titles, administered by the Department of Fair Trading.

The second tier of dispute resolution is the province of specialist tribunals, for example the Singapore Strata Titles Board and Leasehold Valuation Tribunals in England and Wales – which are both heavily used. In some jurisdictions there has also been much litigation brought in the ordinary court system by key actors in multi-owned housing. In the US, McKenzie (Chapter 4) notes that the main regulatory check is provided by civil litigation; for financial reasons, these cases are usually instigated by associations against individual owners. Across different states in the US, different bases for the courts to adjudicate on decisions by homeowner associations apply, including standards of business judgement, reasonableness, and a newly emerging quasi-governmental standard, based on constitutional rights. The case study provided by Sherry (Chapter 10) illustrates how the standard of fiduciary duty applied by the courts to developers, has compensated for the failure of statutory disclosure rules.

Provision of Information to Owners

Many contributors make the point that purchasers of multi-owned property have little idea of what they are buying into and that their position as owners is compromised by asymmetry of information. State attempts to remedy this situation range from compulsory information to be printed on the documentation received by a new purchaser (applies in England and Wales, but only to commonhold developments) to more complex protection mechanisms such as imposing a duty of disclosure on the developer. In her comparison between legislative protection in terms of disclosure between New South Wales and developments in Florida, US, Sherry concludes that further legislation is needed to protect owners in New South Wales. However, McKenzie's chapter indicates that the Florida legislature has also recently needed to strengthen the position of individual owners, but as against association boards, rather than developers.

In relation to owner obligations, problems are caused by unexpected increases in maintenance levies, as Bounds (Chapter 9) shows in New South Wales. This theme is taken up by Alterman (Chapter 5) in relation to Israel, where the 'simple' legal framework requires owners to pay contributions, but provides no enforcement mechanism for this. Alterman concludes that Florida's 'enhanced' law provides more protection for owners by requiring prior disclosure to owners about the likely cost of maintenance in the future. However, as McKenzie shows, other aspects of this legal framework have led to power imbalances between owners and homeowner associations, and Alterman makes the valuable observation that the current economic crisis has revealed the advantages of flexibility inherent in 'simple' type laws.

Differences in Legal and Other Aspects of Culture

It is tempting to look across at other jurisdictions and think that they have effectively solved a particular problem, but the chapters in this book show that no perfect solution has yet been achieved. It is interesting that two contributors (Altermann and Sherry) have selected Florida as a comparator, but McKenzie's research (Chapter 4) indicates that this jurisdiction is by no means unproblematic. Further, experience shows that particular aspects of legal frameworks cannot be merely transplanted into another jurisdiction; the effects will be different. This is partly due to the specific socio-economic context, as indicated by the information given by each contributor to this book, but also has to do with the more amorphous concept of culture, 'a multidimensional and interpretive notion' closely related to power relations (Banakar 2009: 77). Culture is also deeply embedded in social relations: 'Beyond law, there is some empirical basis for claimed differences in national traits in the way people relate to each other' (Hofstedte 1980, cited in Nelken 2009: 119). This point is well illustrated by Alterman's chapter, which attributes both a high level of disputes between Israeli owners and their informal resolution to effective social norms, in a way that would seem impossible to translate to the different culture of, for example, the US.

A key question for the issues raised in this book is whether owners will exercise any legal rights, once they have been given them. This brings in the specific concept of legal culture, which might explain, for example, the high rate of litigation in the US, passive acceptance in Hong Kong and direct action in China, as different responses to common problems in multi-owned housing. However, Nelken (2009) suggests that limited access to lawyers and courts, or limited powers of the court to achieve a satisfactory and lasting solution, may affect these decisions. This certainly goes some way to explaining the position in China, which Wang sets out in detail in Chapter 8. At first it seems surprising that given the seriousness of developer-related problems there, many homeowner associations take no legal action to resolve the problems, although they are not averse to litigation against property management firms. However, Wang's research has established that associations have no legal standing, so cannot bring a lawsuit against developers, but are specifically empowered to take legal action related to property management.

These chapters indicate the importance of detailed research into each jurisdiction, to guard against the apparently easy solution of borrowing aspects of legislation from another, different, context. For example, McKenzie (Chapter 4) and Sherry (Chapter 10) demonstrate the very different approaches taken in the US and New South Wales; Wang (Chapter 8) explores the impact of a rapid transition from state provision to private ownership, highlighting similar issues in a very different context; Robertson (Chapter 3) provides an interesting contrast in approach, as Scotland has recently legislated to end its feudal land ownership system; Cassidy, Guilding and Warnken (Chapter 11) anticipate that frequent legislative review of multi-titled accommodation complex arrangements will be a continuing feature of all Australian state governments for some years to come; and McKenzie (Chapter 4) suggests that the increased state role in regulation of association activities is not matched by a comparable governmental willingness to examine the larger issues.

Conclusions: Issues for a Future Research Agenda

The range of issues canvassed in the book point to the need and potential for further research into a number of topics. While we are not suggesting the research areas discussed below will form a research blueprint, those involved in research into multi-owned housing should find the following areas worthy of further scrutiny.

The conflicts of interests between developers and owners; property managers and owners; on and off-site owners; residential and commercial owners have formed a persistent theme in this book and deserve further attention. In most countries tenants are a group of residents without any rights of participation, and their position is under-researched. These tensions cannot always be readily addressed in legislation or regulation, but the effectiveness of the information now provided to purchasers in multi-owned developments is a key issue. Are owners gradually moving to an understanding of collective rather than individual property rights? Studies are also needed into how to encourage and sustain voluntary participation by owners in day-to-day management, together with the related issue of how this form of private governance might mesh with public local governance through neighbourhood associations and engagement with local councils.

The role of local authorities must be evaluated to understand whether their awareness of the issues connected with multi-owned developments is increasing, particularly the extent to which they are requiring robust legal and financial mechanisms for ensuring the long-term maintenance of complex building structures. The move towards inclusion of sustainable design devices and practices raises important questions too about the respective roles and obligations of individuals as owners and the public in relation to the implementation and long-term maintenance of environmentally sustainable features on private property. Given that at least part of the success of multi-owned housing rests on how well such developments are maintained, issues of long-term maintenance should be a vital component of any future research agenda.

Finally, there are a number of 'big picture' critical questions that remain pressing for researchers in the field of multi-owned housing: Is the expansion of private urban governance the best available alternative in dealing with the issues arising from multi-unit ownership? To what extent, if at all, should local authorities or the national state intervene in what could be considered private matters? And at a broader level are we seeing the erosion of the mandate and responsibilities of the local state and the increasing willingness and capacity of private legal entities to take over management and control?

The role of the state in multi-owned housing is not only an important area for future research, but one that is fast-changing. Rapid social, environmental and technological change is creating a pressing need for regular reviews of legislation as it affects building codes, on-going management and changing social and environmental values. Therefore research is needed to monitor the proliferating legislation and court decisions, alongside close-grained empirical work to explore relationships between the key actors in multi-owned housing. As this book amply demonstrates, a combination of studies undertaken at all scales holds the key to understanding this increasingly important phenomenon of multi-owned housing.

References

Banakar, R. 2009. Power, Culture and Method in Comparative Law. *International Journal of Law in Context*, 5(1), 69–85.

Barton, S.E. and Silverman, C. 1994. *Common Interest Communities: Private Governments and the Public Interest*. Berkeley, CA: Institute of Governmental Studies.

Blandy, S., Dixon, J. and Dupuis, A. 2006. Theorising Power Relationships in Multi-owned Residential Developments: Unpacking the Bundle of Rights. *Urban Studies*, 43(13), 2365–83.

Clarke, D. 1998. Occupying 'Cheek by Jowl': Property Issues Arising from Communal Living, in *Land Law: Themes and Perspectives*, edited by S. Bright and J. Dewar. Oxford: Oxford University Press, 377–405.

Hofstedte, G. 1980. *Culture's Consequences: International Differences in Work Related Values*. Beverley Hills, CA: Sage.

Mahon, M. and Ó Cinnéide, M. 2009. *Legislating for Planning and Residential Development in Ireland: Exploring the Democratic Deficit*. Paper to the European Network for Housing Research conference, 'Changing Housing Markets: Integration and Segmentation', Prague, 28 June–1 July 2009.

McKenzie, E. 2006. Emerging Trends in State Regulation of Private Communities in the USA. *GeoJournal*, 66(1–2), 89–102.

Nelken, D. 2009. Defining and Using the Concept of Legal Culture, in *Comparative Law: A Handbook*, edited by E. Örücü and D. Nelken. Oxford: Hart, 109–32.

Index